I0755842

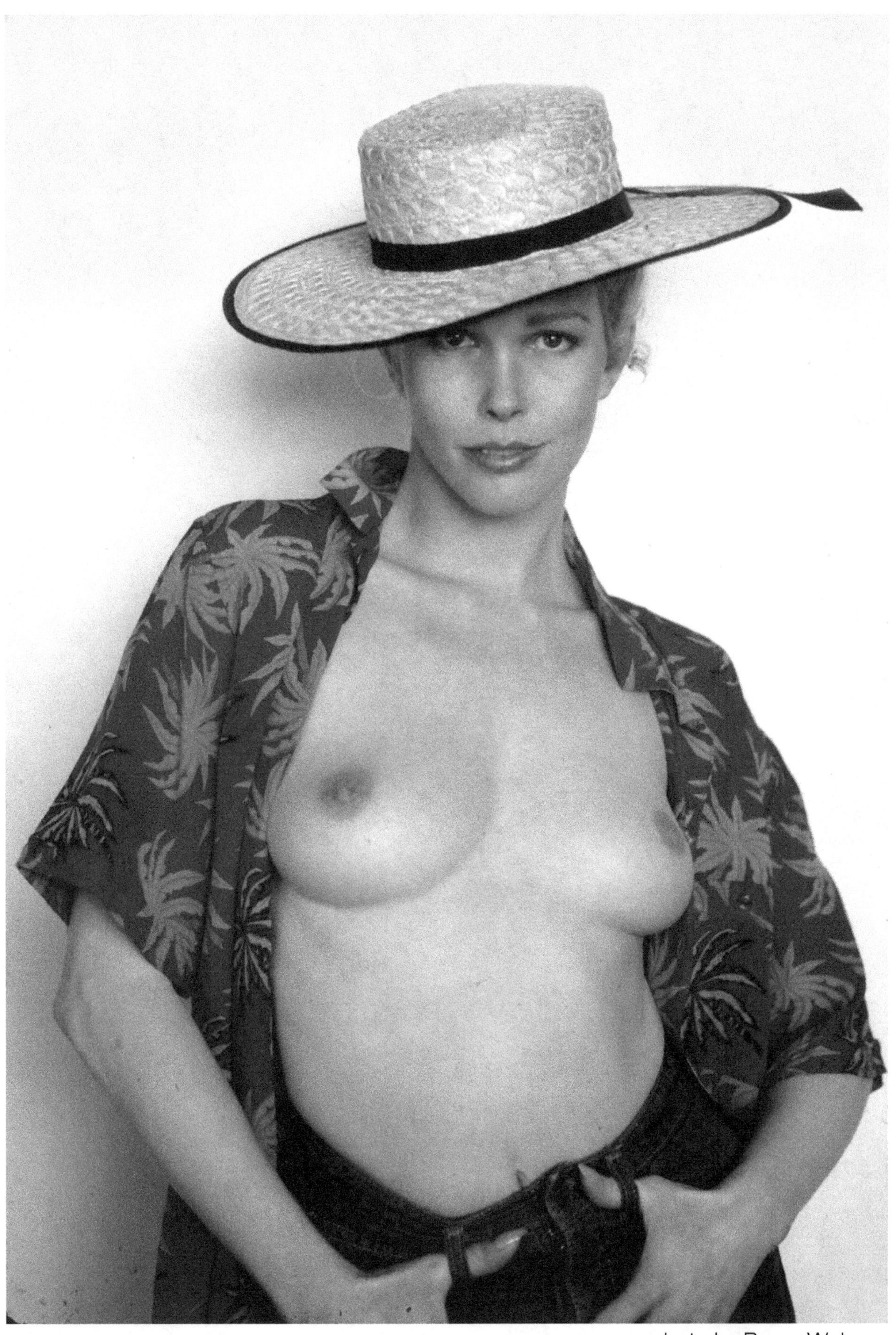

photo by Baron Wolman

Songs of Silence

by

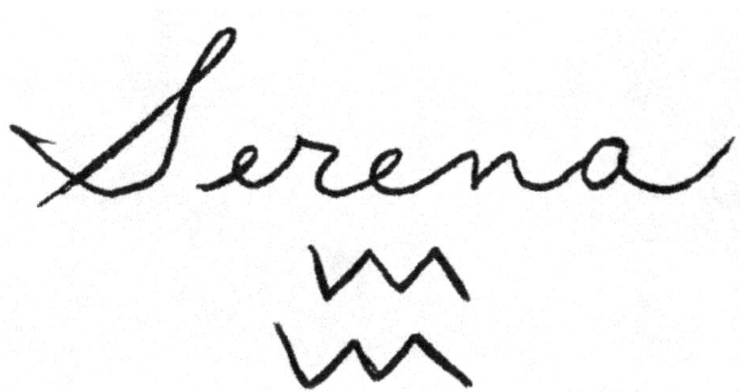

All Art by Serena Czarnecki
Photos not credited are by Serena
or in her Collection.

Cover and Interior design by Vinnie Corbo

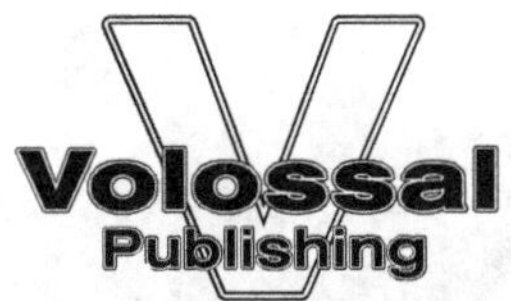

Published by Volossal Publishing
www.volossal.com

ISBN 979-8-9850796-6-1

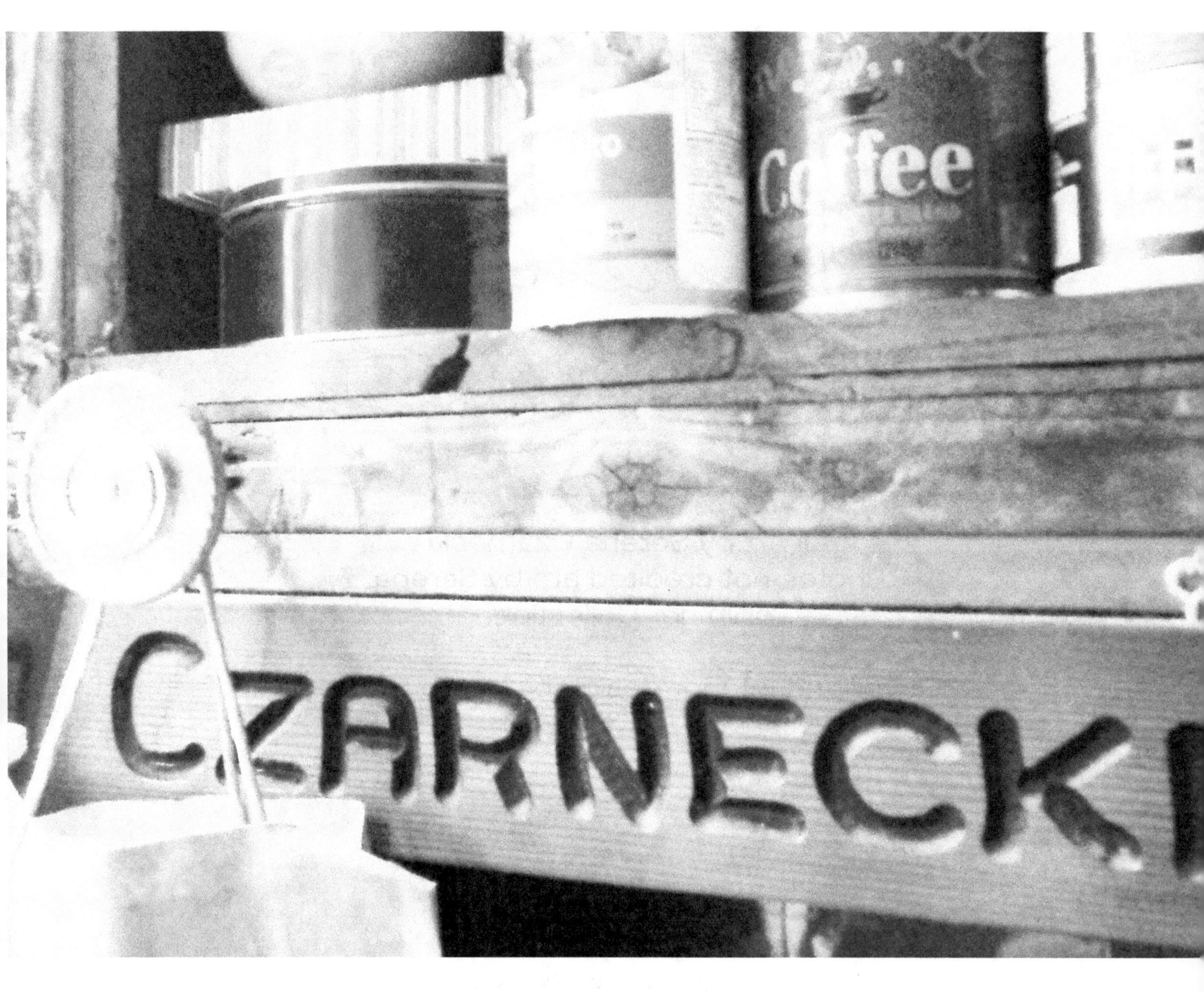
Coffee
CZARNECKI

Table of Contents

Dedication

For all the Essential Workers who have kept us alive.

Many thanks to my sister Cyryla, who tells me wonderful stories...

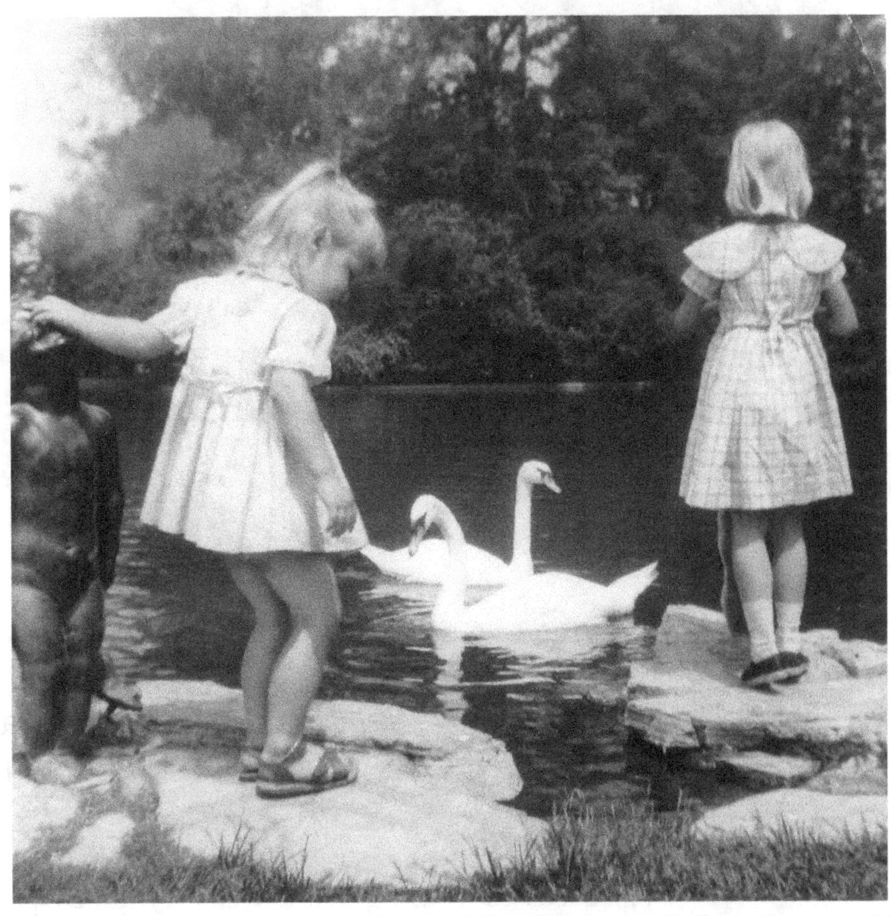

Photo of the sisters by James Czarnecki

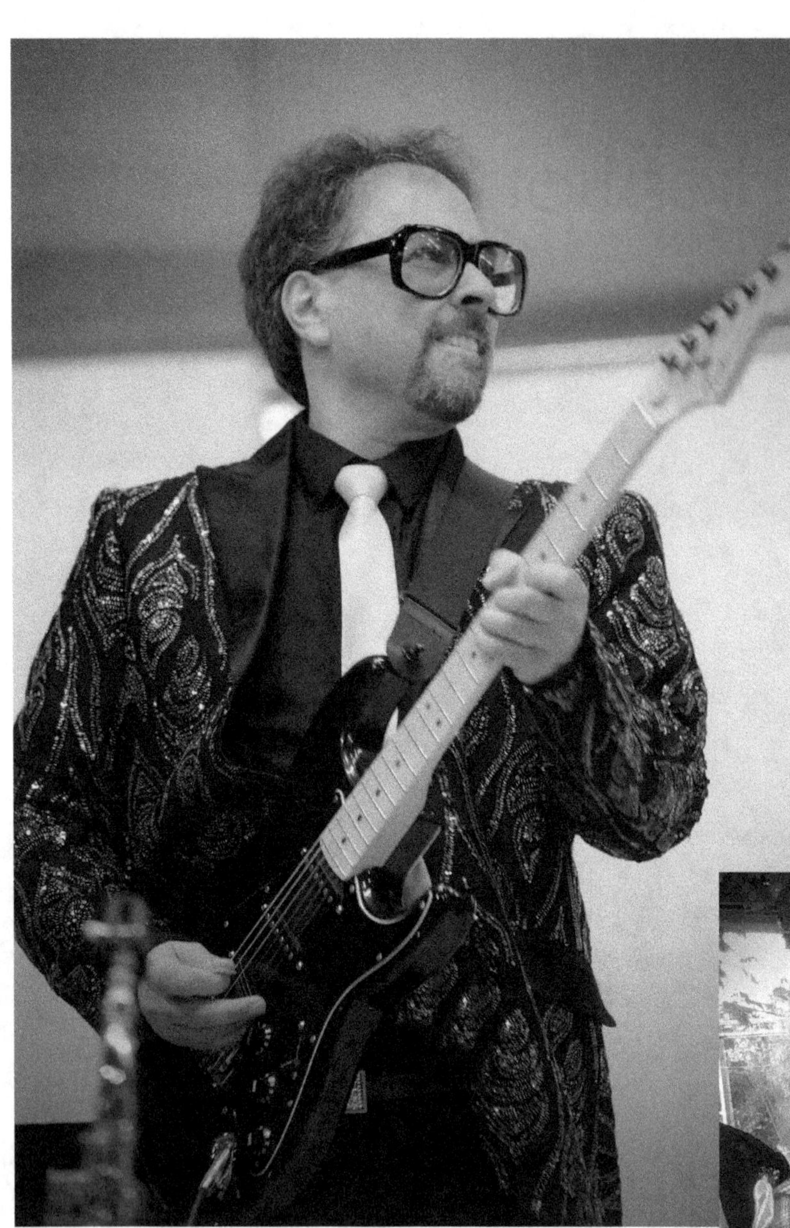

...and to Vinnie Corbo,
who knows the Songs.

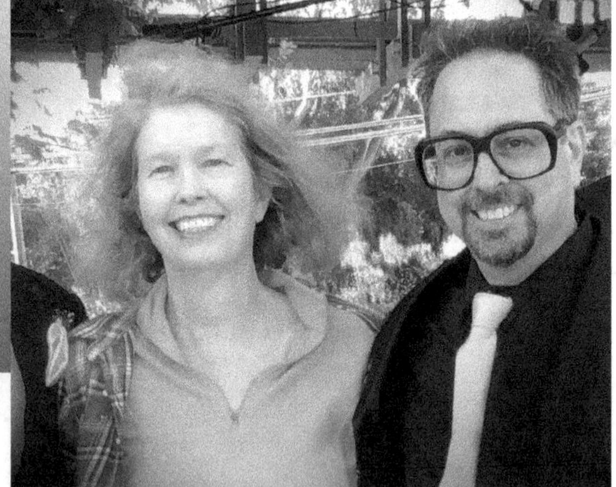

Special Thanks to Rockstar Randy,
who plays the songs.

Thanks to the Artistic Family Group, Steve Zambrano
and Baron Wolman for the use of photos.

Introduction

Since living in San Francisco on Polk Street

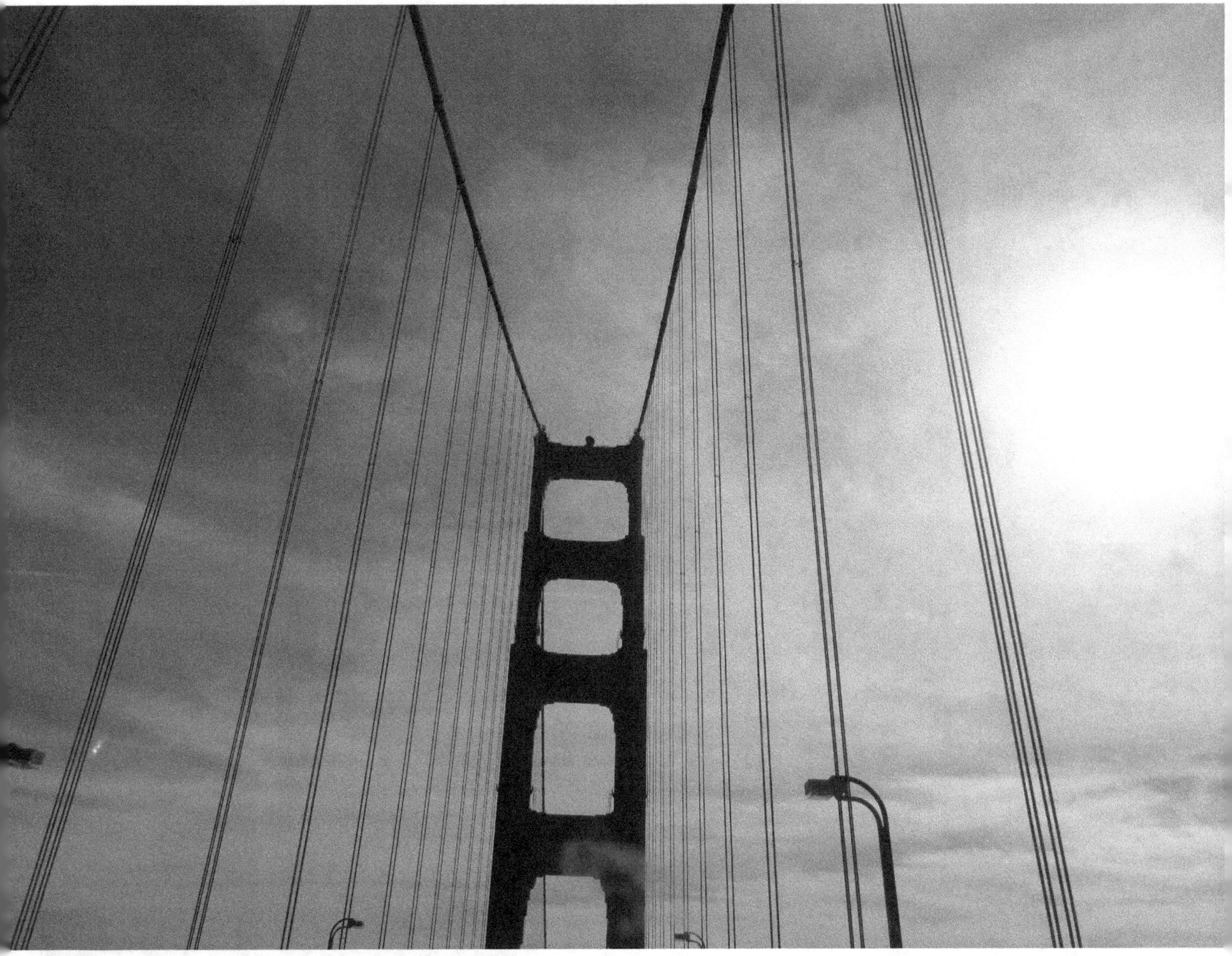

I have traveled.

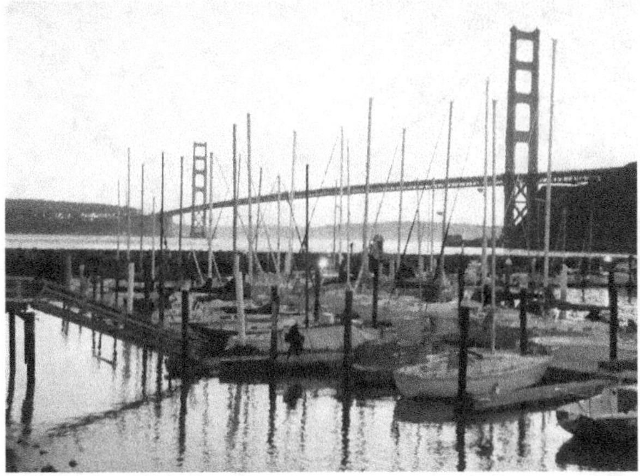

I've lived in Mexico,

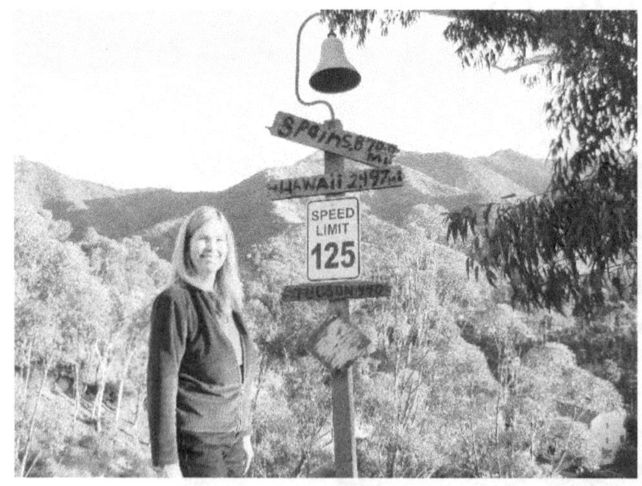

New York City,

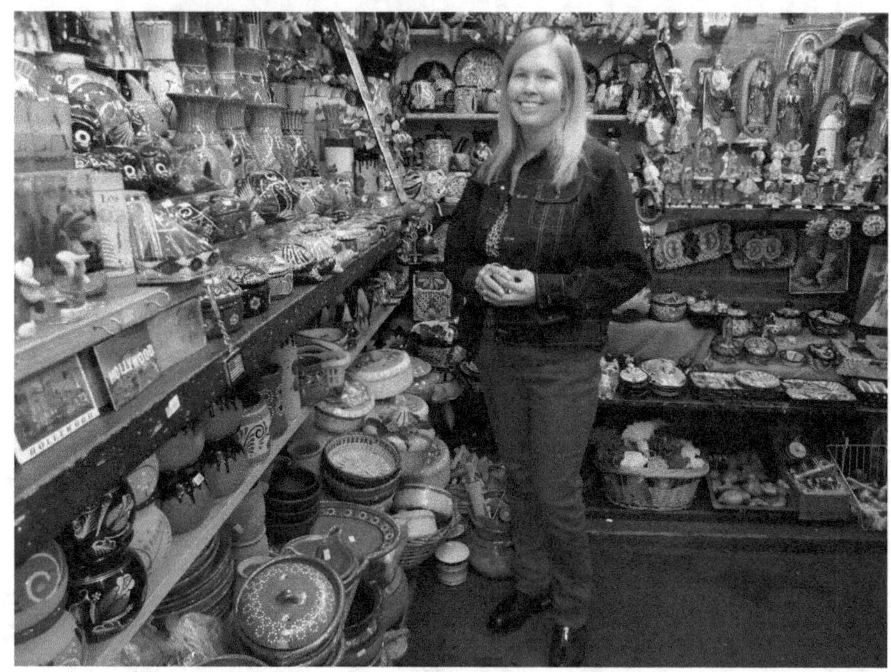

and in the country
by the beautiful San Francisco Bay.

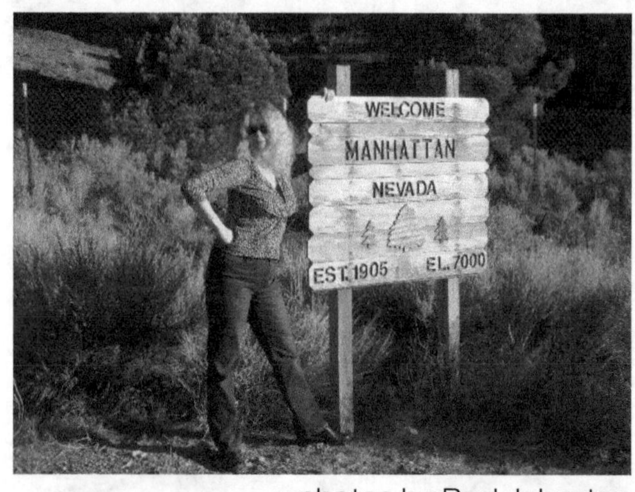

photos by Paul Johnston

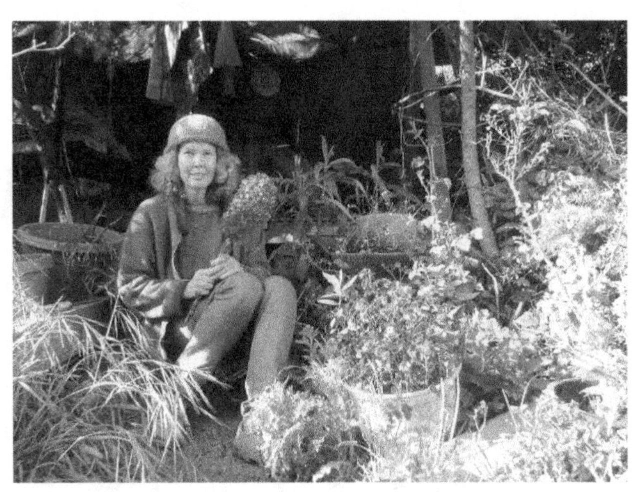

I've settled in with my 3rd husband,
My True Love - Paul.

We are well suited for each other. We each have our own passions, and keep space between ourselves to indulge in our separate devotions. I fall more in Love every day. He acts his love out for me each day. He truly is the cutest thing I've ever seen.

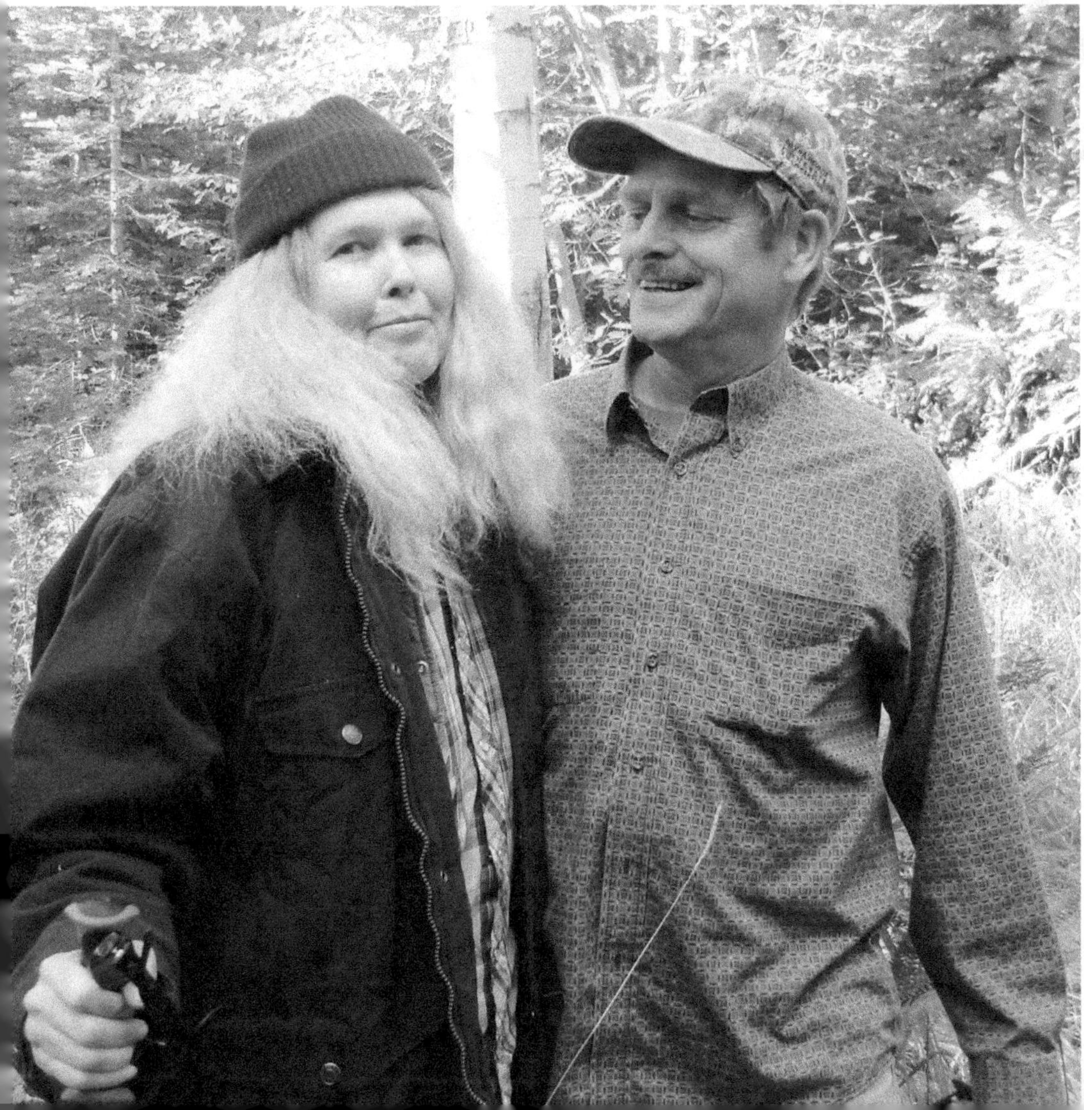

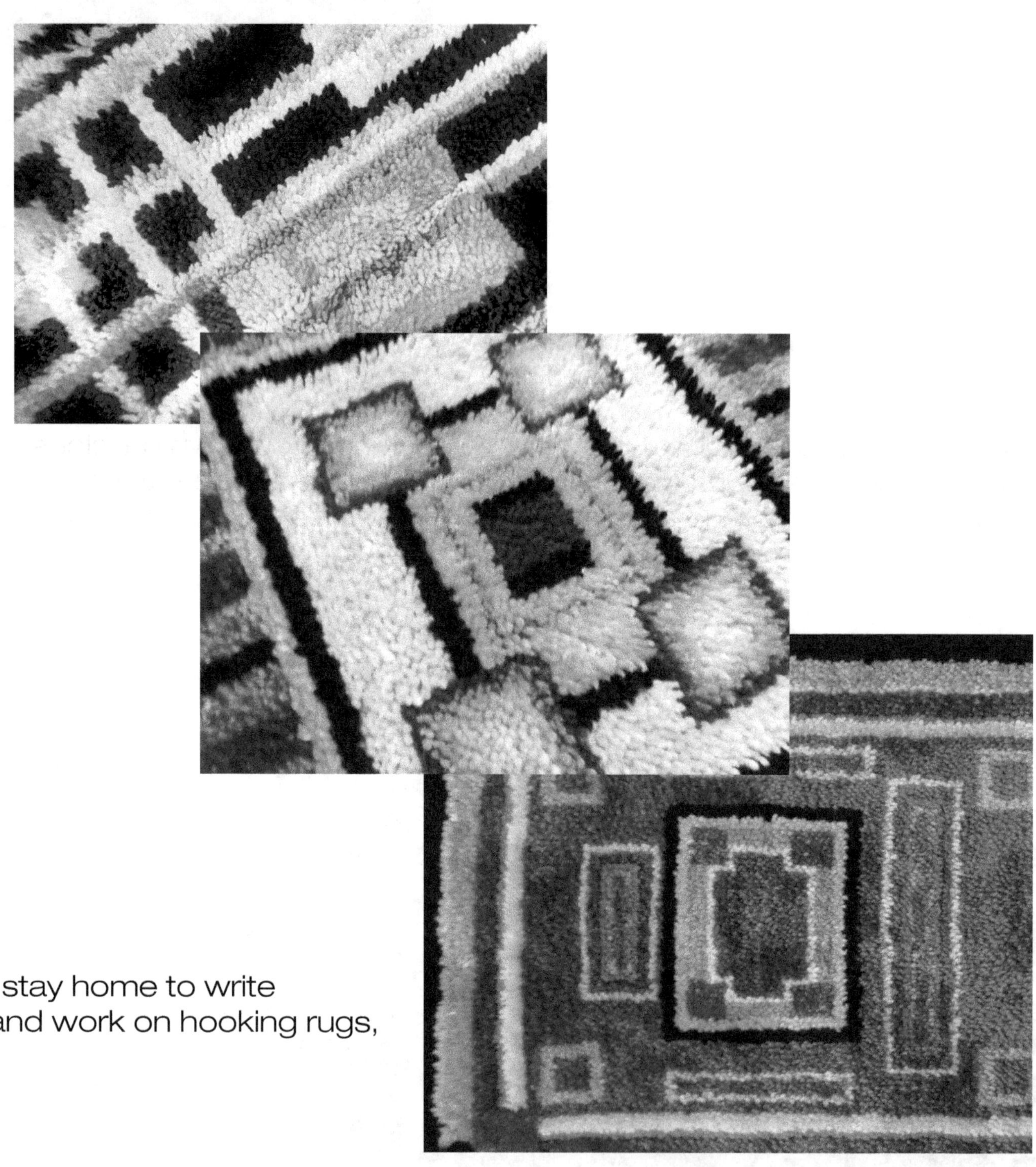

I stay home to write
and work on hooking rugs,

and doing artworks of watercolor, pencil and pastels.

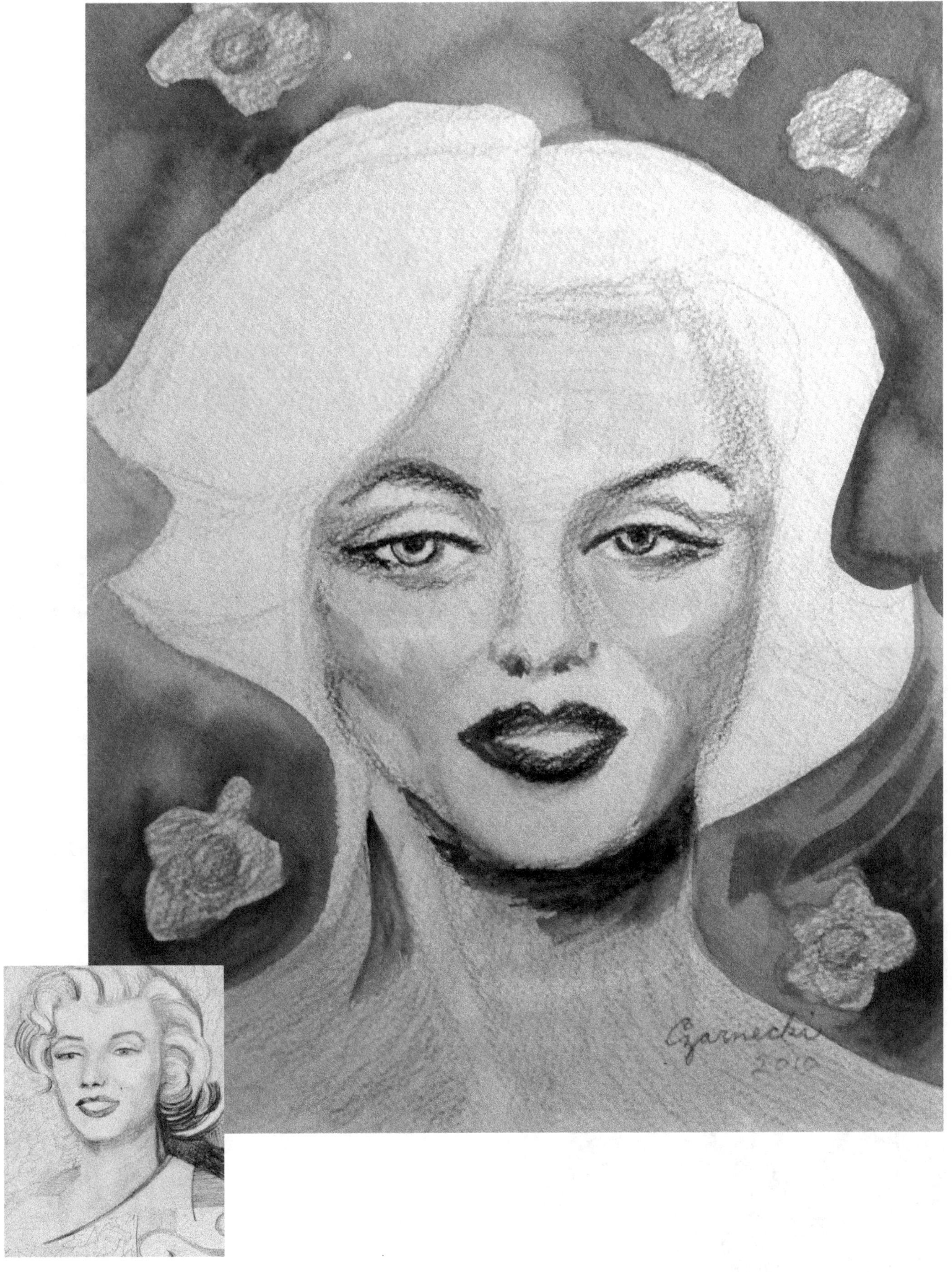

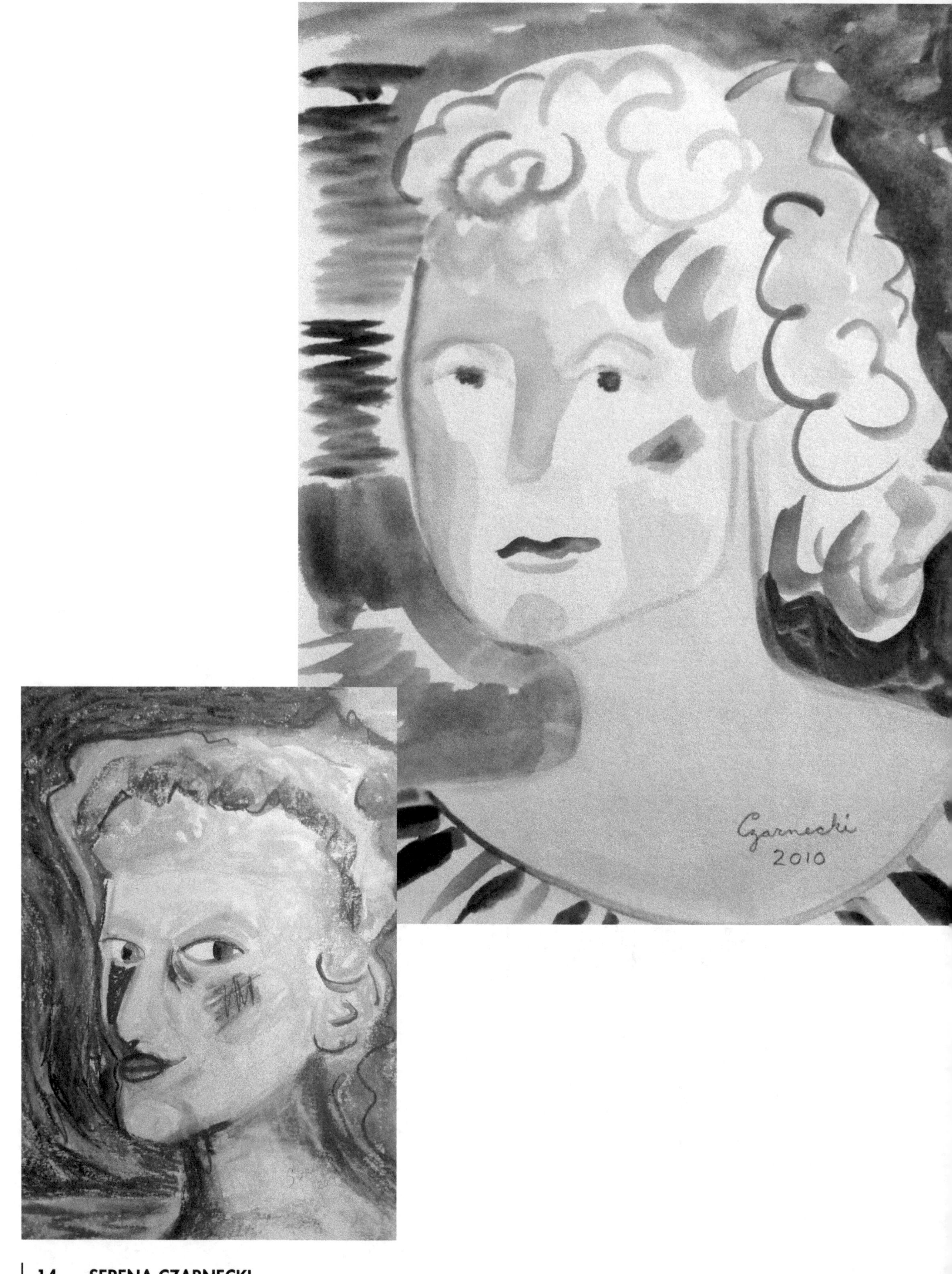
Czarnecki
2010

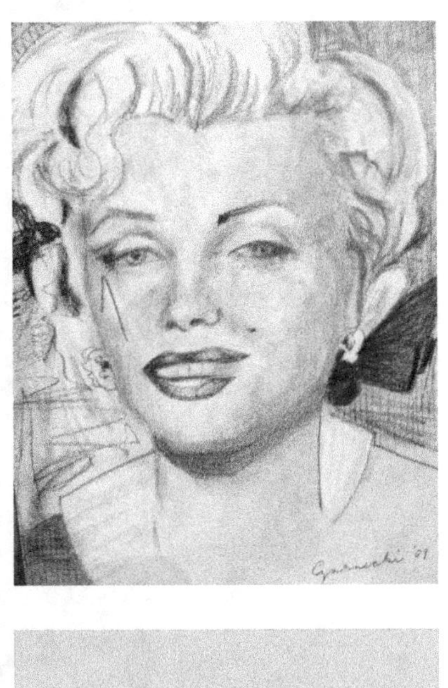

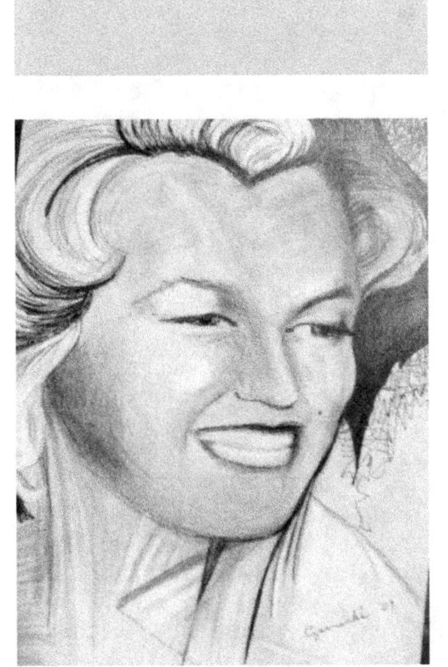

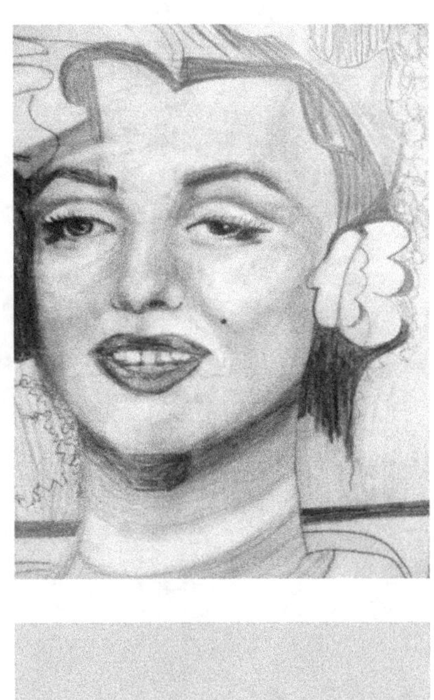

Covid 19 has changed the world,
but my world is pretty much the same as it ever was - I stay home.

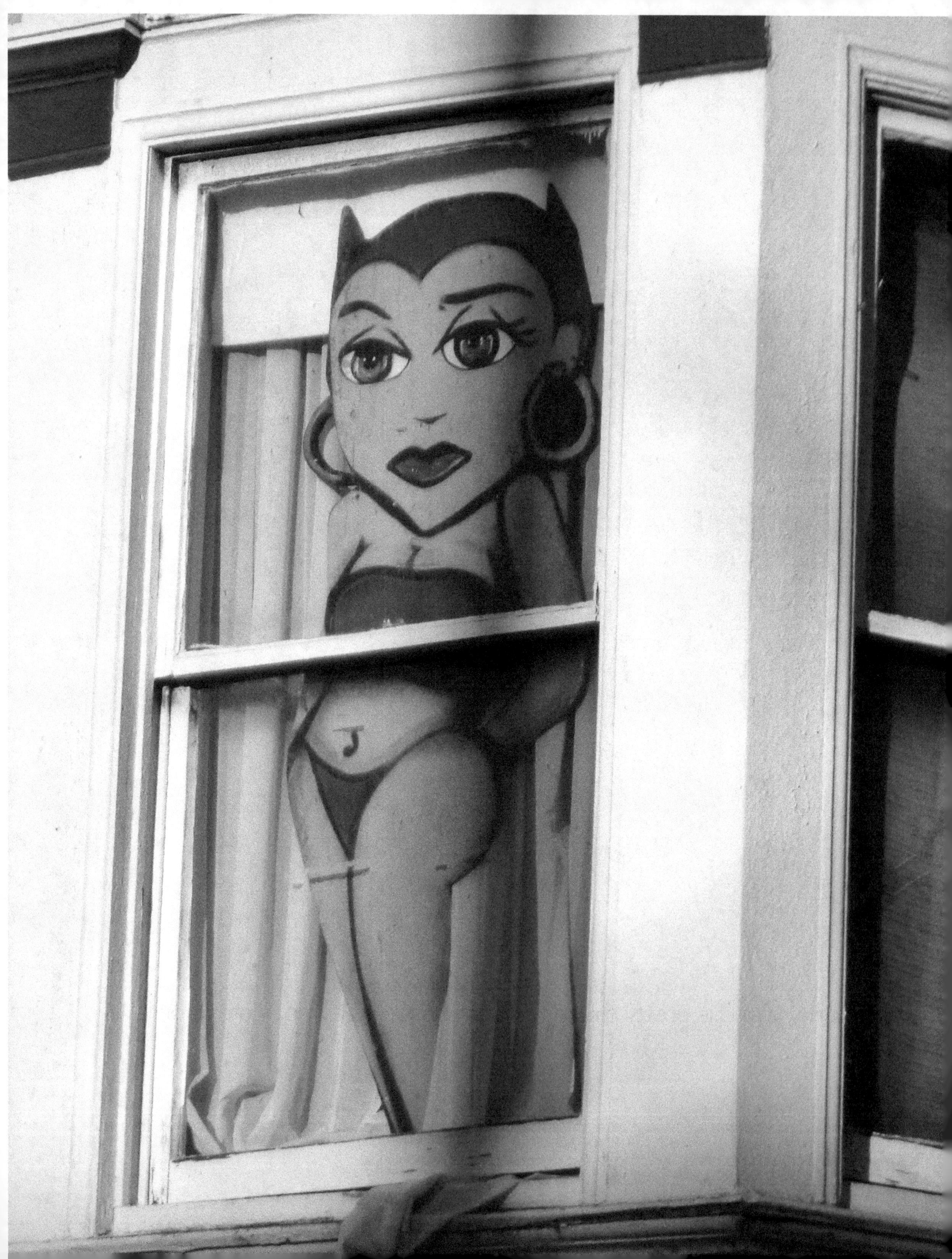

Hooking rugs has been soothing to me during the Pandemic. Some folks baked sourdough bread. I made warm and cozy throw rugs. I've made rugs for years and years.

First I'd crochet them. I made those for everyone in my family. They were done with two strands of yarn so they were bulky; much heavier than a sweater or scarf.

Then I began haunting the thrift stores and buying up old sheets. Preferably not white sheets! I'd tear the sheets into one and a half inch strips. All the strips would be sewn together, then I wind them into balls. I made a storage house full of these balls. They were multi-colored. I don't like white sheets! I really hoped that one day I would turn all this work into an installation artwork.

What I did was braid three strands from three balls together. Once I had a nice flat, colorful braid, I then sewed them together into oval rugs. Colonial style. The old way of disposing of rags. (I've also made quilts, but that's another story...)

Then I happened upon a rug kit. I made one for my sister CC and one for myself. I knew she'd like it because it had daisies pictured on it; her favorite flower. She loves yellow, and this rug pattern had lovely yellows. It is the base rug in my living room with other rugs I've hooked over it.

Rugs keep me warm here where we are unprotected by insulation from the outside cold. It is beautiful here, but as Mark Twain said, "The coldest winter I ever spent was a summer in San Francisco." Historians say Twain was most likely NOT the first person to say this, but every year people quote that and attribute it to him.

I love the fog. It is mysterious. Fog can hide mountains and flows with the currents of air. Maybe because I'm an air sign I feel close to the fog. I feel at home here. When I was a child, Los Angeles was even smoggier than it is today. I had earaches and coughs and colds. I vowed I'd move away from there. When the Hippie Movement washed over me as a teen, I could only think of moving to San Francisco. And this Beauty By the Bay welcomed me. The views threw their arms about me and I was home.

I, of course, got vaccinated as soon as I was eligible. Scientists were able to figure out three vaccines so quickly and we all are indebted to their knowledge. I wear a mask when going out and I feel so much safer knowing I got "The Jab." Didn't hurt at all. I did lay around all day the day after my second shot, but no big deal. The Covid Booster was an additional relief.

I've controlled, with medication, the huge dips into depression, and the ultimate inevitable excesses of my bipolar disorder. I still ride the roller coaster, but with an even keel. Asking only for peace, I temper my furious anger. Each day I try to be better...and do better.

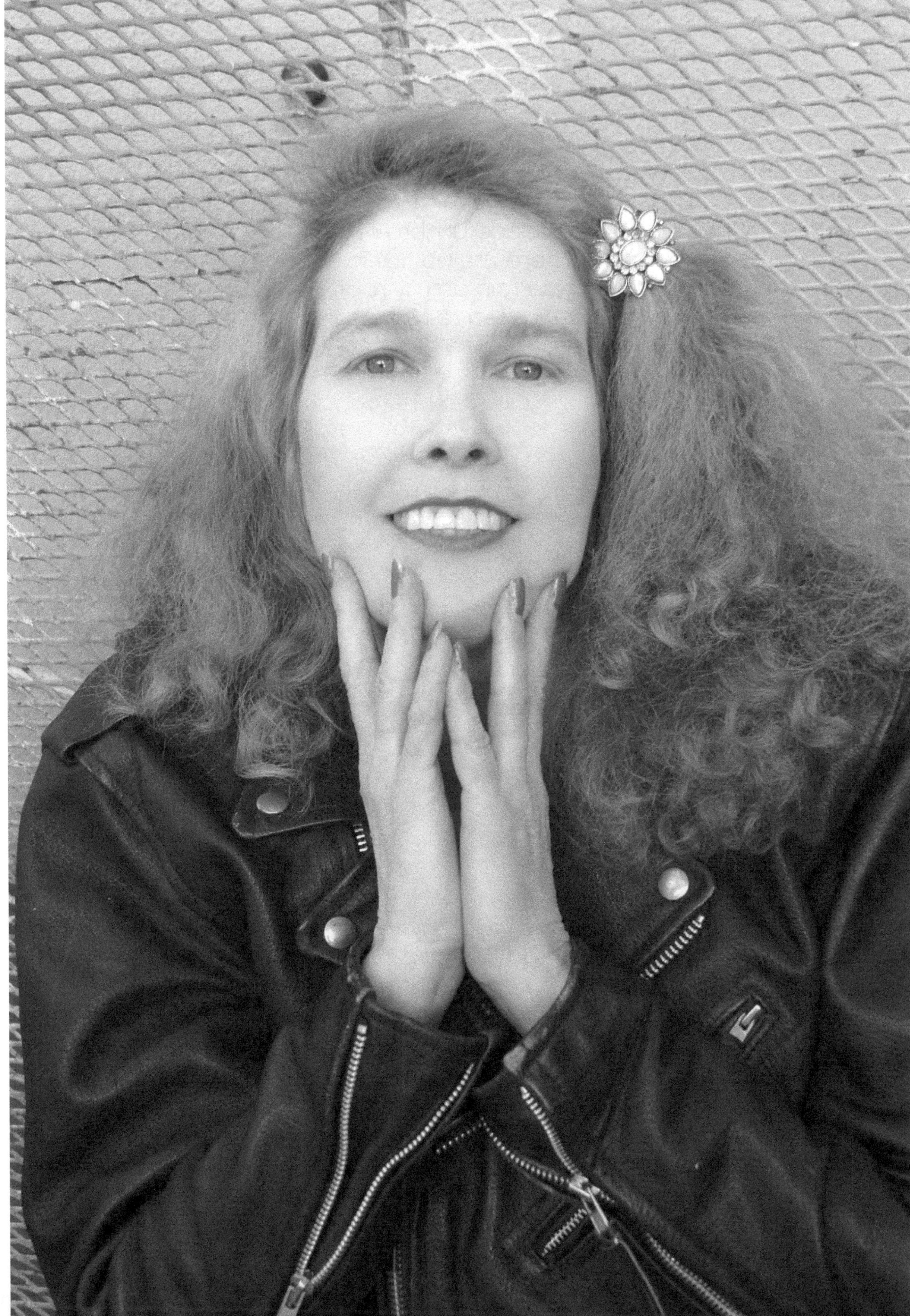
Photo by Steve Zambrano

Being quiet and finding calm is my achievement and my reward for living.

I find it so very peaceful here in the redwoods where we reside. There are no traffic sounds. I love to hear the birds and the rain on my roof. I even wrote a book of poems, Dedicated to Mount Tamalpais and to "my" Paul.

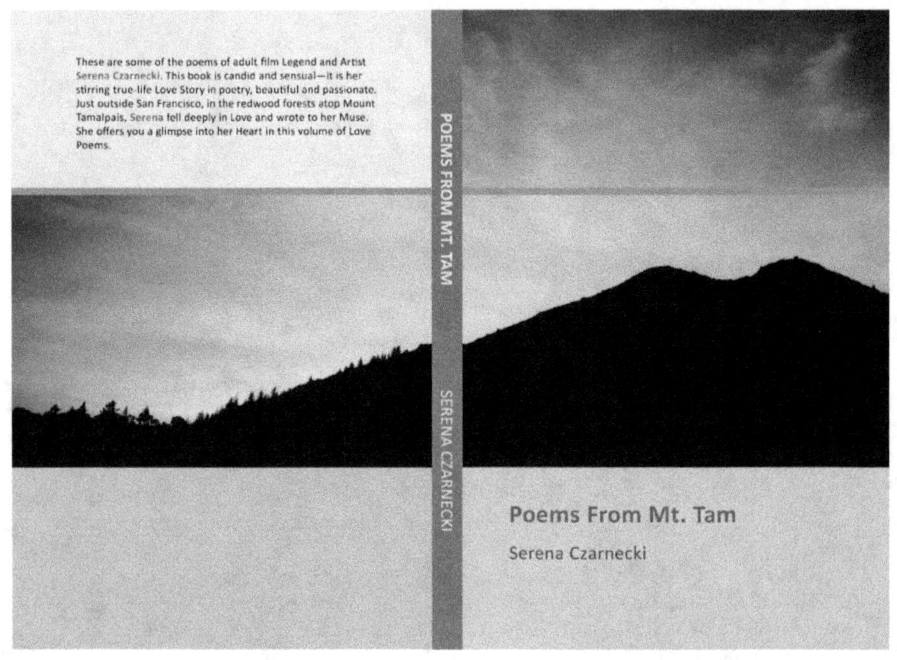

Book design by Bo Gorzelak Pedersen, who edited this book of poems.

Photo of the mountain by Serena Czarnecki

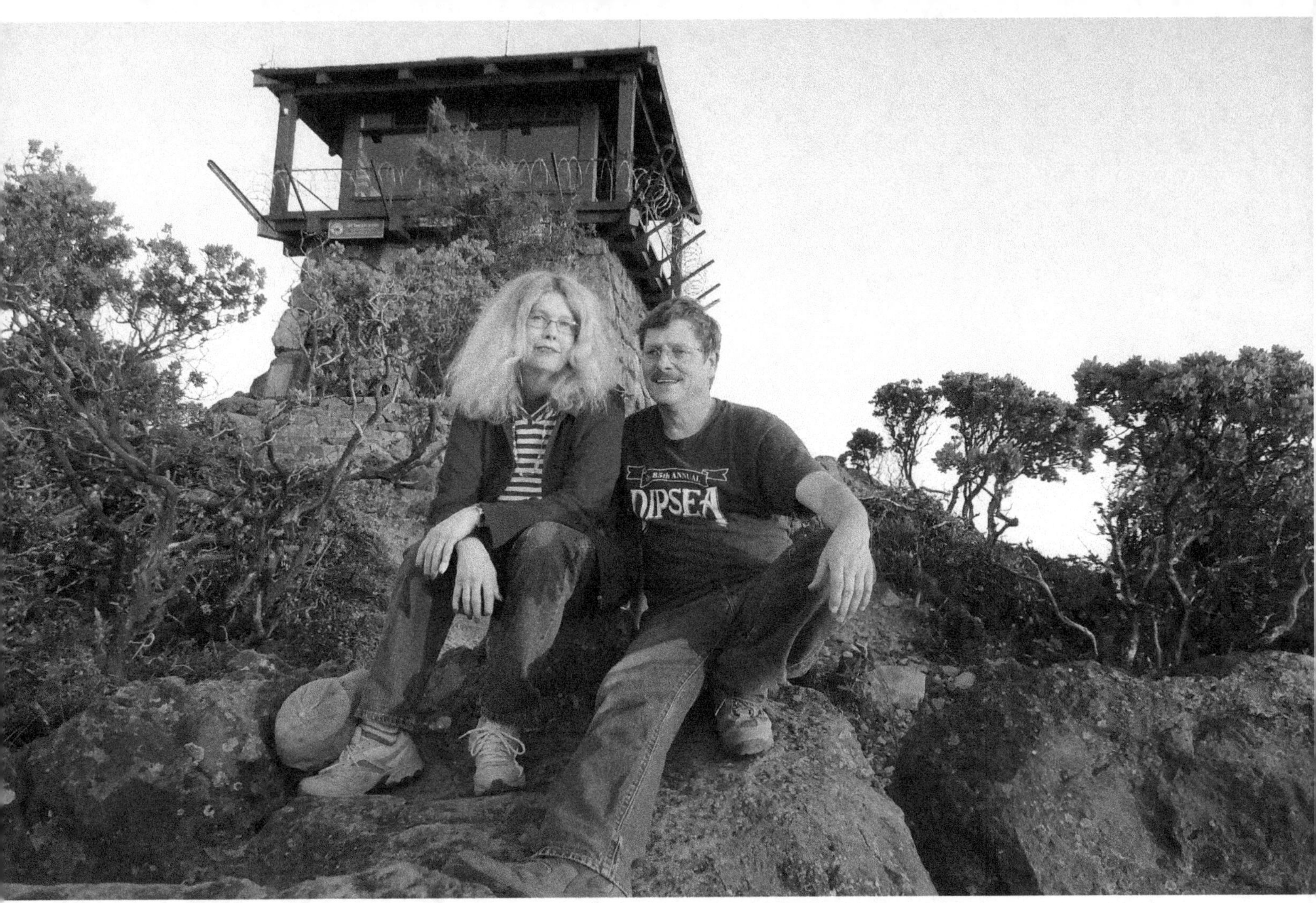

I've always claimed to be a cheap date. While not being in any way cheap, it doesn't take much to make me amused. When I smoked marijuana (started as a young teen) in joints, I didn't ever want much. For the last twenty years I've smoked out of a small bowled pipe. But one puff will get me coughing. I never did learn how to smoke! I'd take a puff and immediately my lungs would explode in a coughing fit. But even what I managed to inhale would be plenty for me. I'd stay high until I would eat to come down.

Thank the Goddess for Edibles! Glad to stop hurting my air intake, stopping smoking Pot was easy. Quitting cigarettes was the hardest thing I've ever done. I now eat just a teeny bit of an Edible. Like one fourth of a gummy bear. I don't want to get so high I get paranoid, which happened frequently when I smoked. I wish to take the hard edge off Life. I like to be positive. I don't want to see how cruel Life can be. Having negative thoughts nudges me into Depression. And being bipolar, Depression is a deep, dark, horrifying place. I don't think to eat a bite of Edible often, and I wonder why not! Not a hit, just a bit. This is my way of taking my medicine, I should remember to take it more often! Not to get high, really, just to achieve a sense of peace. I may need a reminder, but as I believe in a Peaceful Soul, I need just a small reminder. I certainly wish to remain aware and functioning.

Lucy and I were separated for years. When I attempted to serve Custody Papers on her father, I was shot at, which made the front page of the SF Chronicle. But since she turned 18, we've been mending fences, and have become friends over time. She has always been the Diamond in My Eye.

She is a lovely person; happily married now with three beautiful, smart kids. Paul and I have visited her and Mike and their children many times. He is the best cook I've ever known. He does it all in the kitchen. He smokes his own salmon overnight. Paul does cook very good simple food for me too. But Mike is the Chef!

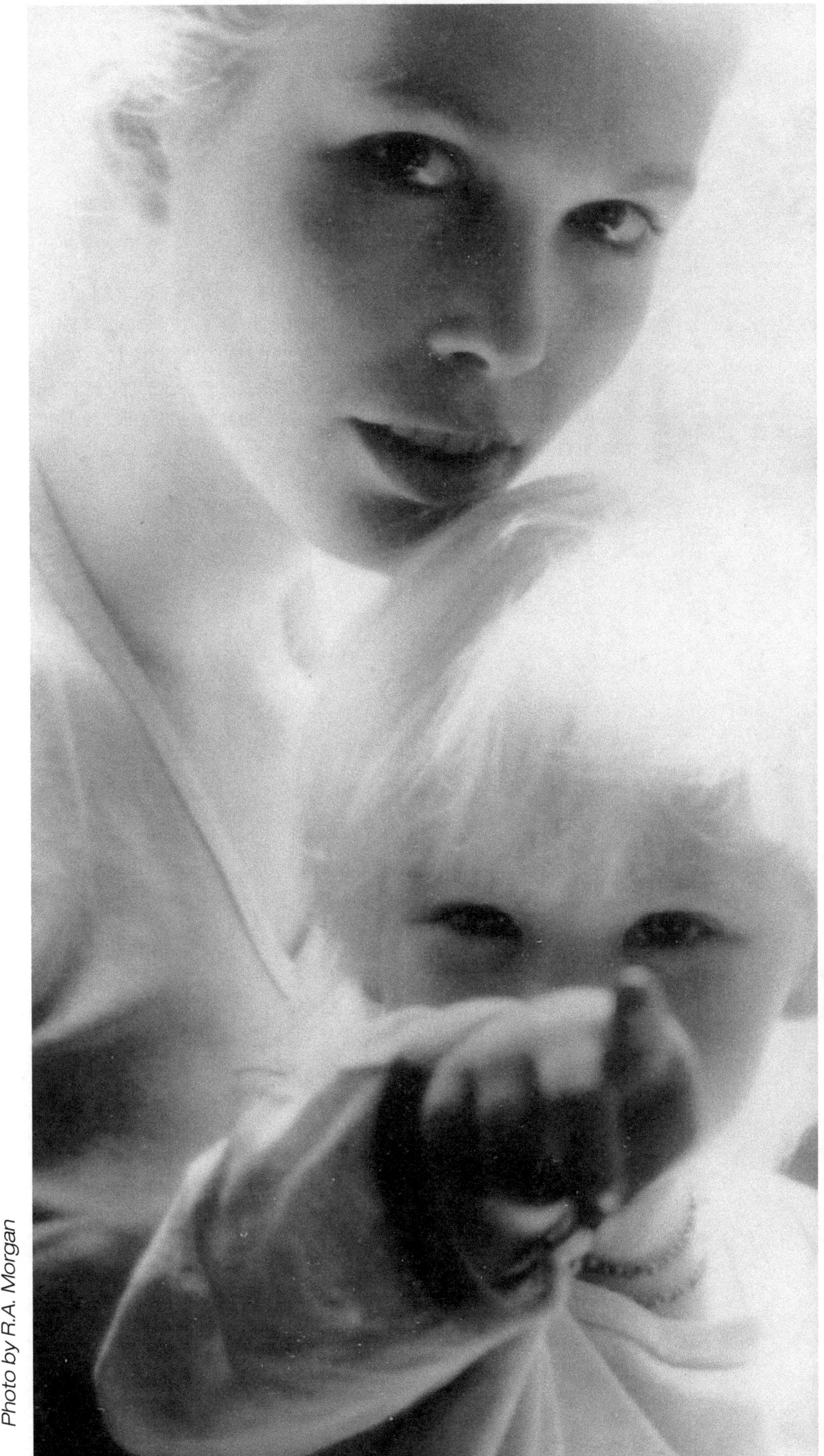

Photo by R.A. Morgan

So I keep on keepin' on. Time and Life go on. I want to leave a mark that I lived, through my artistic achievements, so I present this book to you. I am the Energizer Bunny of Creation. So much flows from my fingertips. I am blessed and just allow the Art to come through.

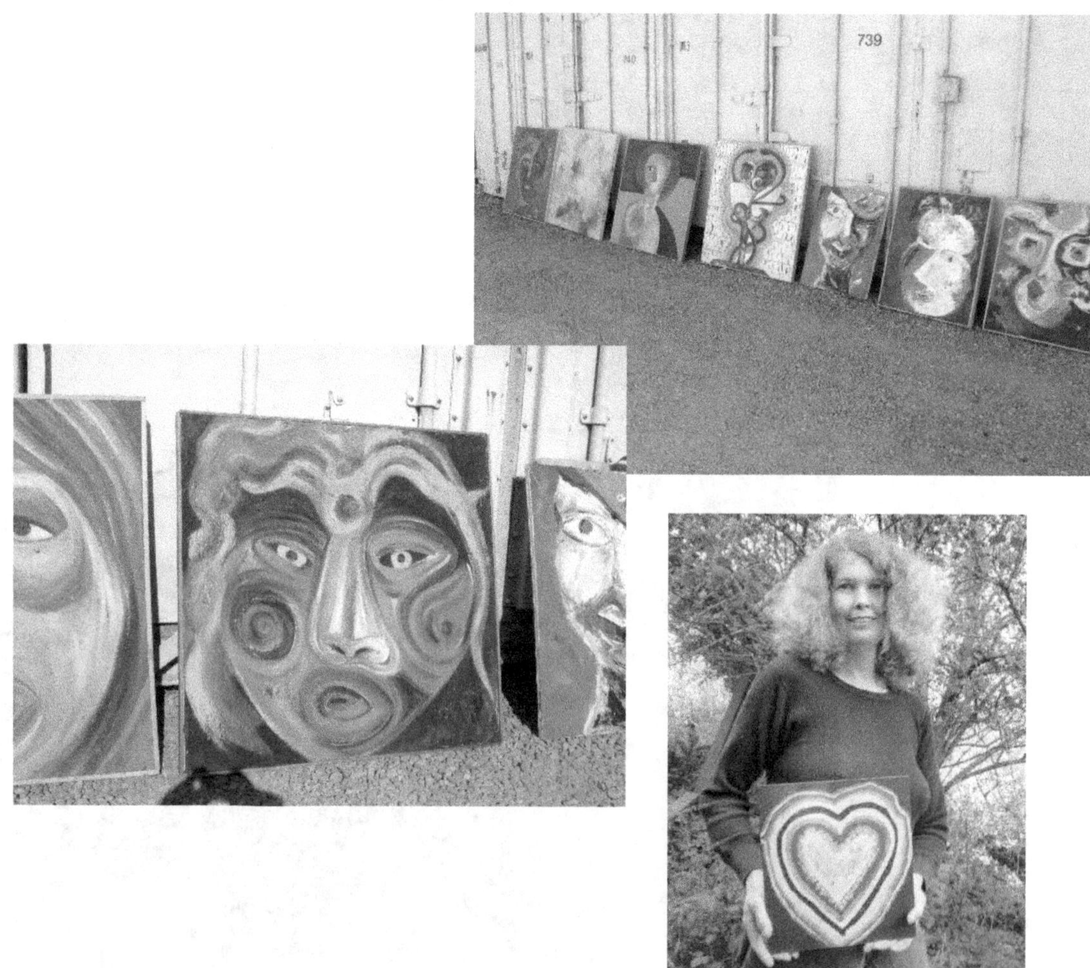

Prologue

To protect myself I keep my world quite small. So that I may deal with it through my Bipolar Disorder. If dealing with too many voices, circumstances, people, I can get confused. When confused, I get frazzled. When frazzled the Furies can descend on me. So I stay in Peace. The Death Cult have indulged themselves in the End Days. Not believing in their god, I see a better path ahead. I see the Evil side of the coin flip to the shiny side of Existence. I live my life with purpose, on purpose.

I do see a young girl named Greta attempting to tell the world it needs to change our route of destruction to our exquisite planet. We need to make huge changes now, already the Climate is raving out of control with floods and droughts and fires. Through our reaching, our achieving, our industrialization, we have lost contact with the natural way of things. We have forgotten the basic truth that every single thing is connected. If we poison, the planet gets poisoned.

We are connected to everything, and we with it. We are the air we breathe, the water that washes us, the light that falls upon us. We are the whole. We each may be on our separate path, but all paths make up the whole. I remember sometimes that I am dreaming of a butterfly, and that I am the butterfly.

Songs in the Silence

"Silence is the language of god,
all else is poor translation."
- Rumi

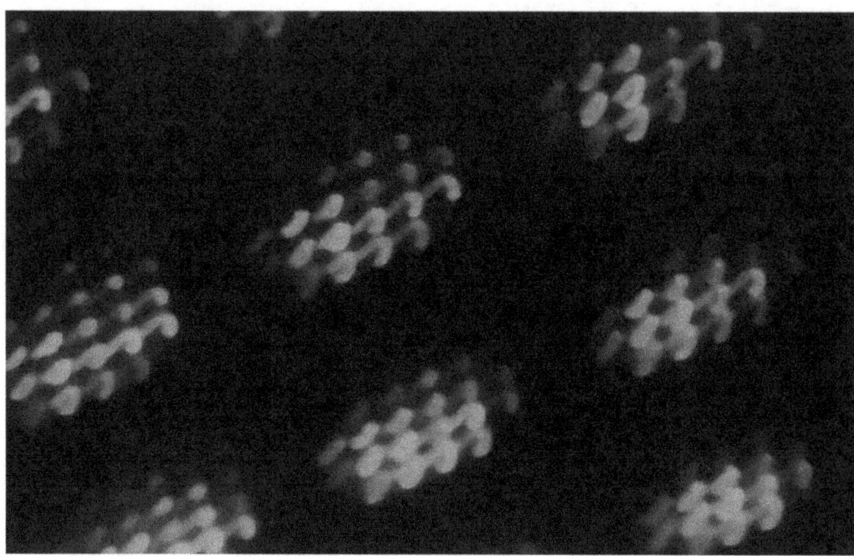

The Silence is the non-thing that makes up the glue between all things.

The Silence is where you might
delve in meditation,
when thought has quieted
and left you still.

The Silence is the place
between waking and sleeping,
before the dreams,
after the business of action.

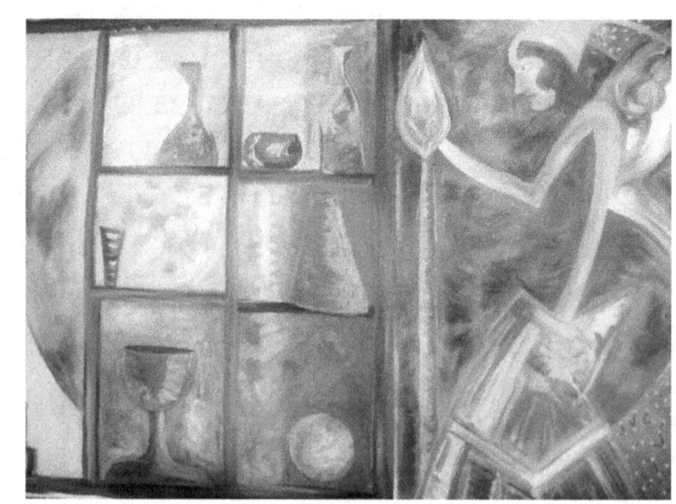

Silence can be filled by many thoughts, dreams, and more Silence.

Silence is what we never hear. But there are songs in the Silence.

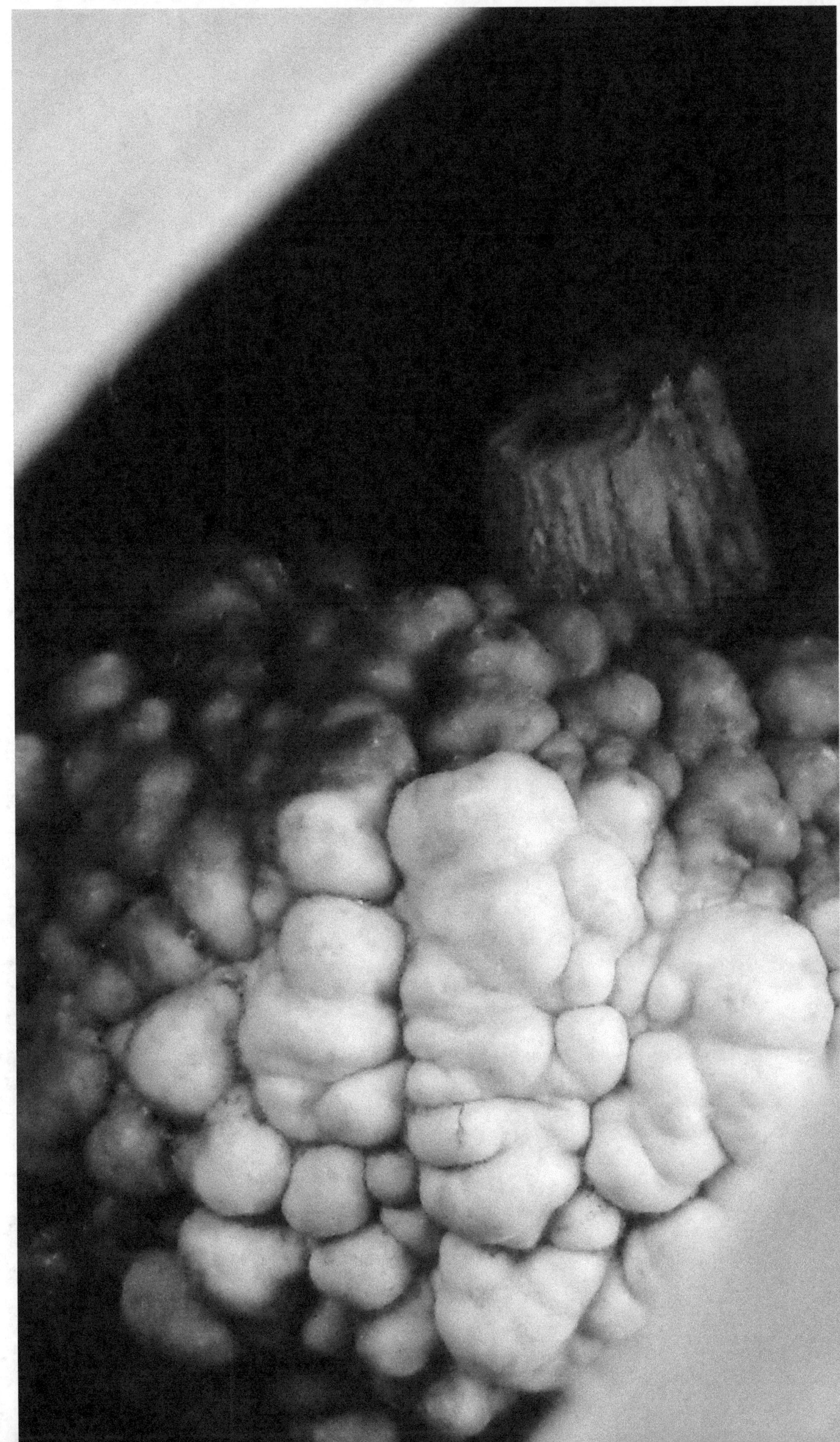

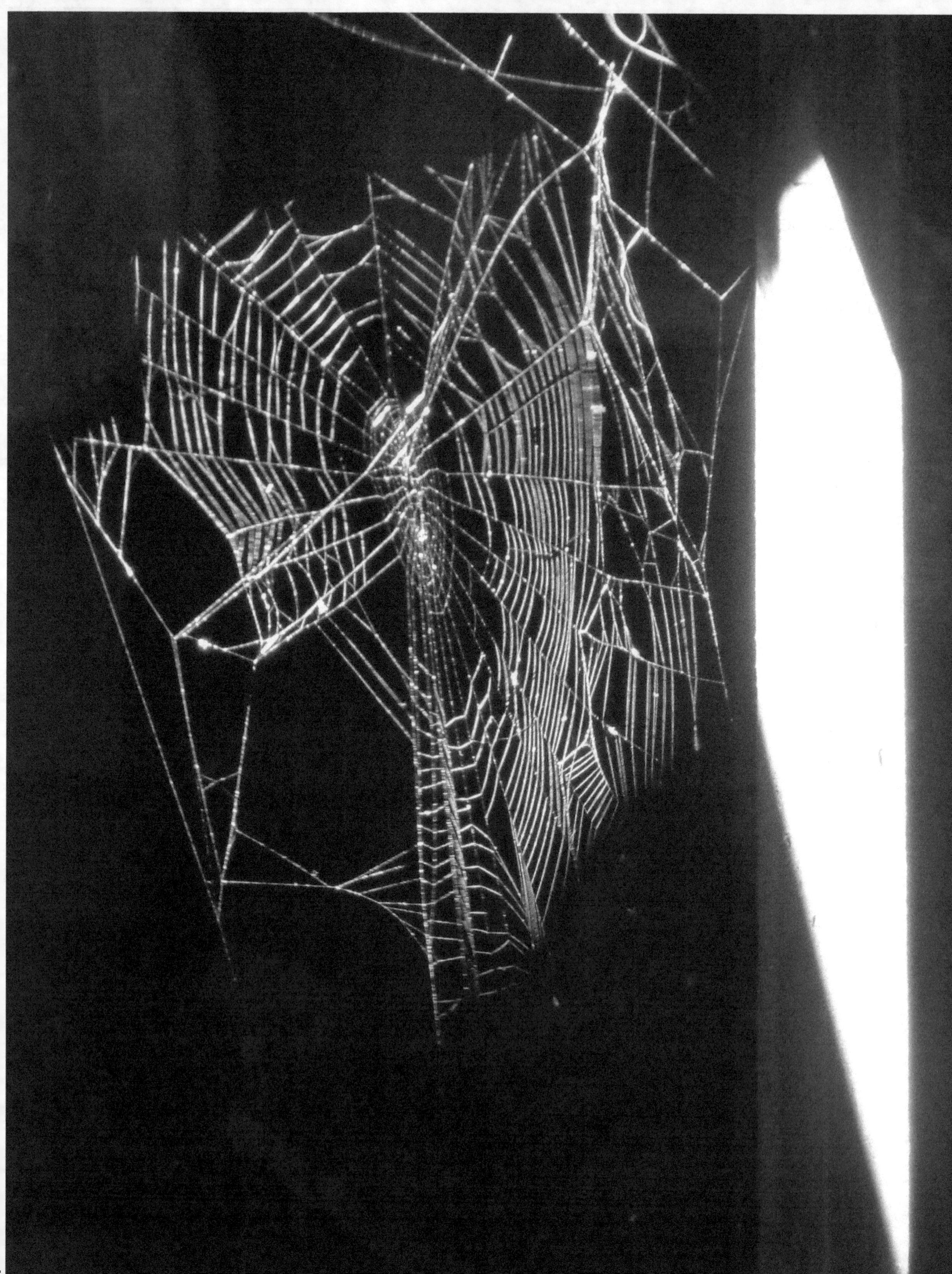

Silence is the ringing out of all from nothing.

Silence must be enjoyed, there is so little of it.
Crowded are the places between Silence.

The Silence is the breath of Divinity.
Silence is the Source.

Silence is both a noun and a verb.
The noun can be peaceful, the verb can be violent.

As with most things,
opposites touch to complete a full circle.

I hope that Silence as a noun has been around longer!

Silence is said to be golden,
which is a nice way of saying shut-up, please.

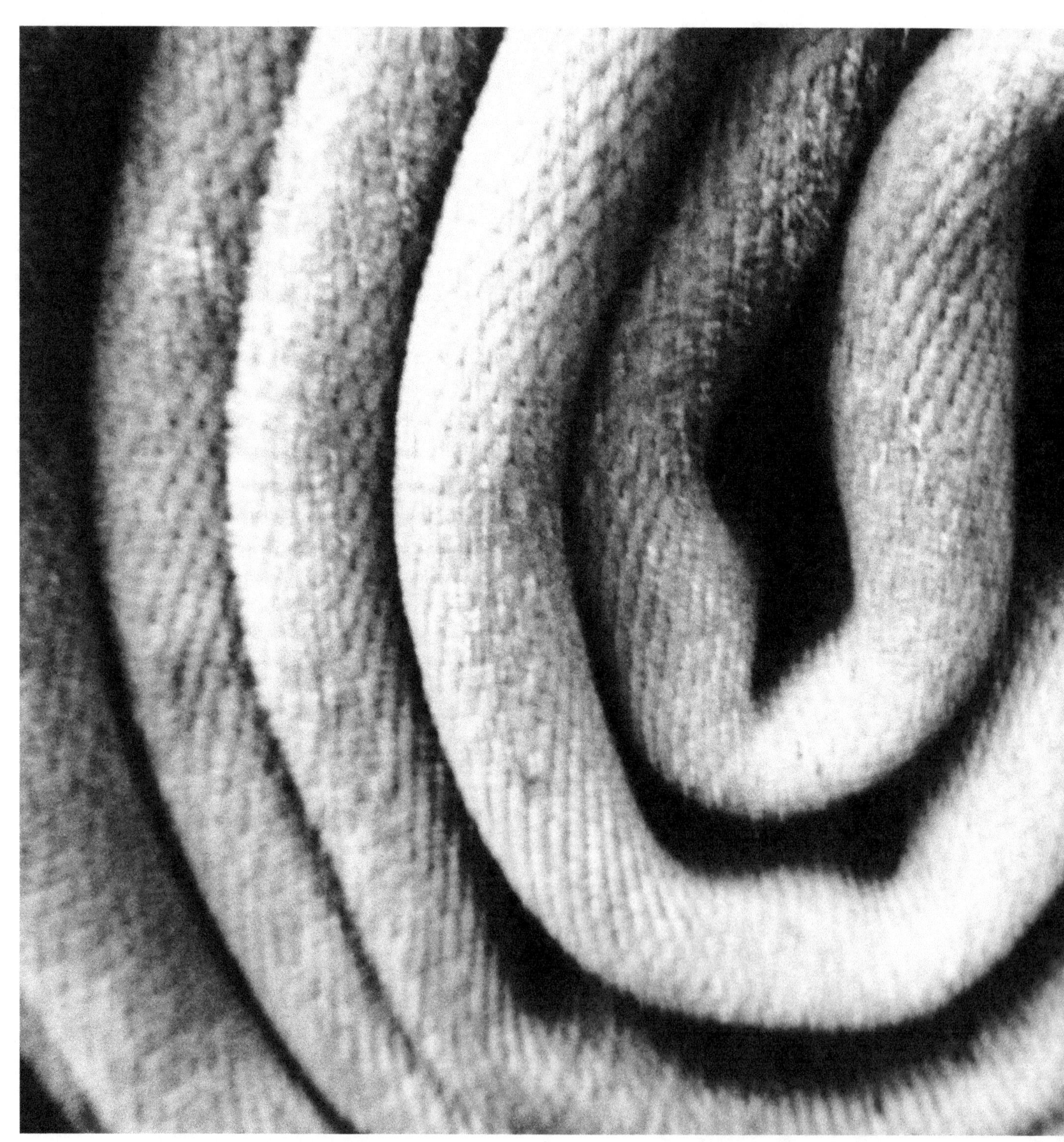

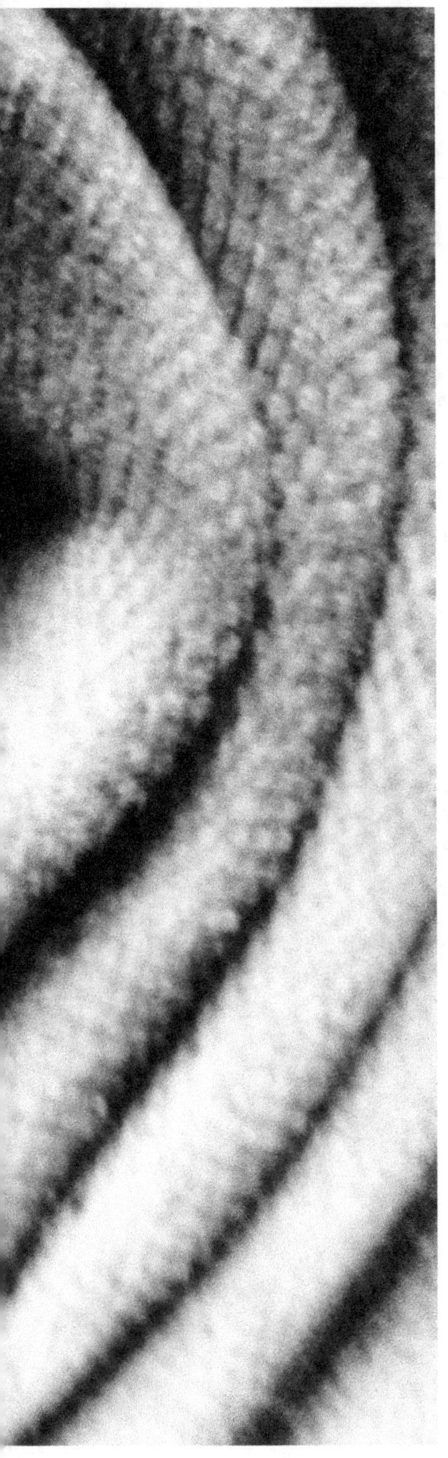

Dusk is like the Silence, the slot of the day that seems to hold it's breath in anticipation of the night.

Between the bright sun and the stars, the dusk is Silent and has no color, only the shadow pale.

"The music is not in the notes,
but in the silence between."
- Wolfgang Amadeus Mozart

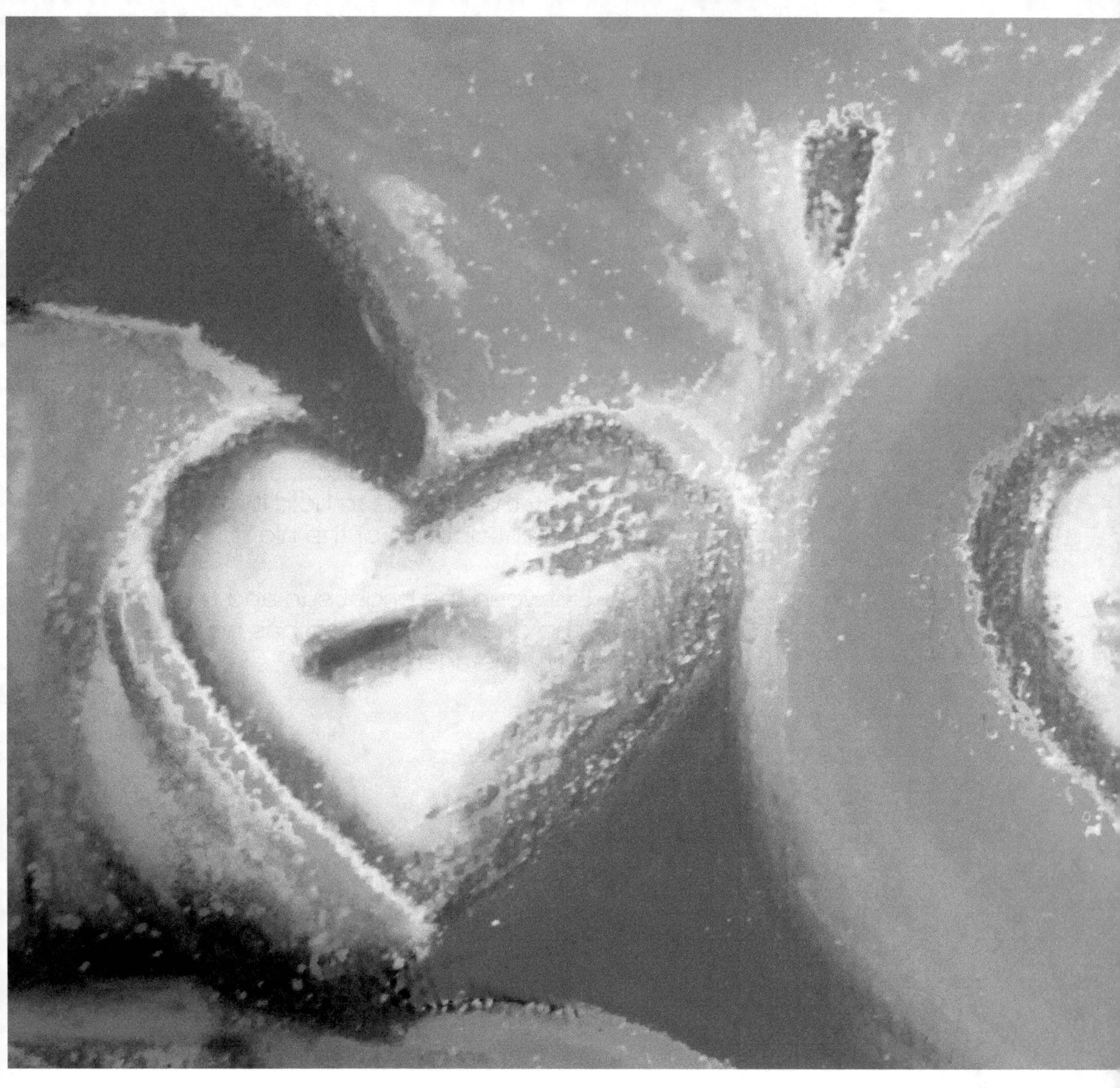

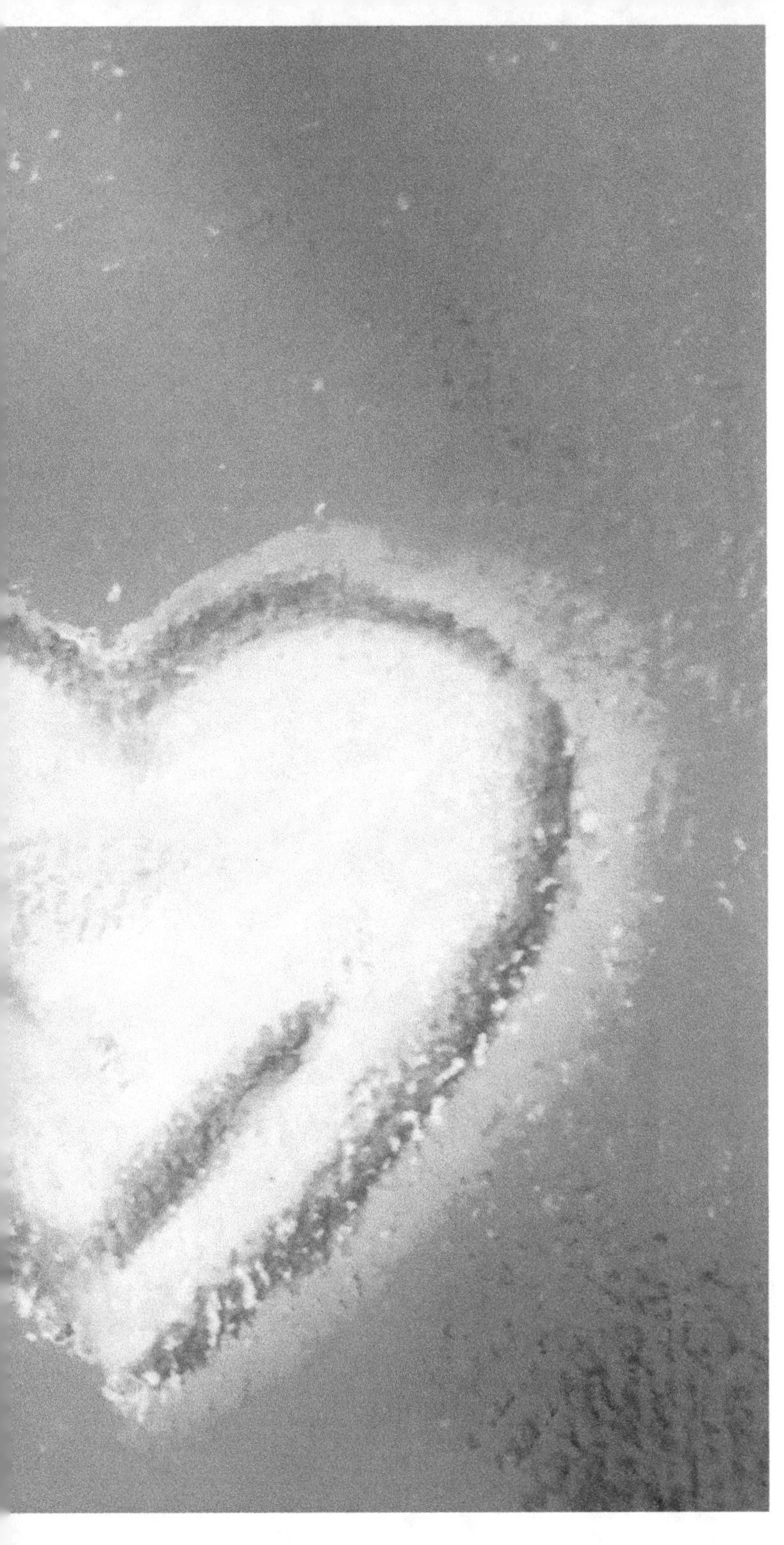

A Poem

I find myself to find me sobbing,
Only regret can cause these heaves.
Not having said something, done something.
If you are still crying,
You need to stop sobbing now.

Section One

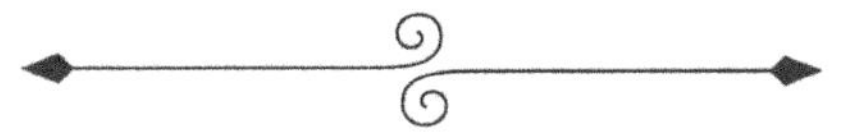

What I have learned

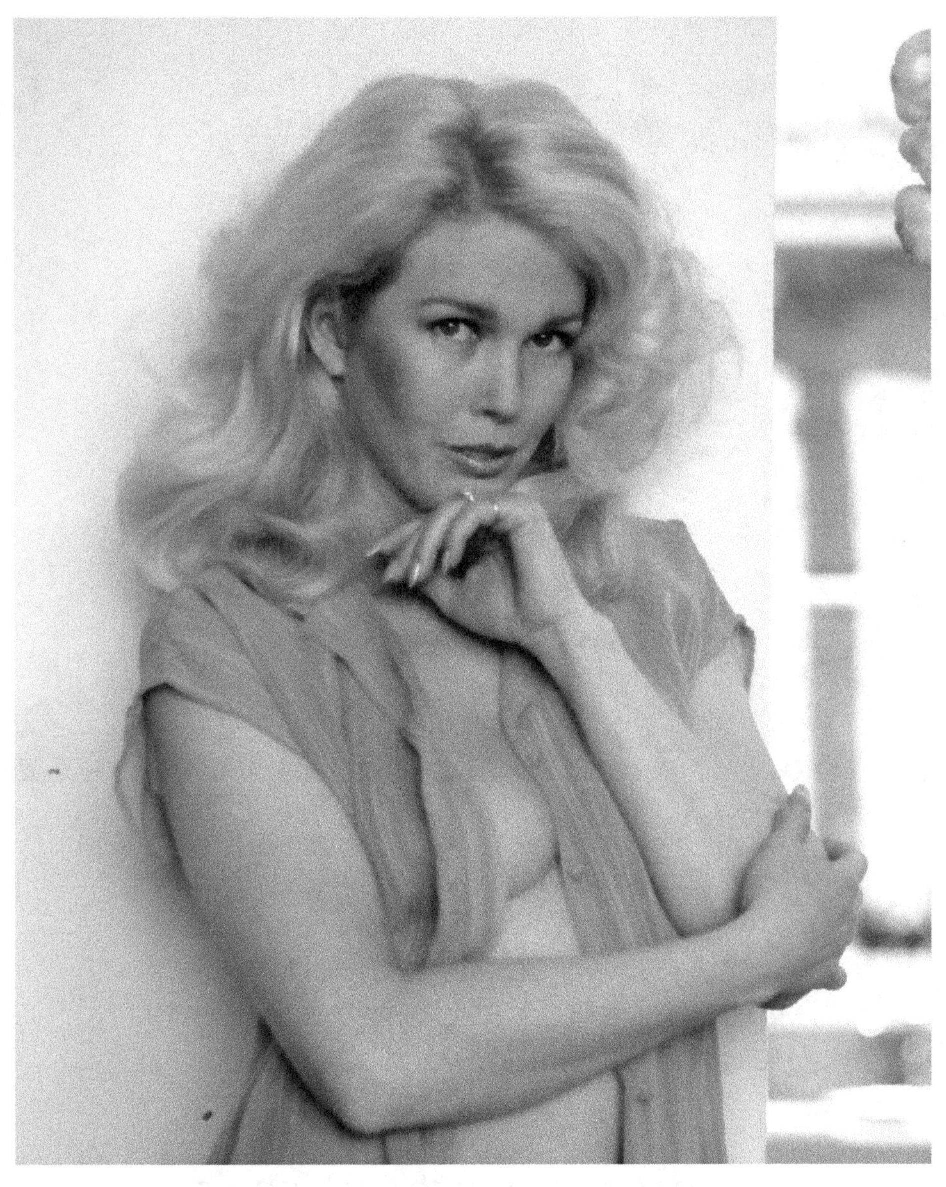

What I have learned *from Lovers*

"All you need is Love. Love is all you need."
- The Beatles

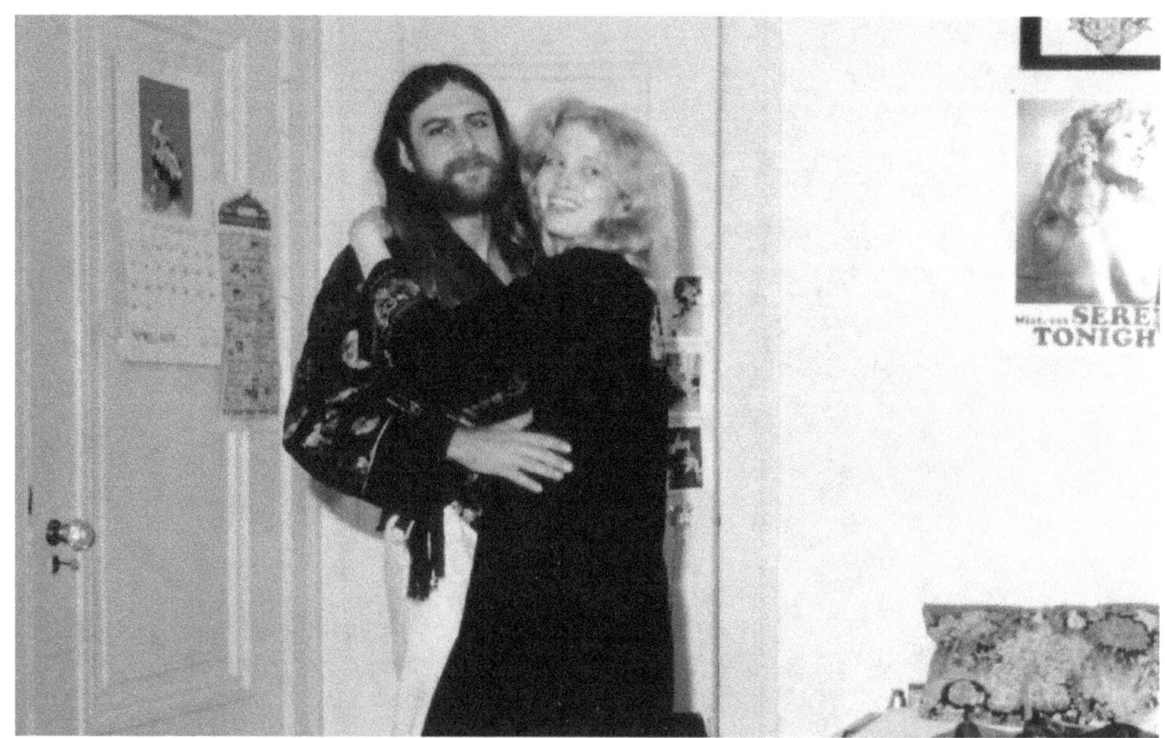

First Husband

I loved you too much.
I was unable to handle my emotions.
Though we can't seem to get along,
I thank you for our daughter.

Serena Czarnecki with first husband.

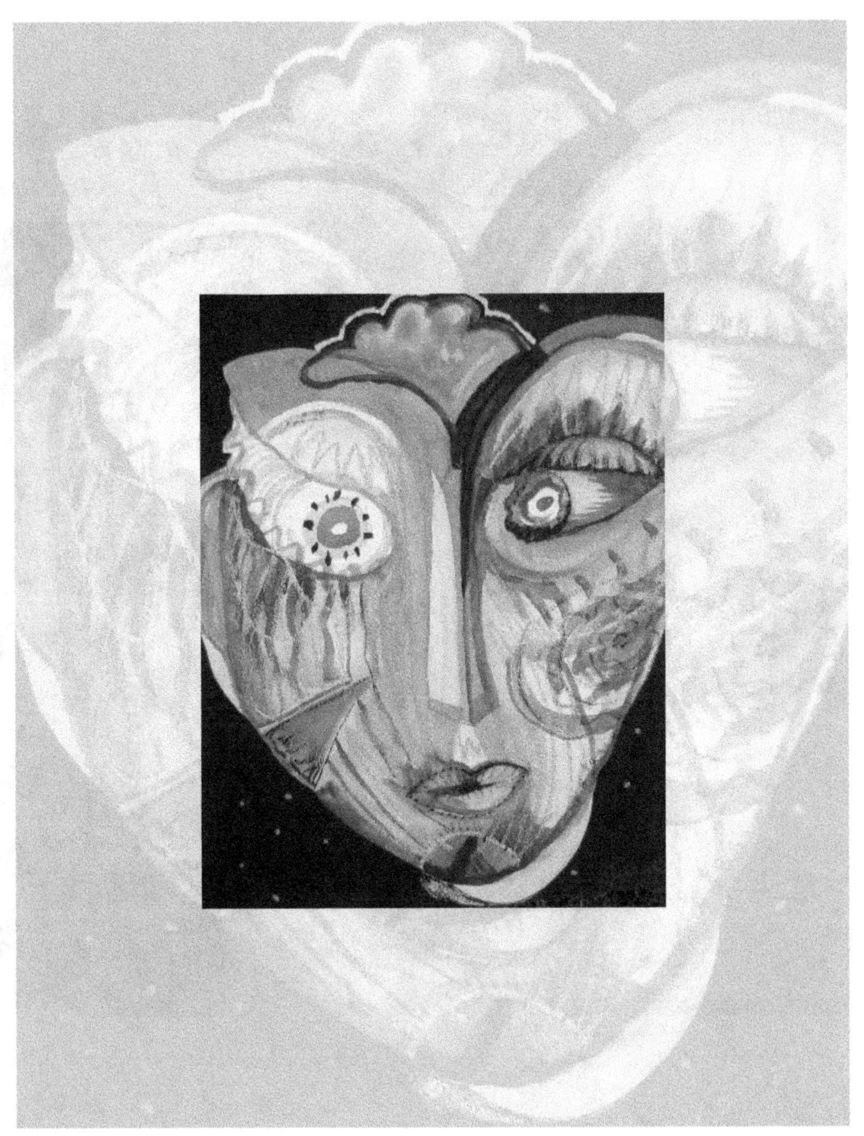

Second Husband

Do *not* believe everything you are told.

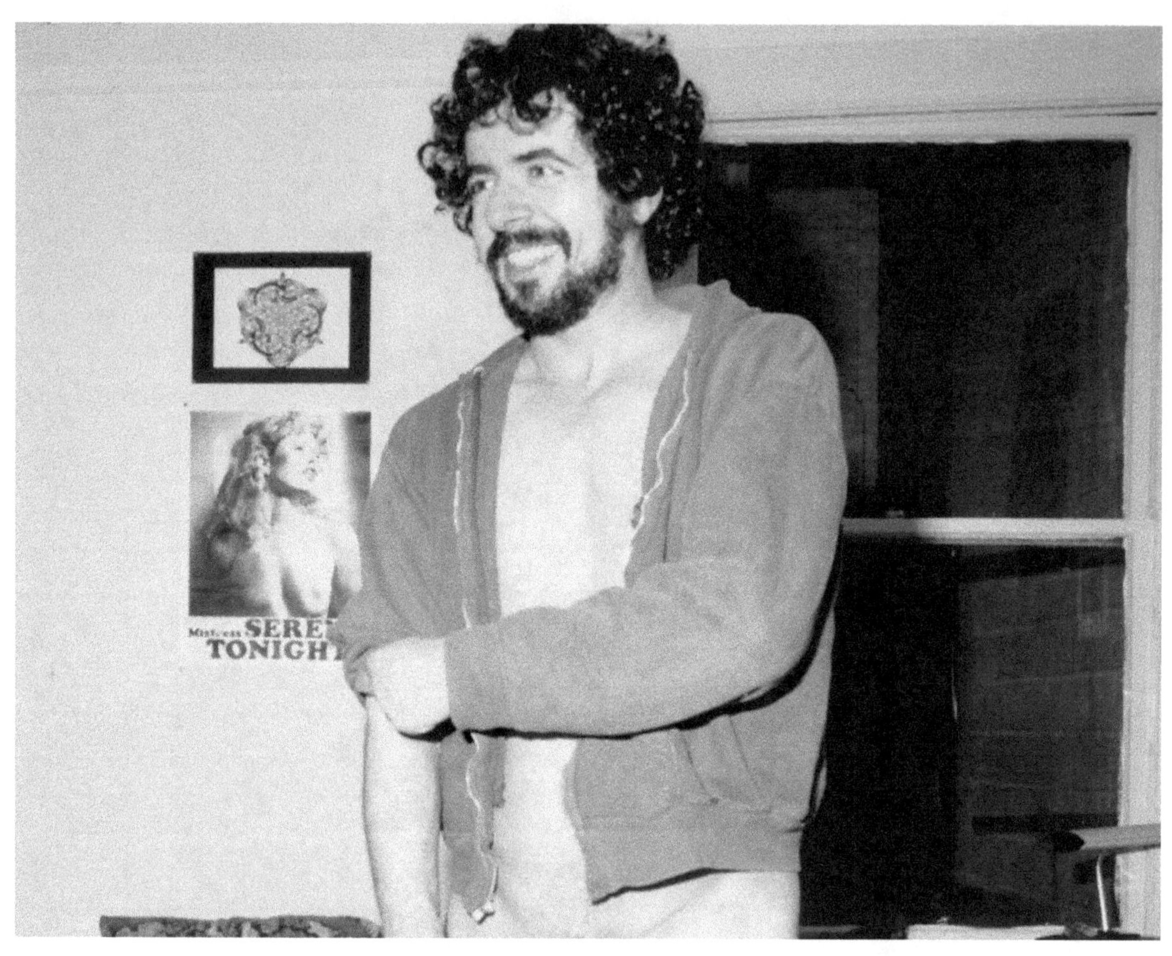

Jamie Gillis, XXX Super-Star

That you can be gentle while doing bondage.

That you can be charming and a beast at the same time.

That you can die of Cancer from smoking cigarettes.

Photo by R.A. Morgan

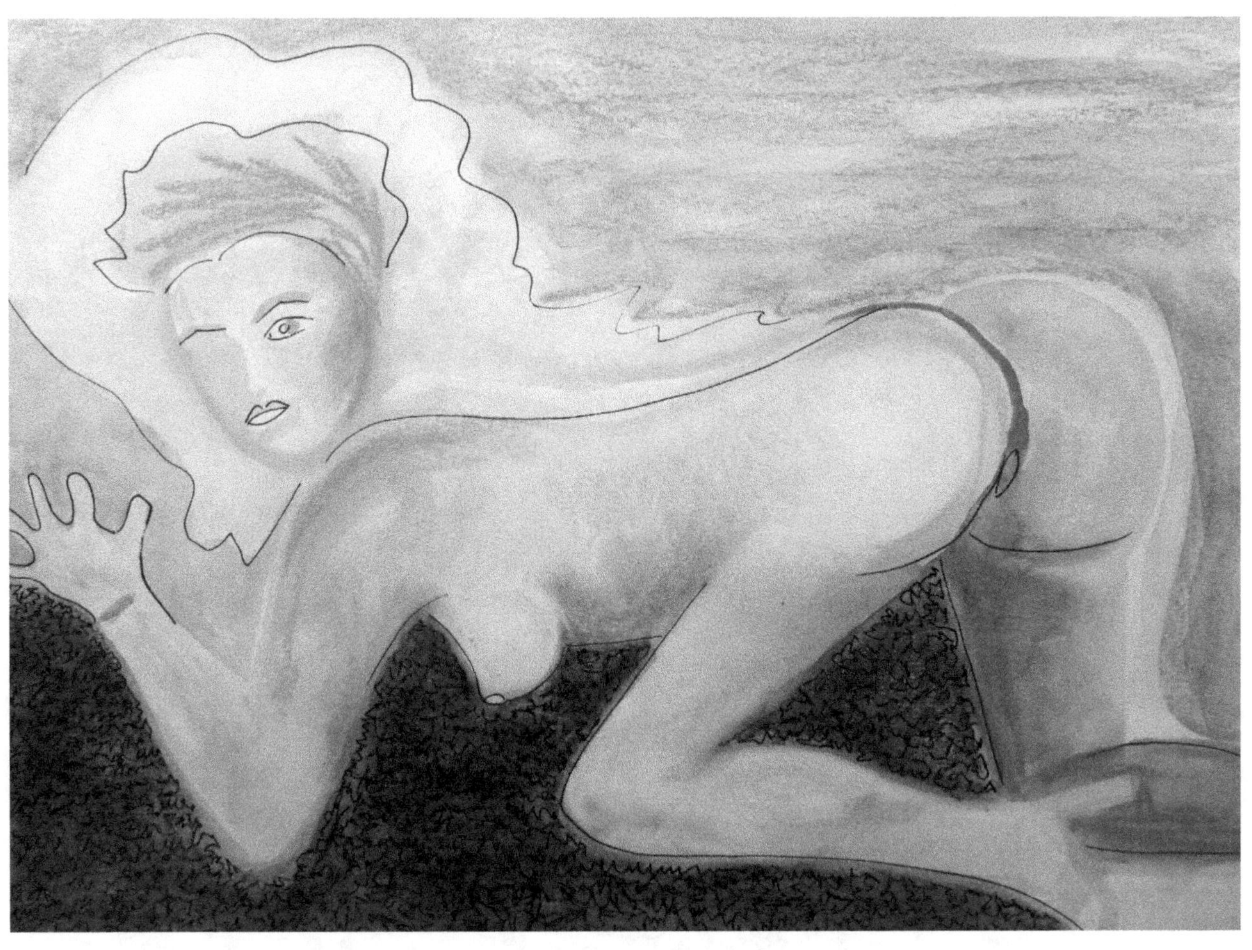

Diana

Taught me how to make love with a woman on her living room floor.

Watercolor with Pen and Pastel on paper by Serena Czarnecki

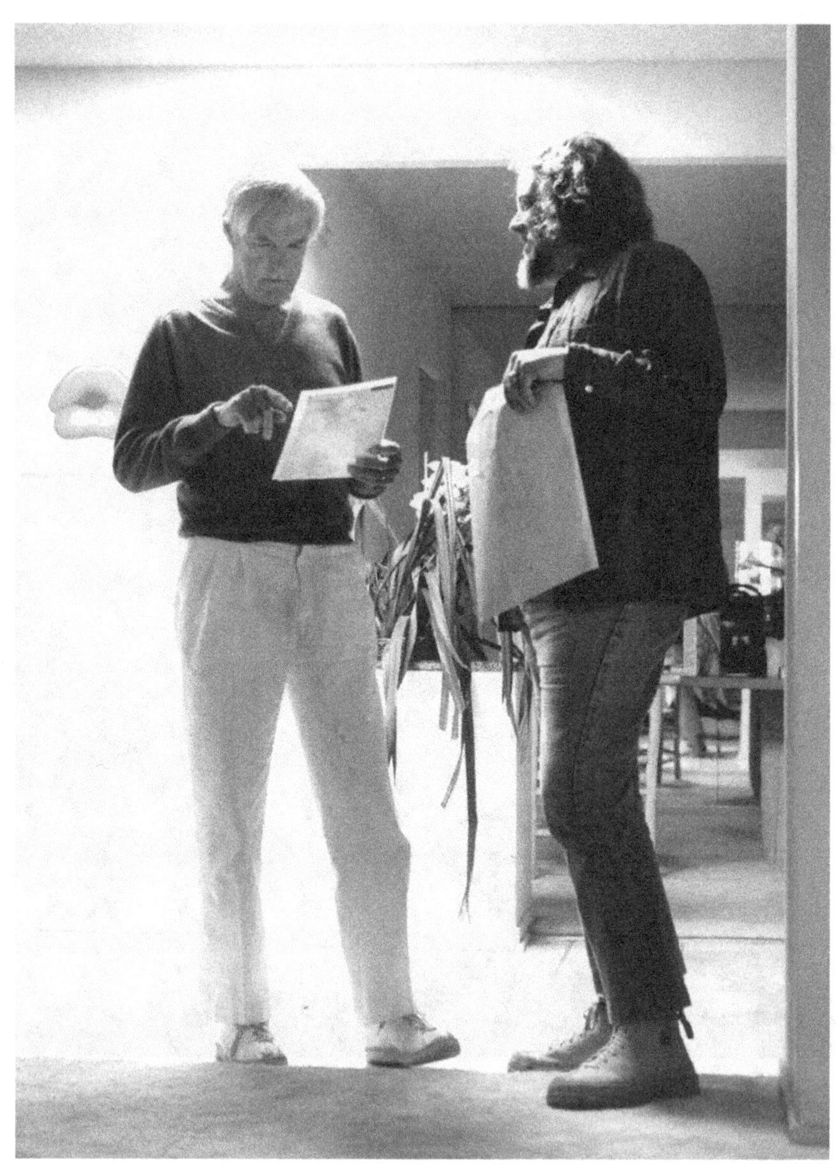

Michael Bowen, Visual Artist

Michael coined the phrase "human be in" that led to the 1967 counterculture event that drew Hippies to San Francisco. The event in San Francisco's Golden Gate Park inspired a string of 60's era endeavors such as Rowan and Martin's Laugh-In and John and Yoko's Bed-In.

Michael taught me in Mexico to scrape your fingernails across the soap when washing your hands. And how to open a garlic clove by smashing it with the flat of a knife. He introduced me to many famous people.

Photo of Timothy Leary and Michael Bowen by Serena Czarnecki

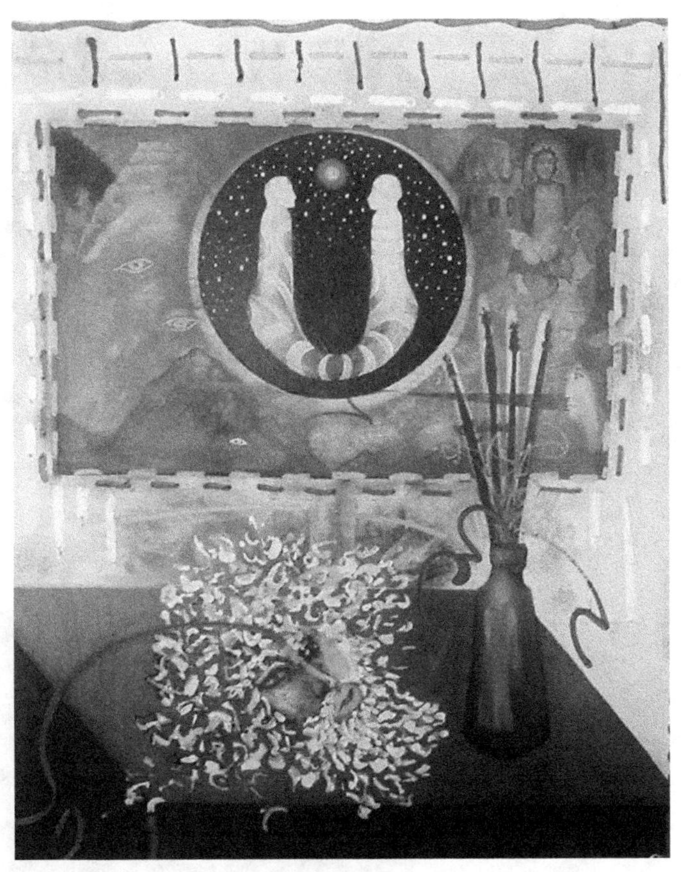

He did teach me about Art, I was his Apprentice.
I've always admired his paintings.

I, alas, also learned many bad habits from him.

But I love his children as my own.

Painting by Michael Bowen, owned by Serena Czarnecki

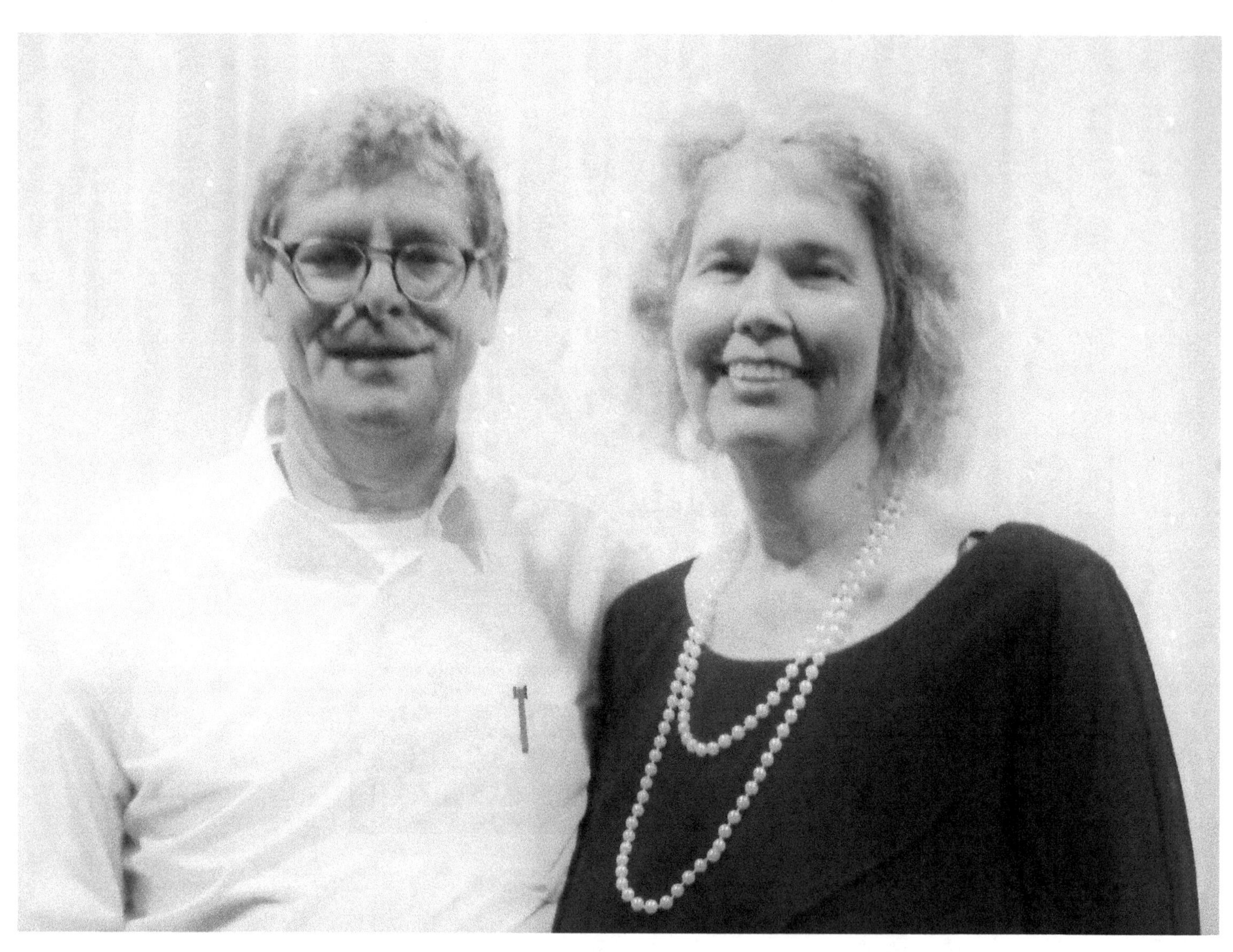

My Paul

To not follow, but to walk beside your friend.

Paul and I, taken at my daughter's wedding.

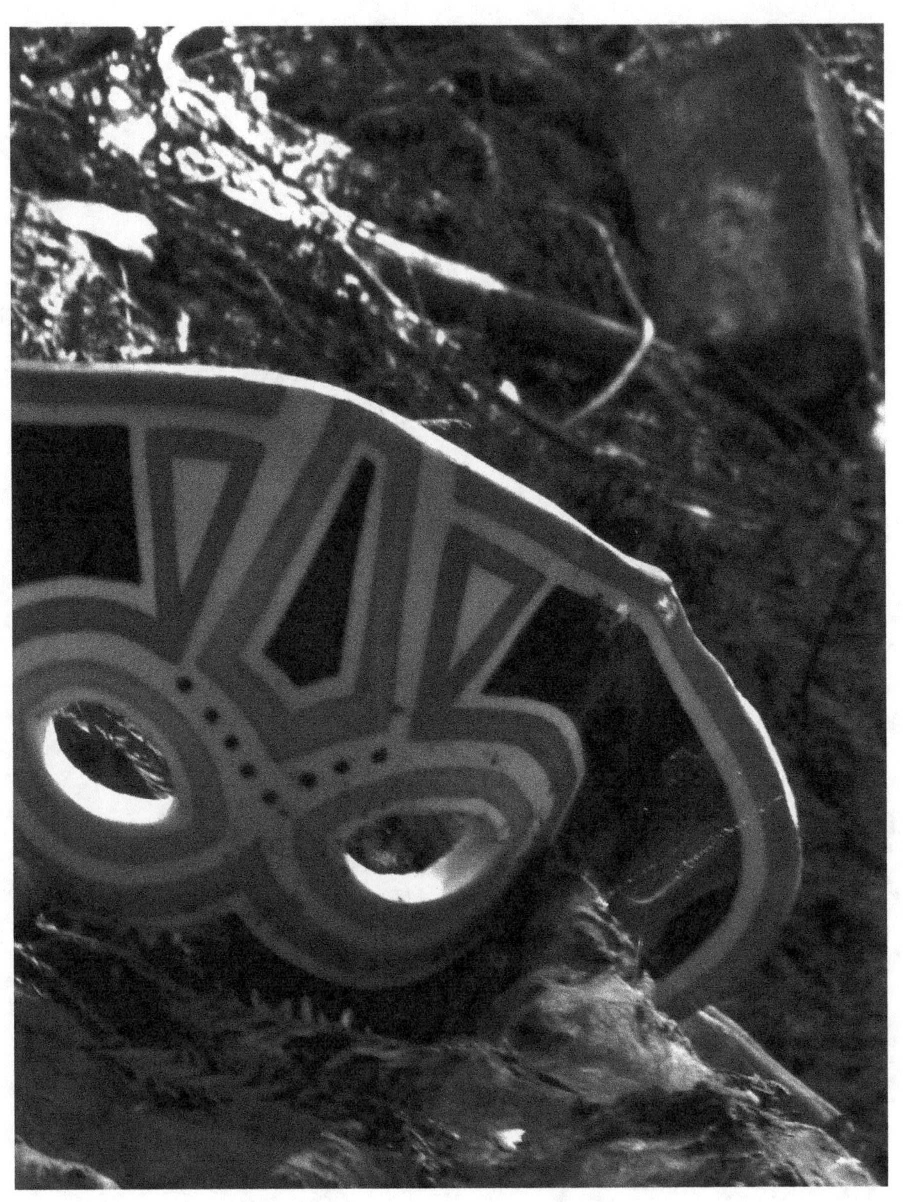

Tanya

That black is indeed beautiful.

Sculpture by Serena Czarnecki

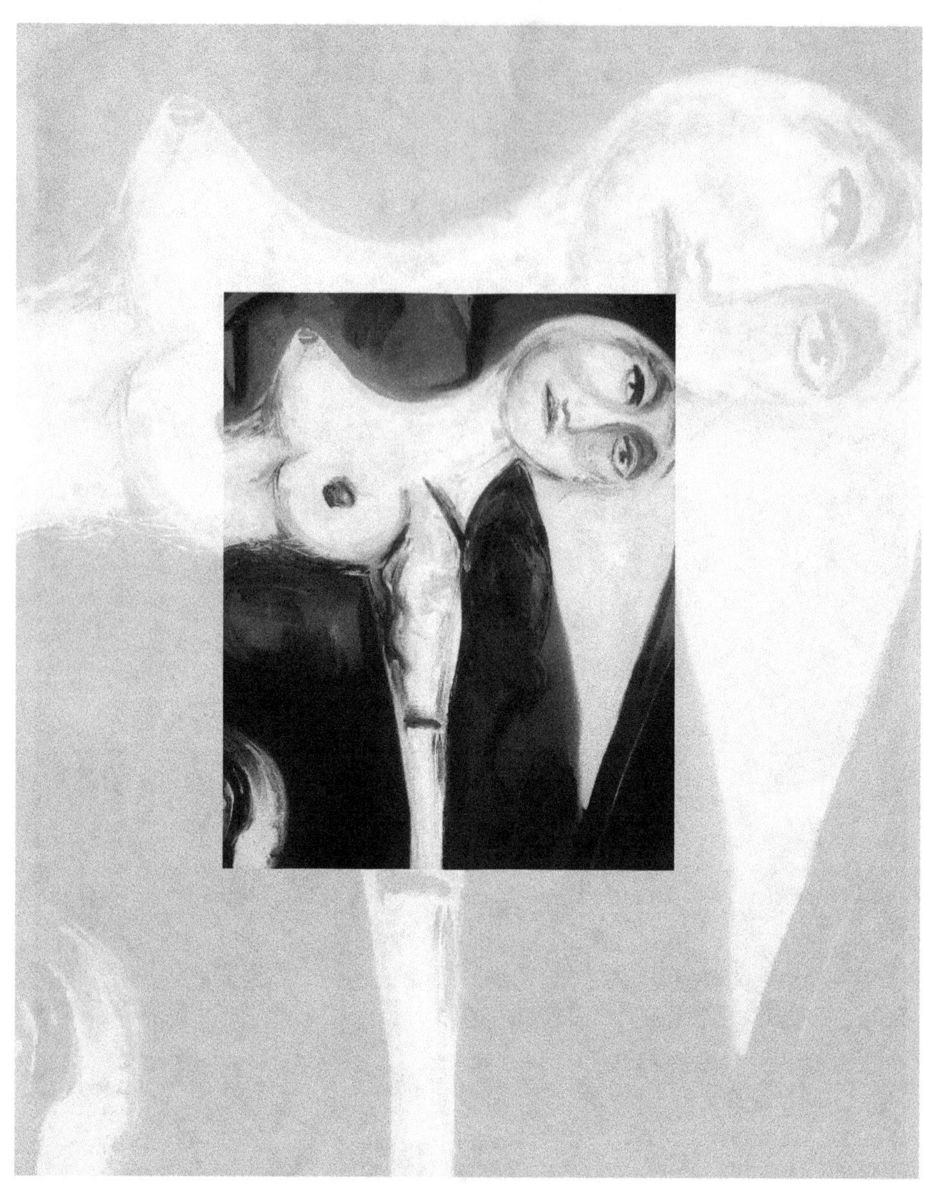

Wicked Wanda

Great things come in small packages.
Lots of love can be in a tiny body.

Oil painting on canvas by Serena Czarnecki.

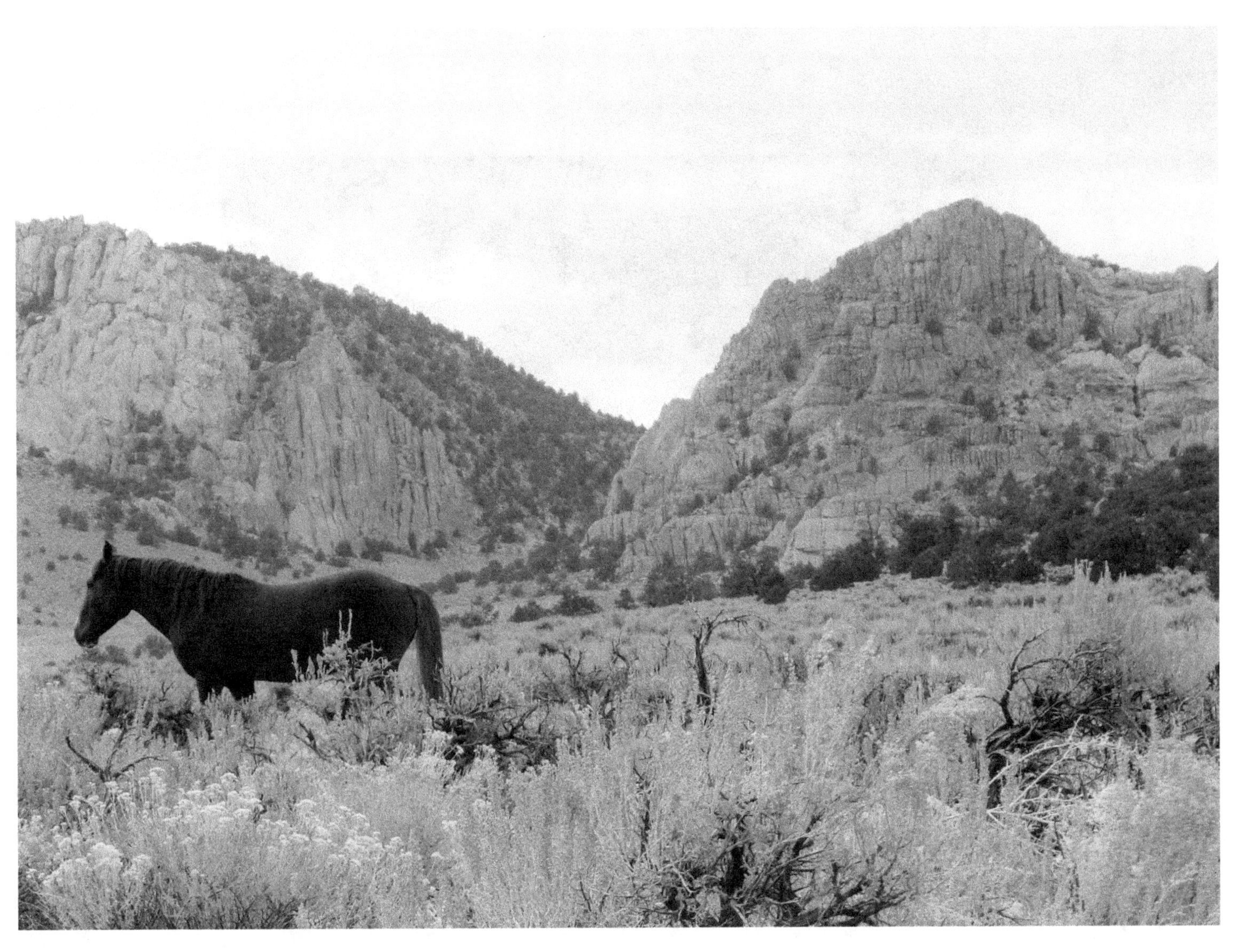

Morgan

Wild horses couldn't drag me away.

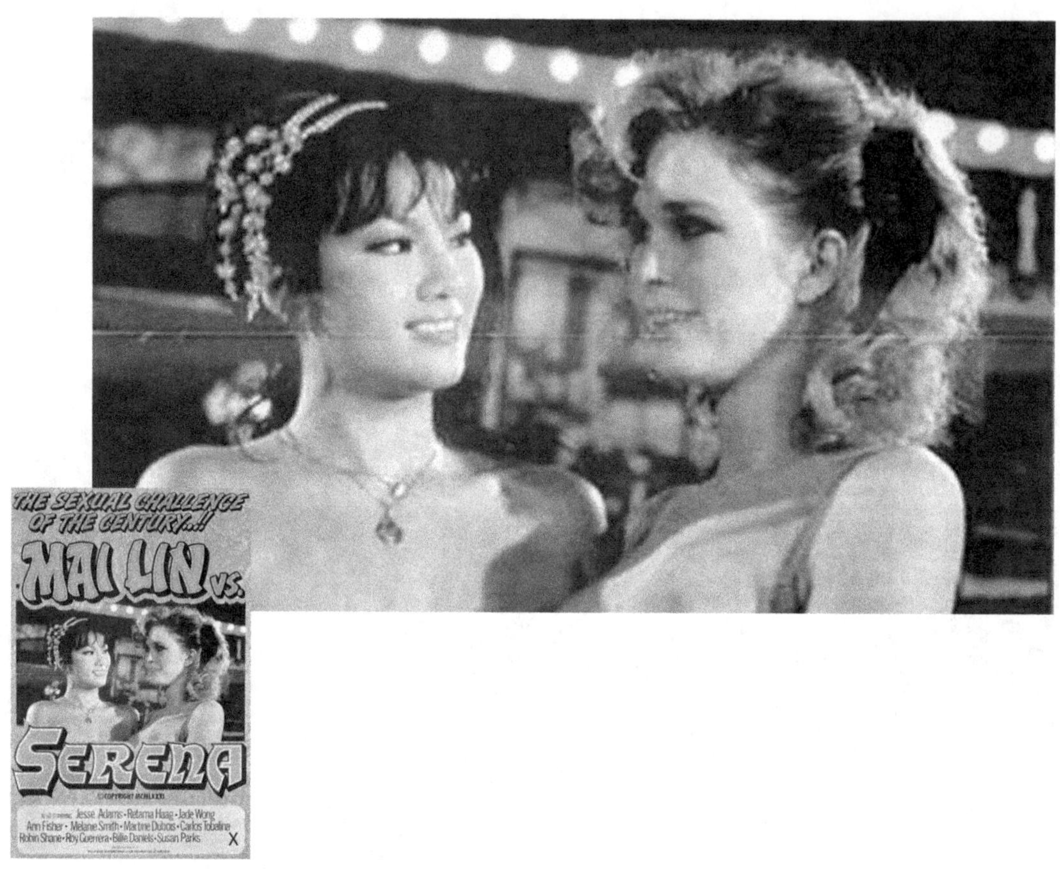

Mai Lin, XXX Star

That you can be bright, pretty and submissive.

We made movies with each other in Los Angeles.
We danced together at the Mitchell Brothers O'Farrell Theatre in San Francisco. We had fun!

Mai Lin vs. Serena box cover.

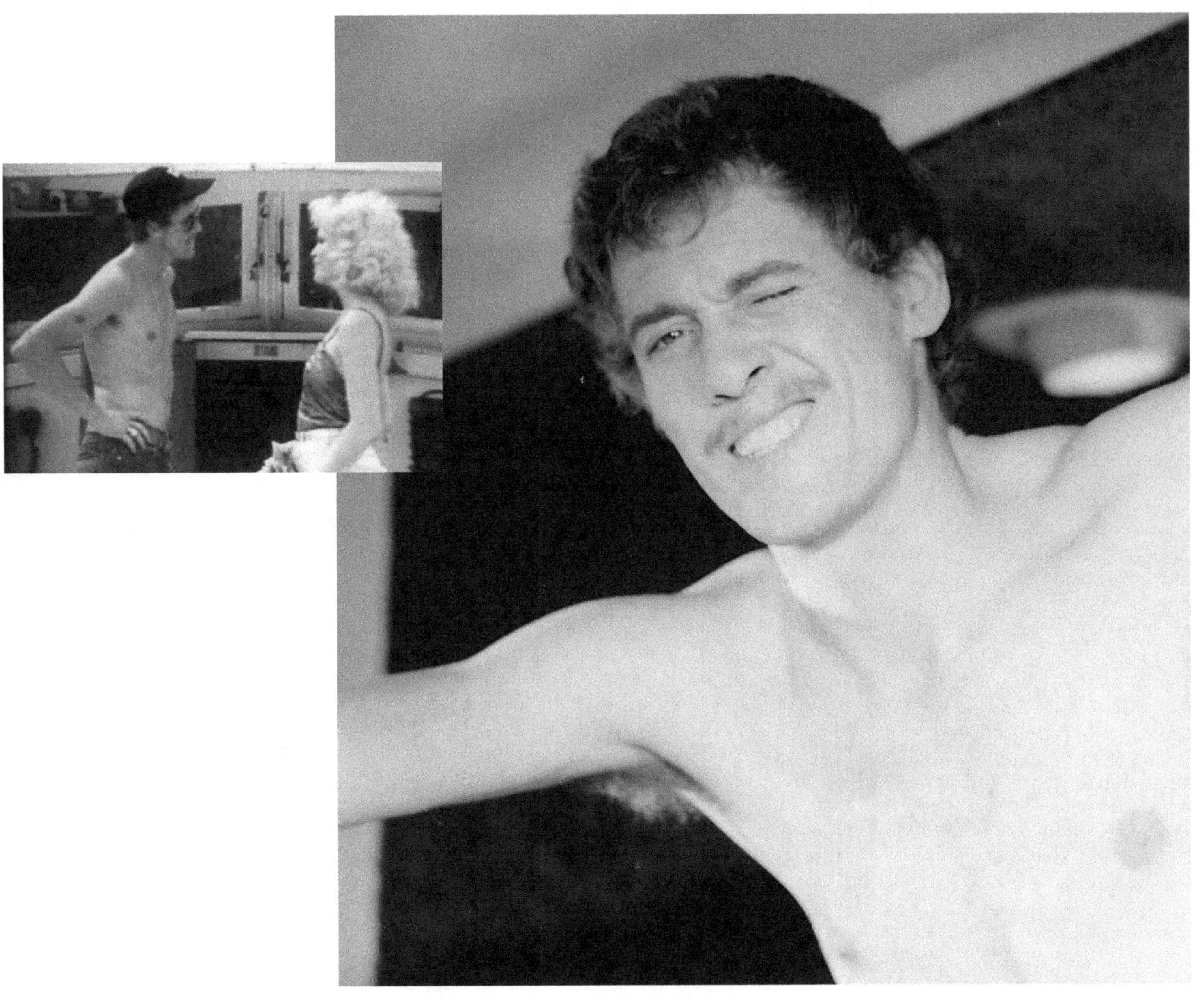

John Holmes, XXX Super-Star

You can make a good living by using the gift with which you were born.

John and Serena discussing a scene.

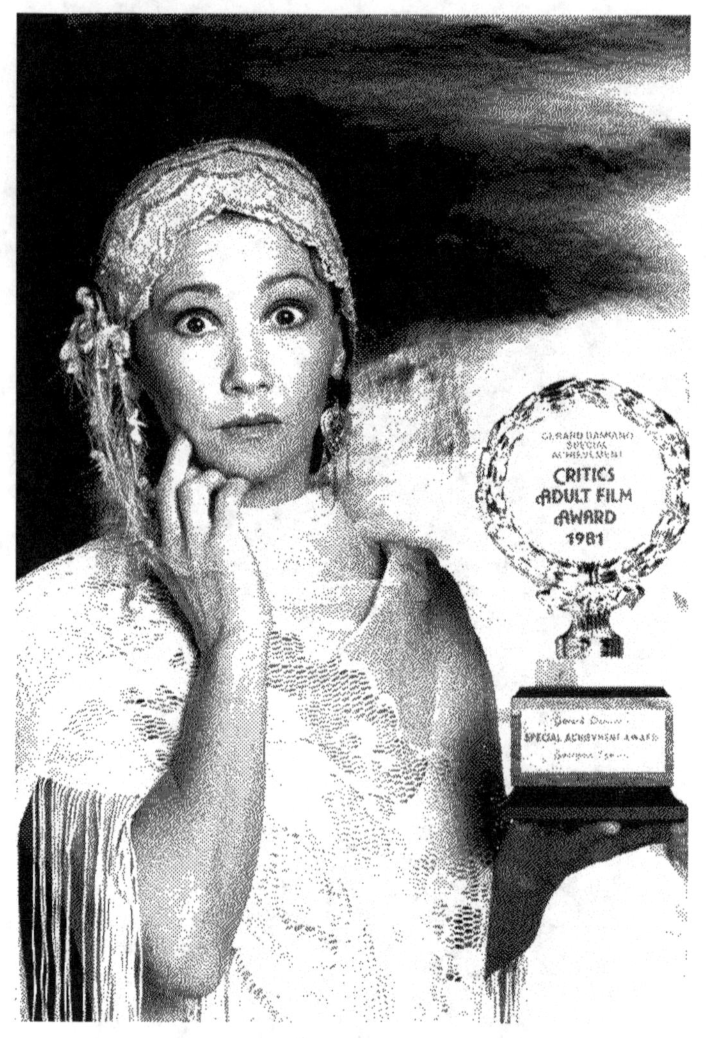

Georgina Spelvin, Actor, XXX SuperStar

I learned so very much from this woman!
She was a great actress and
chose to work with her sexual body.

I delighted in her presence, and her pussy!

Thanks, Georgina, for the use of the photo!

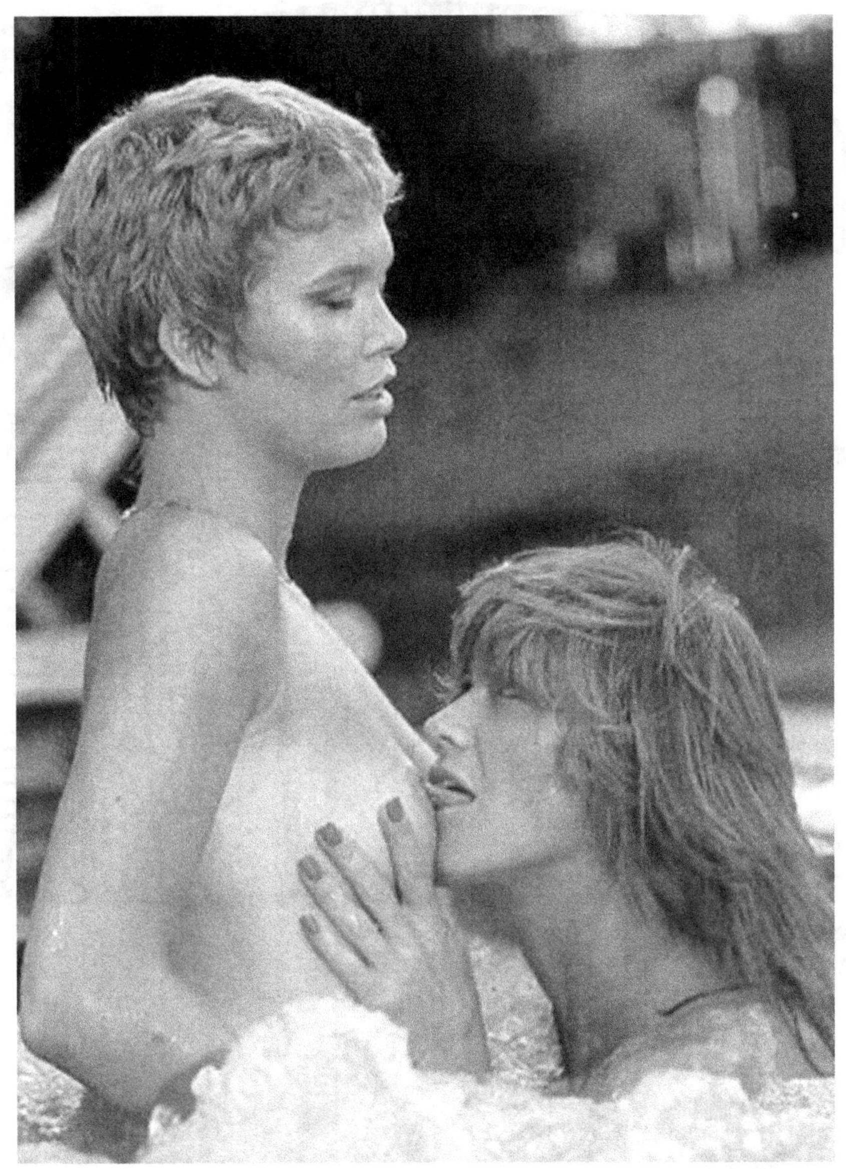

Marilyn Chambers, XXX SuperStar

She used the fountainhead of physical pleasure as the creative force.

Androgenous is hot, hot, hot.

Photo used with permission of McKenna Taylor

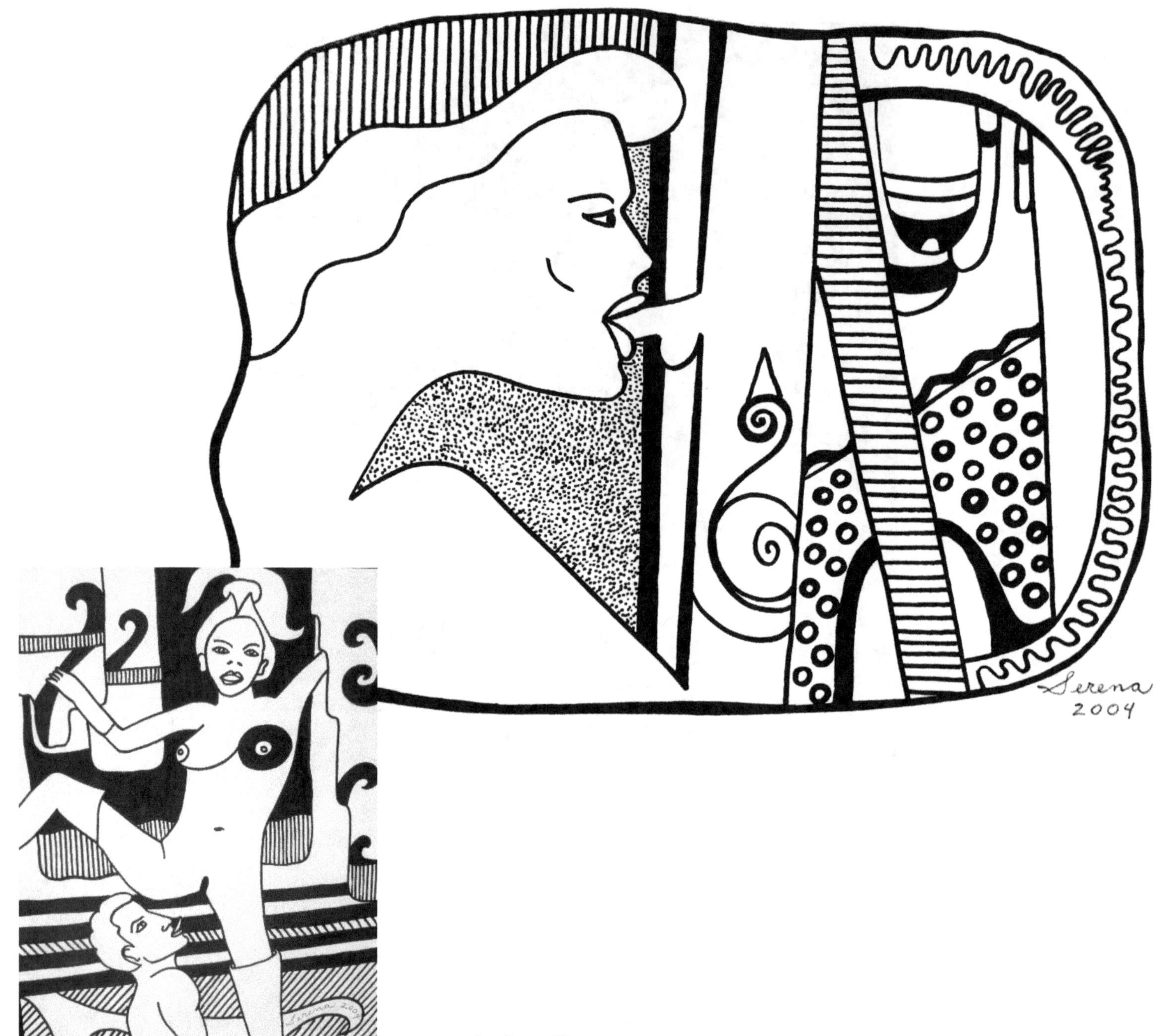

John Seeman

Erotica's "Go-To Cock"

I learned that hot stuff can be packaged
in a brown paper wrapping.

Pen and Ink by Serena Czarnecki

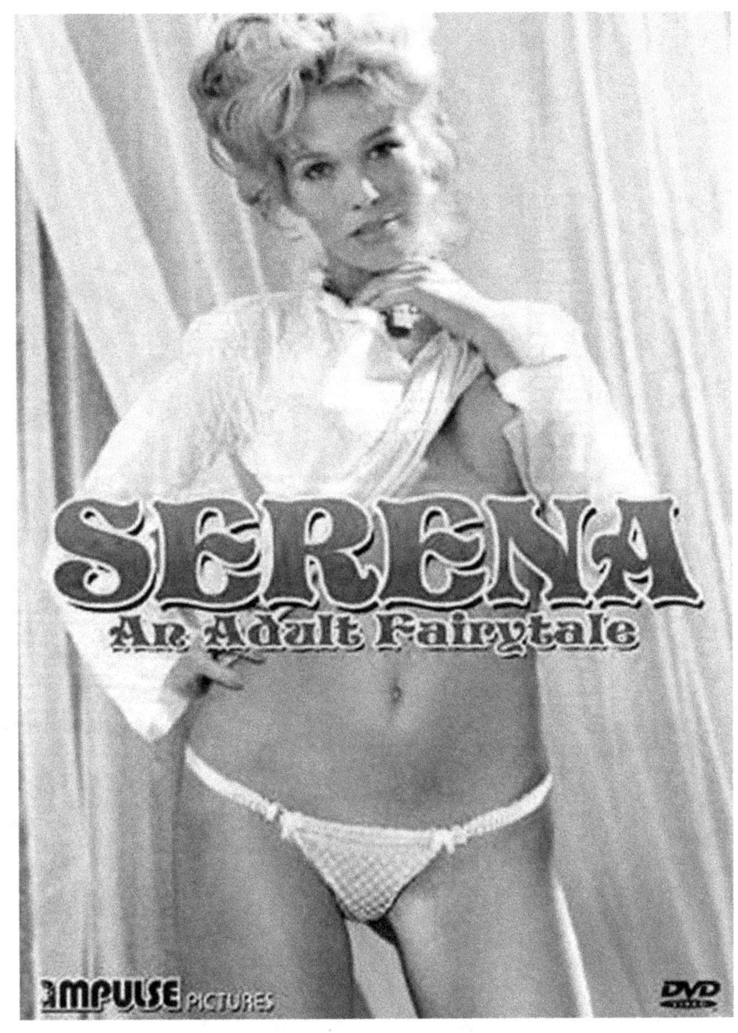

Paul Thomas, XXX Star

I learned you can be a beautiful man.

He played the role of Prince Charming in "Serena" - a Cinderella story.

Photo used with permission of Impulse Pictures

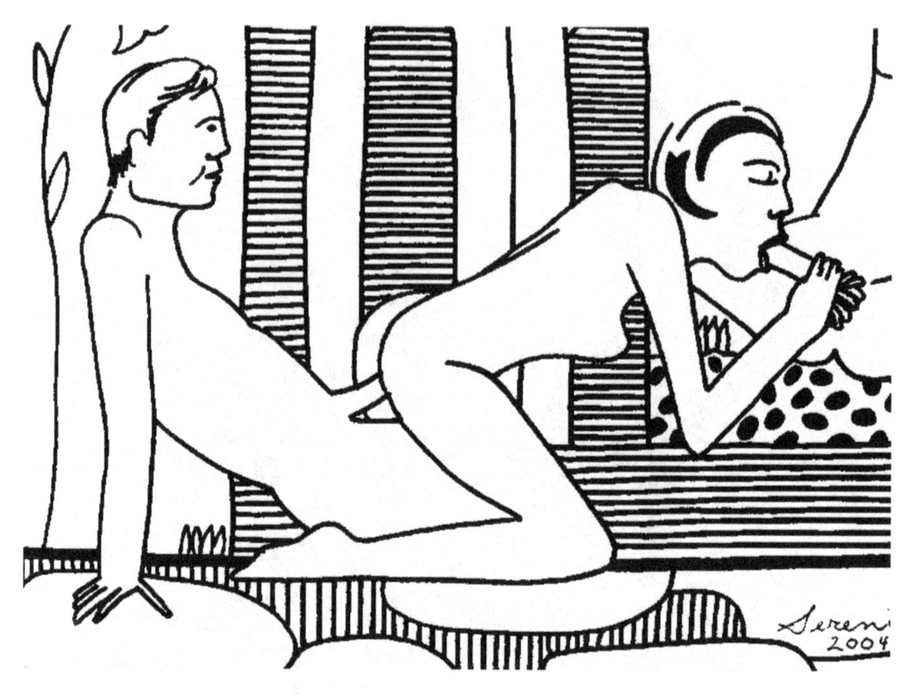

Aunt Peg, XXX Star

No matter what Life hands you, have FUN.

Pen and Ink by Serena Czarnecki

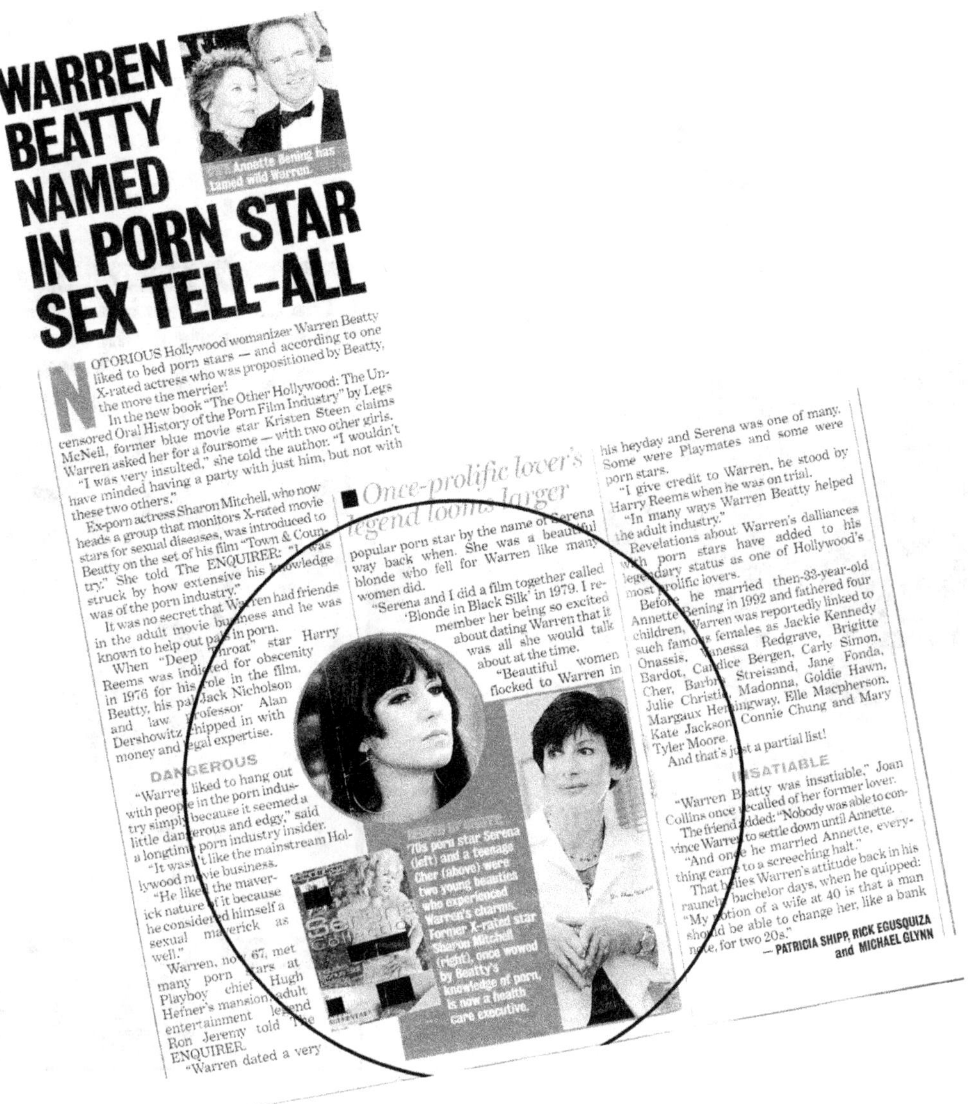

WARREN BEATTY NAMED IN PORN STAR SEX TELL-ALL

Annette Bening has tamed wild Warren.

NOTORIOUS Hollywood womanizer Warren Beatty liked to bed porn stars — and according to one X-rated actress who was propositioned by Beatty, the more the merrier!

In the new book "The Other Hollywood: The Uncensored Oral History of the Porn Film Industry" by Legs McNeil, former blue movie star Kristen Steen claims Warren asked her for a foursome — with two other girls.

"I was very insulted," she told the author. "I wouldn't have minded having a party with just him, but not with these two others."

Ex-porn actress Sharon Mitchell, who now heads a group that monitors X-rated movie stars for sexual diseases, was introduced to Beatty on the set of his film "Town & Country." She told The ENQUIRER: "I was struck by how extensive his knowledge was of the porn industry."

It was no secret that Warren had friends in the adult movie business and he was known to help out pals in porn.

When "Deep Throat" star Harry Reems was indicted for obscenity in 1976 for his role in the film, Beatty, his pal Jack Nicholson and law professor Alan Dershowitz chipped in with money and legal expertise.

DANGEROUS

"Warren liked to hang out with people in the porn industry simply because it seemed a little dangerous and edgy," said a longtime porn industry insider.

"It wasn't like the mainstream Hollywood movie business.

"He liked the maverick nature of it because he considered himself a sexual maverick as well."

Warren, now 67, met many porn stars at Playboy chief Hugh Hefner's mansion, adult entertainment legend Ron Jeremy told The ENQUIRER.

"Warren dated a very popular porn star by the name of Serena way back when. She was a beautiful blonde who fell for Warren like many women did.

"Serena and I did a film together called 'Blonde in Black Silk' in 1979. I remember her being so excited about dating Warren that it was all she would talk about at the time.

"Beautiful women flocked to Warren in his heyday and Serena was one of many. Some were Playmates and some were porn stars.

"I give credit to Warren, he stood by Harry Reems when he was on trial.

"In many ways Warren Beatty helped the adult industry."

Revelations about Warren's dalliances with porn stars have added to his legendary status as one of Hollywood's most prolific lovers.

Before he married then-33-year-old Annette Bening in 1992 and fathered four children, Warren was reportedly linked to such famous females as Jackie Kennedy Onassis, Vanessa Redgrave, Brigitte Bardot, Candice Bergen, Carly Simon, Cher, Barbra Streisand, Jane Fonda, Julie Christie, Madonna, Goldie Hawn, Margaux Hemingway, Elle Macpherson, Kate Jackson, Connie Chung and Mary Tyler Moore.

And that's just a partial list!

INSATIABLE

"Warren Beatty was insatiable," Joan Collins once recalled of her former lover.

The friend added: "Nobody was able to convince Warren to settle down until Annette.

"And once he married Annette, everything came to a screeching halt."

That belies Warren's attitude back in his raunchy bachelor days, when he quipped: "My notion of a wife at 40 is that a man should be able to change her, like a bank note, for two 20s."

— PATRICIA SHIPP, RICK EGUSQUIZA and MICHAEL GLYNN

■ Once-prolific lover's legend looms larger

'70s porn star Serena (left) and a teenage Cher (above) were two young beauties who experienced Warren's charms. Former X-rated star Sharon Mitchell (right), once wowed by Beatty's knowledge of porn, is now a health care executive.

Warren Beatty, Actor

I learned that sex is hot, but so is conversation.

from the Enquirer Newspaper

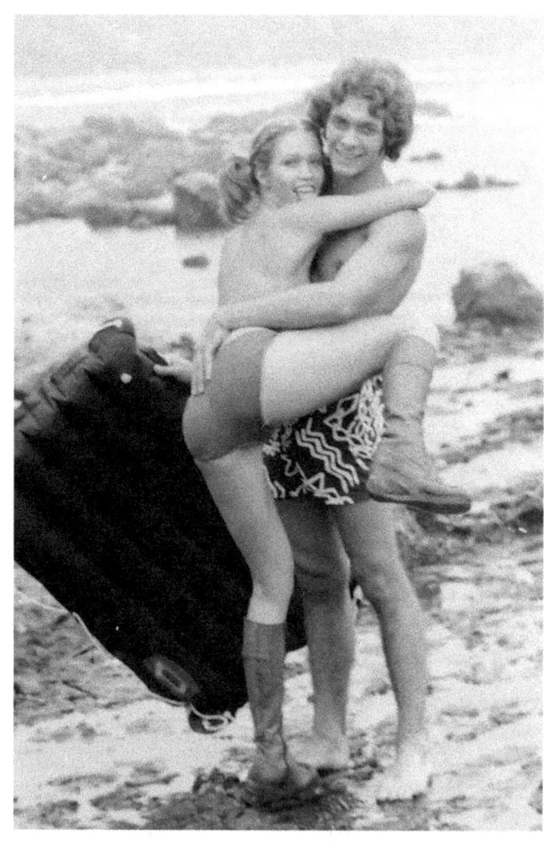

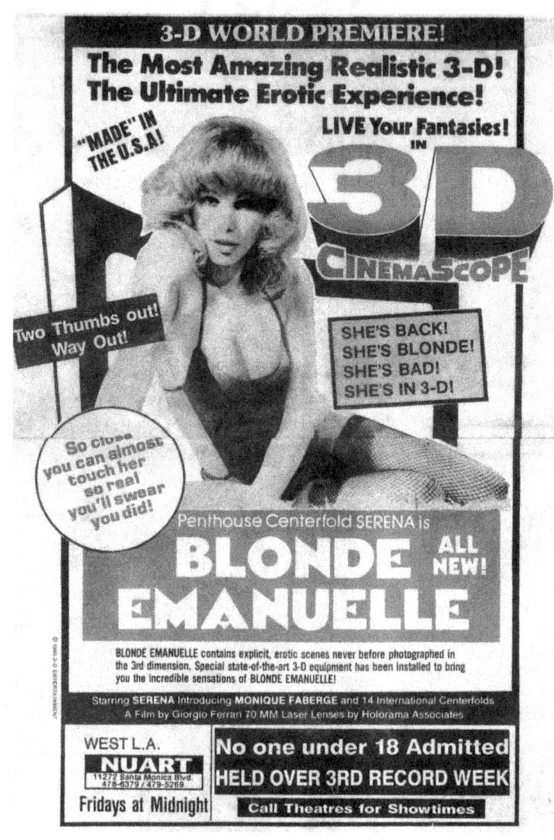

Mike Ranger, XXX Star

He taught me passionate fucking gets you high.
Once we took MDA together, so we were high while fucking!

Photo of Mike and I in our 3D appearance in film.

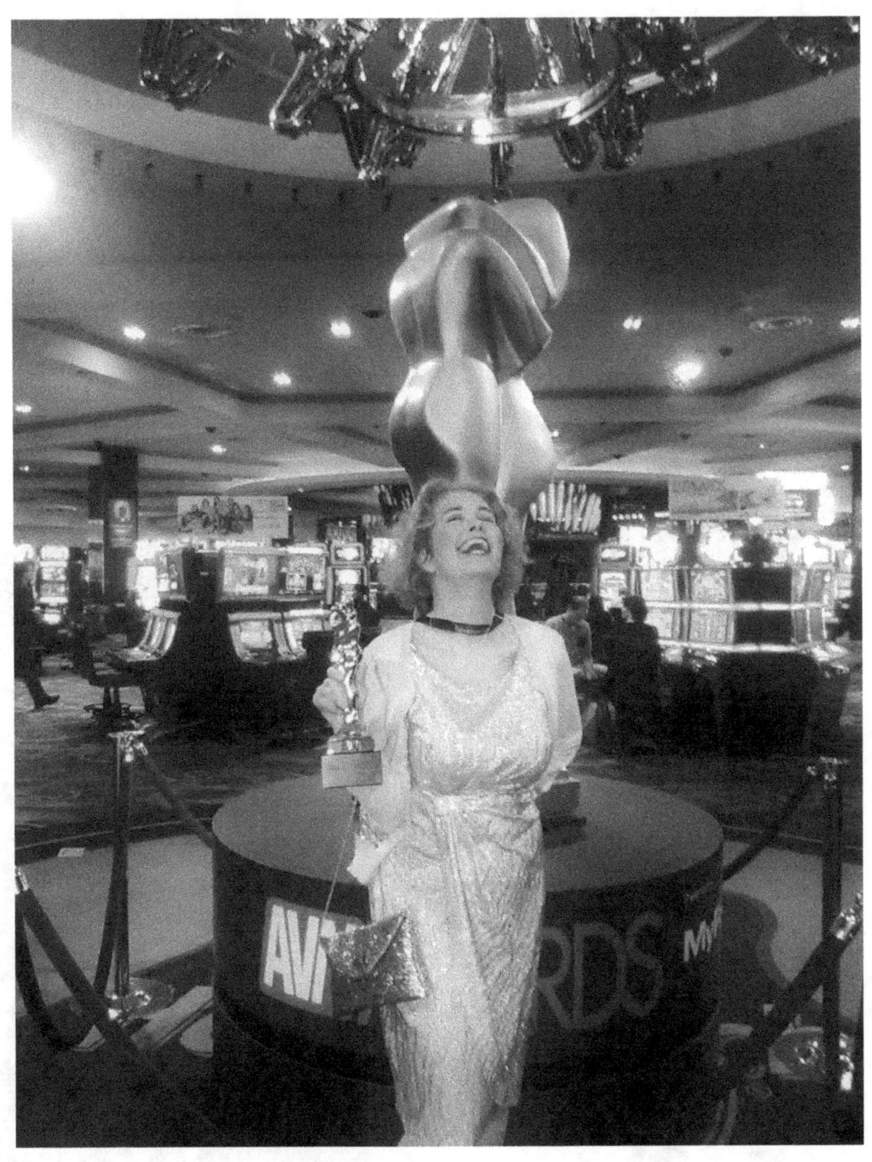

Mark Stevens, XXX Star

He was so kind to me.
I learned to make money in fun ways.
We danced, covered in golden paint, to Chubby Checker, Live!

Mark and I were Inducted into the AVN Hall of Fame in 2019.

Photo of Serena with her AVN Hall of Fame Award by Cyryla Czarnecki

What I have learned *from the Actors of XXX*

I let loose with enjoyment with them!

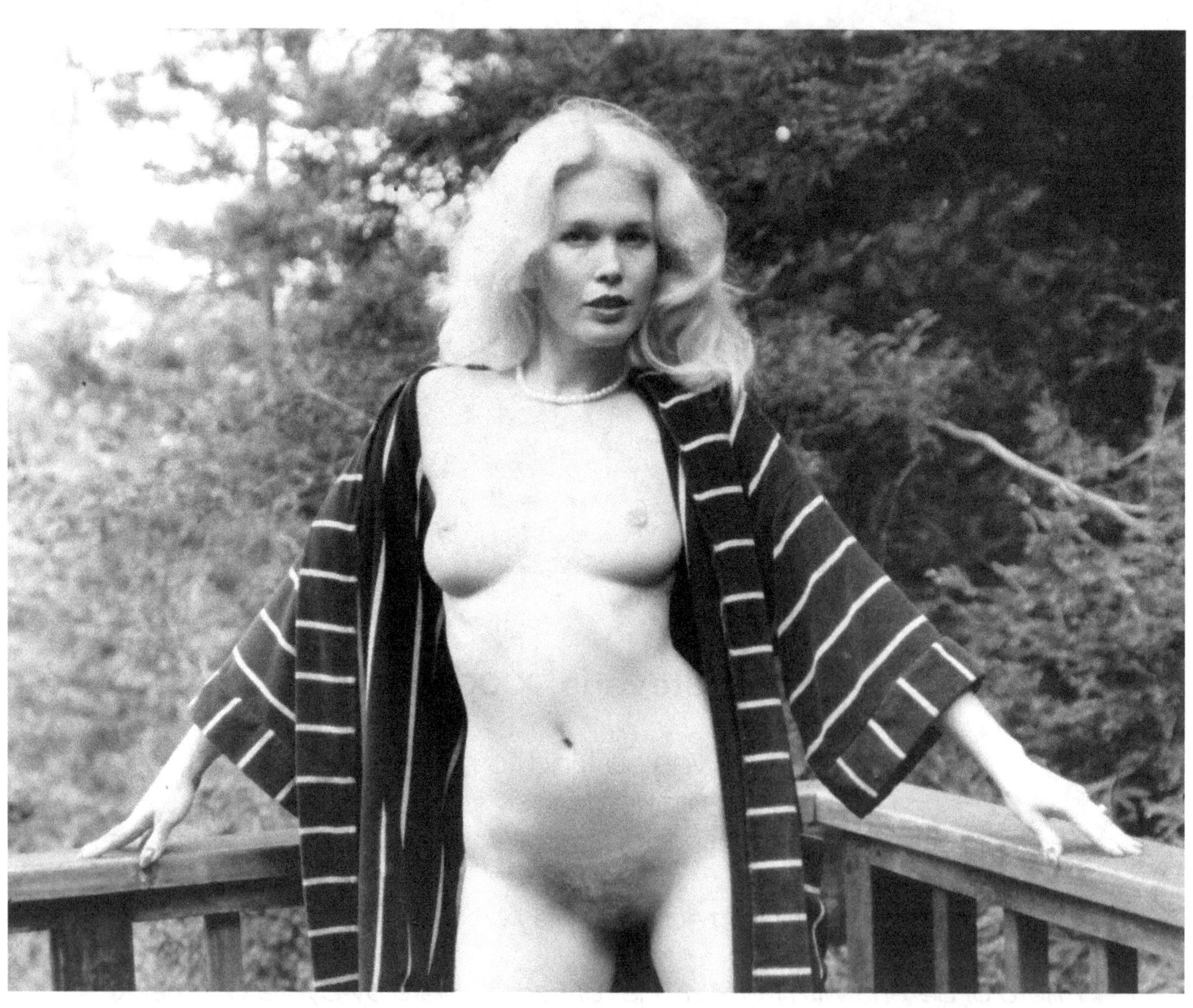

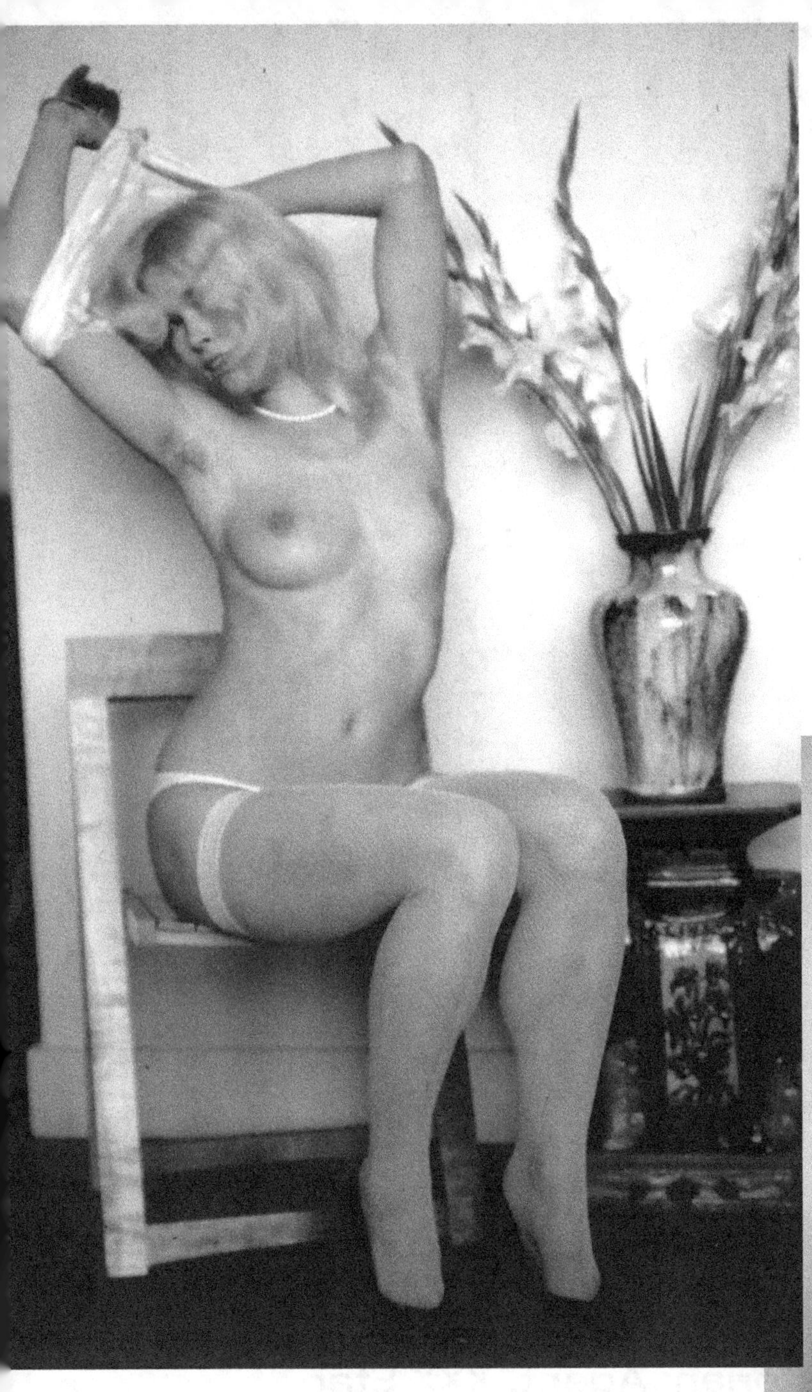

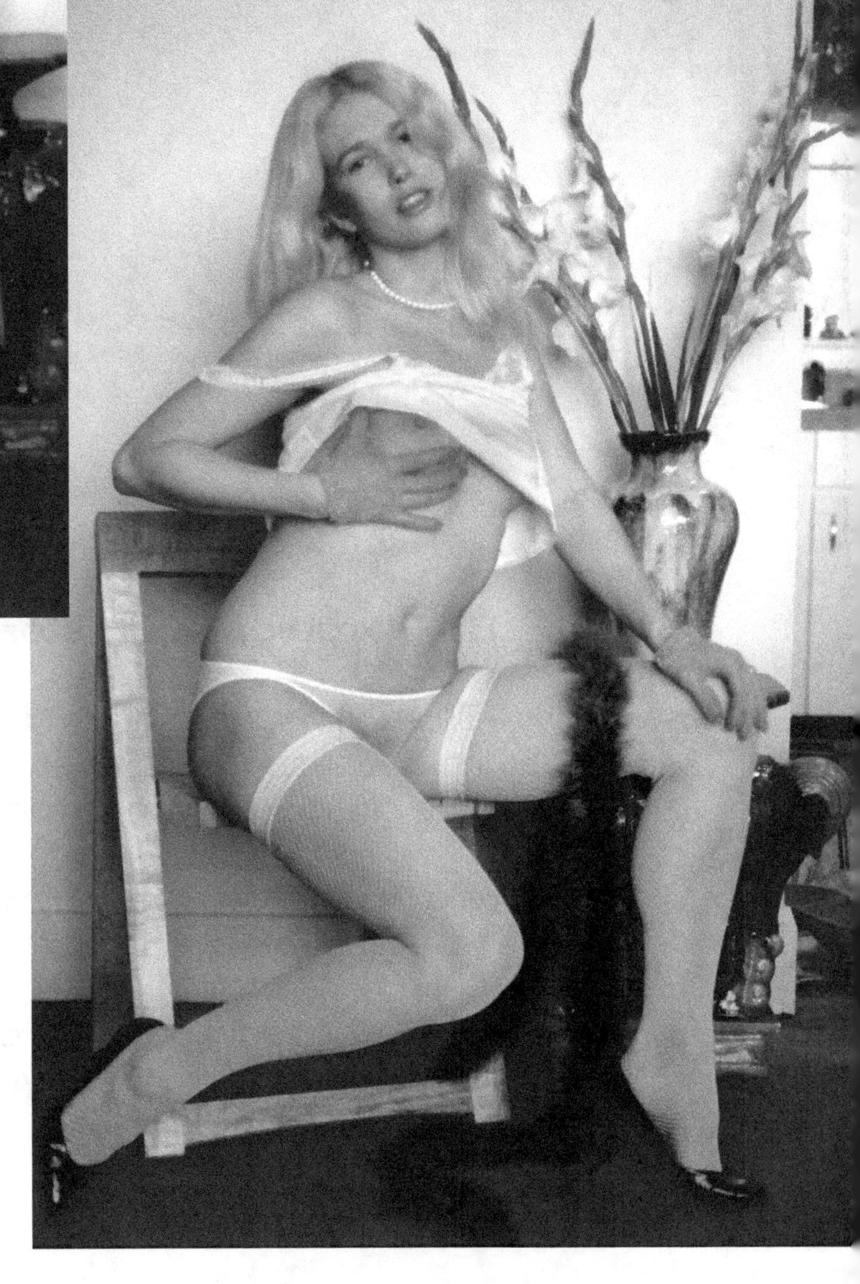

Photos of Serena by Baron Wolman

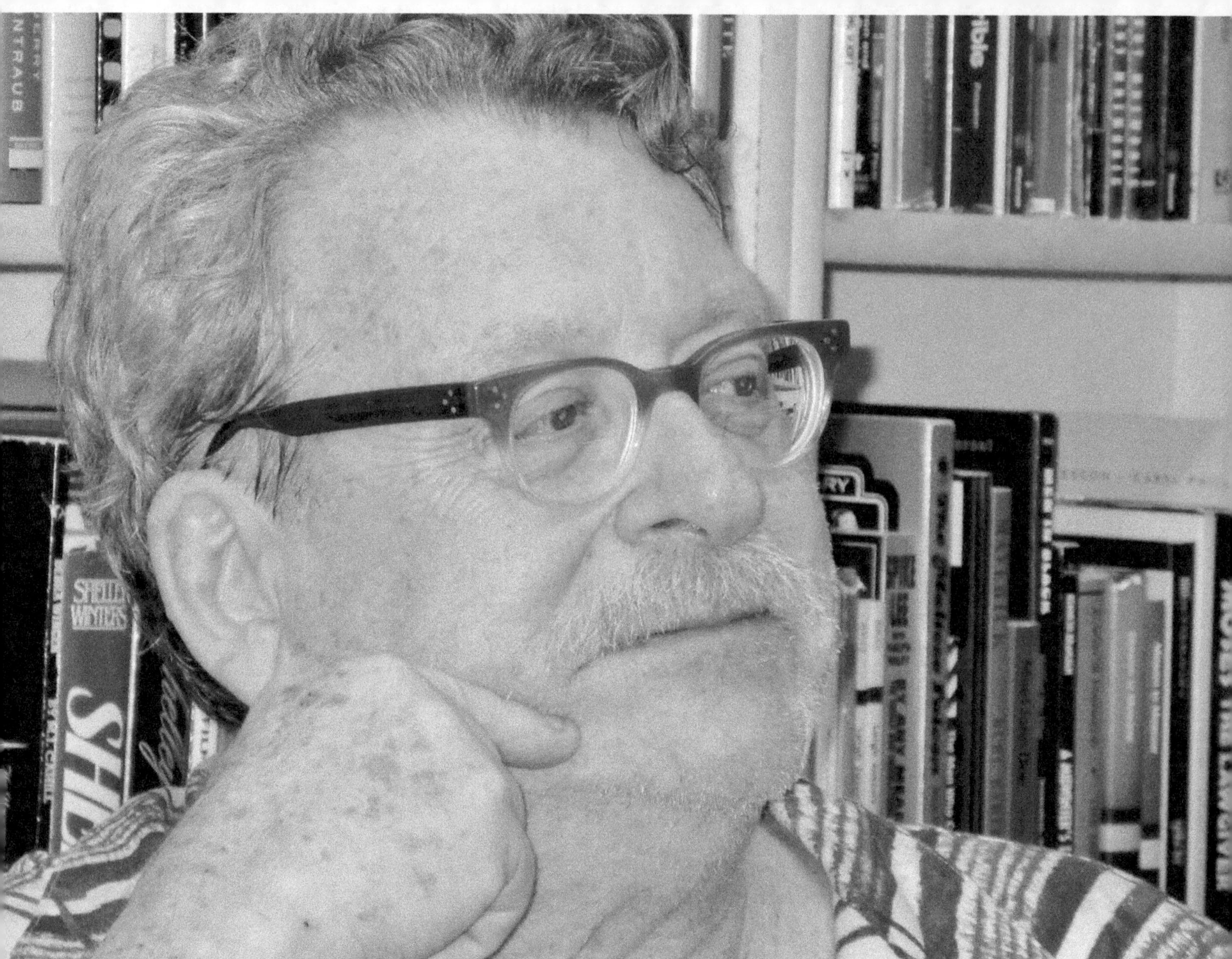

Bill Margold, XXX Historian, Agent, XXX Star

Bill and I hugged the minute we met each other.
A long squeeze that forever cemented our relationship.
He was the closest person to me during the years I did Erotica.

We'd "work" together, but were always best friends.
He was my Agent always. I spoke with him on his radio program.

He died during the radio program one day, interviewing someone,
doing what he loved to do, TALK!

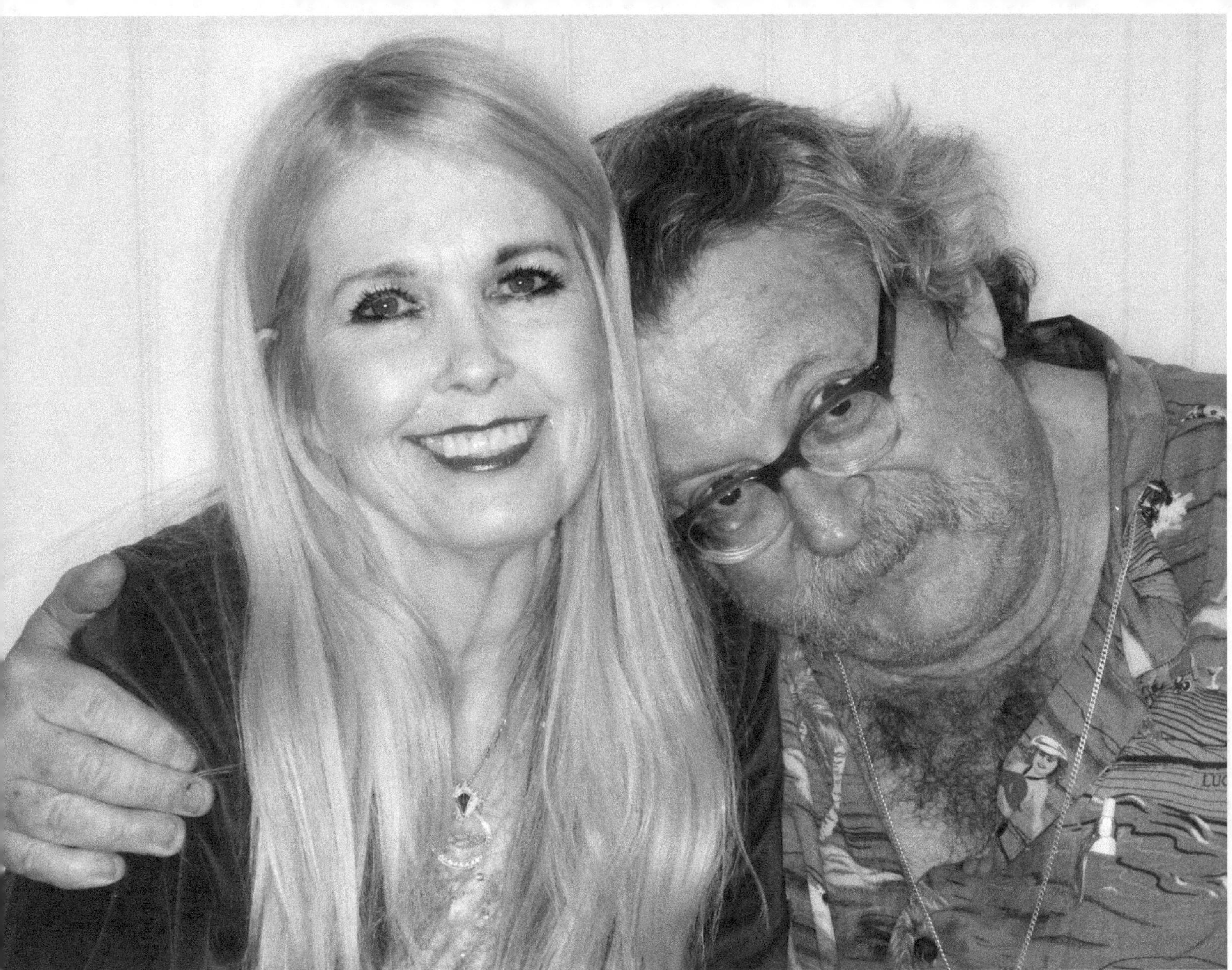

He loved me so much that when he found out I adored the movie "The Wind and The Lion," he got all the set photos (enlarged, on board) and presented them to me. This is one of the greatest gifts I've ever been given.

Thank you, Darling William. I always called him "Marygold or William" What do you say about the person who loved you and protected you from the moment he met you???

Photo by Steve Zambrano

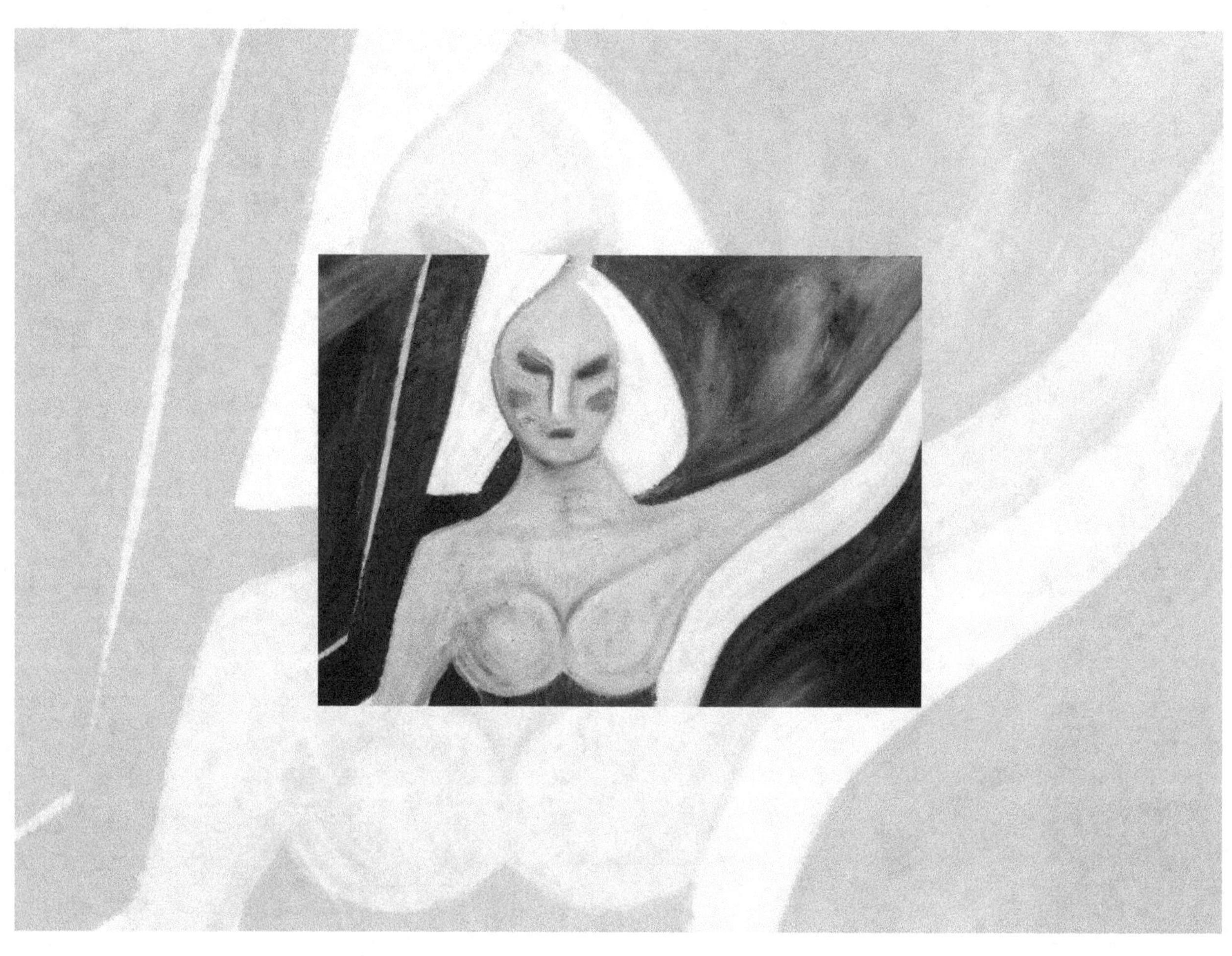

Nina Hartley, XXX Star

She speaks well for all of us outsiders. She is a real trooper.

Detail of "Big Woman" oil painting by Serena Czarnecki

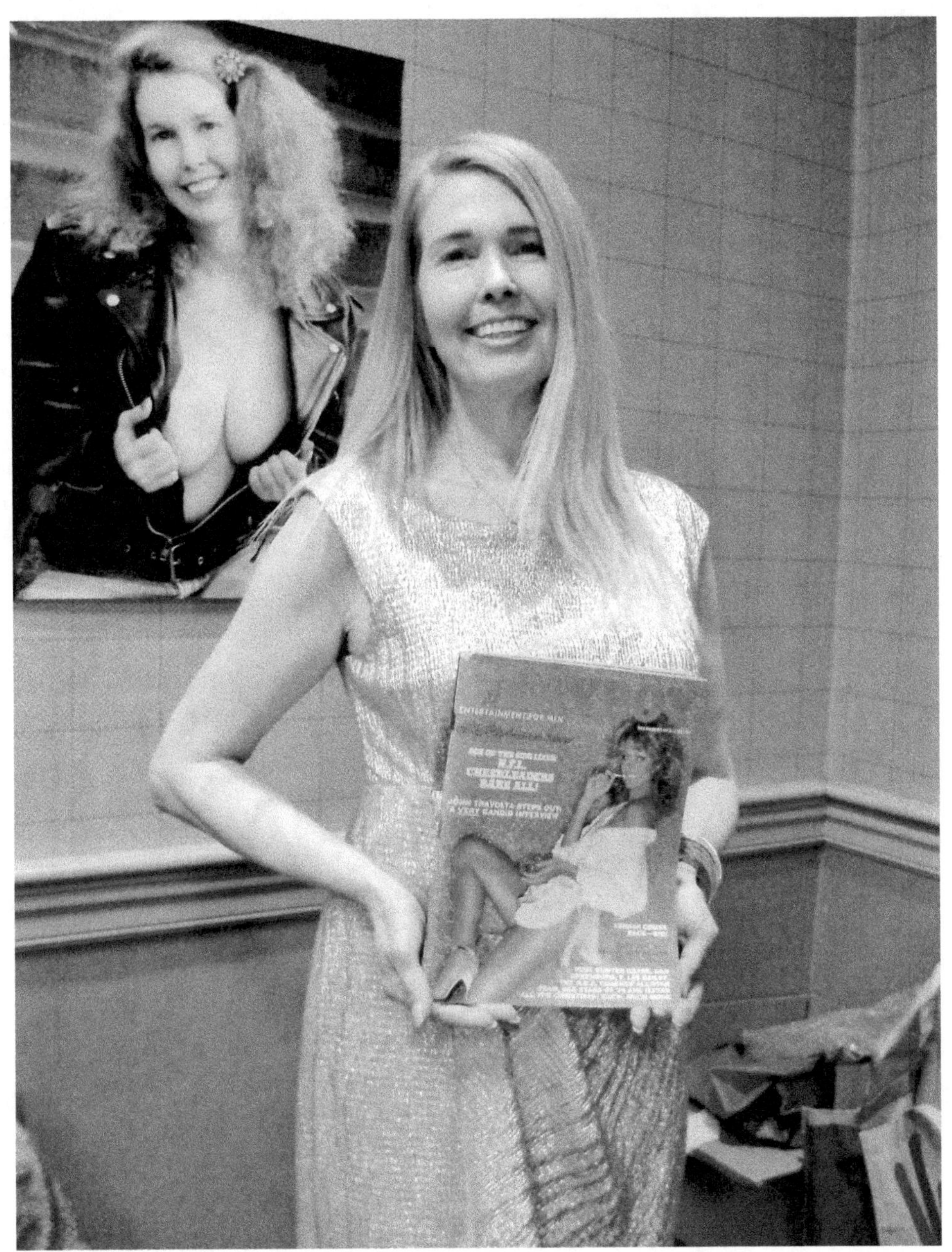

Hugh Hefner, Playboy

You can read about my night of passion with this great man
in my Memory Book "Bright Lights, Lonely Nights."
I was photographed for Playboy Magazine for four issues.

Photo of Serena holding one of the Playboys she's pictured in

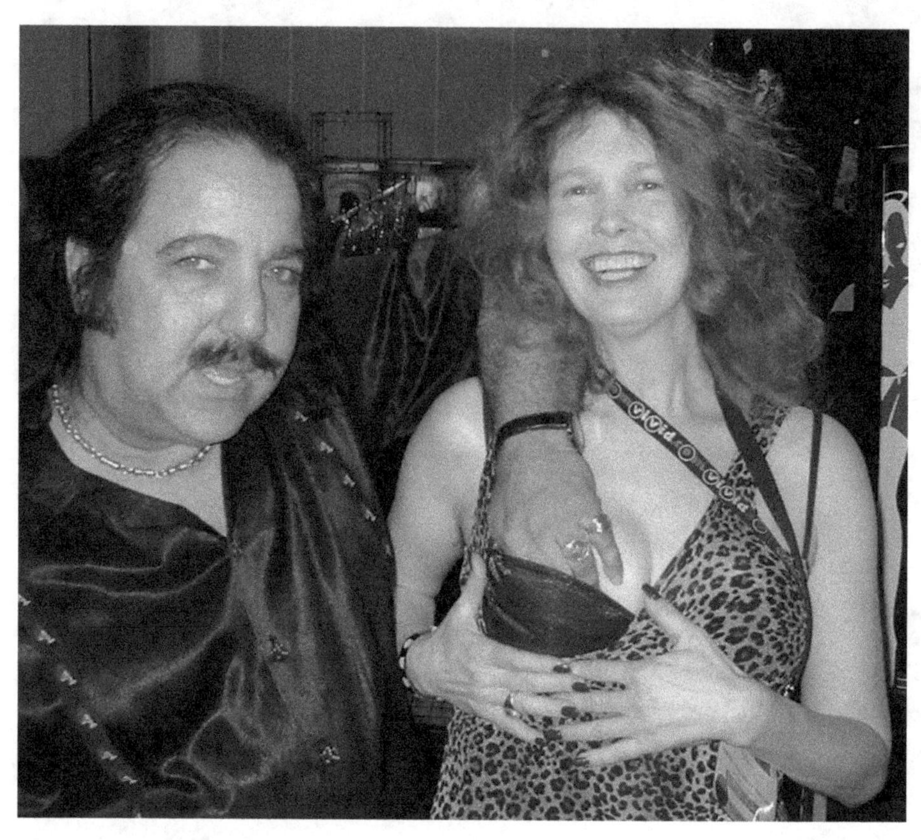

Ron Jeremy, XXX Star

He was always ready to get a feel.

Photo in the collection of Serena Czarnecki

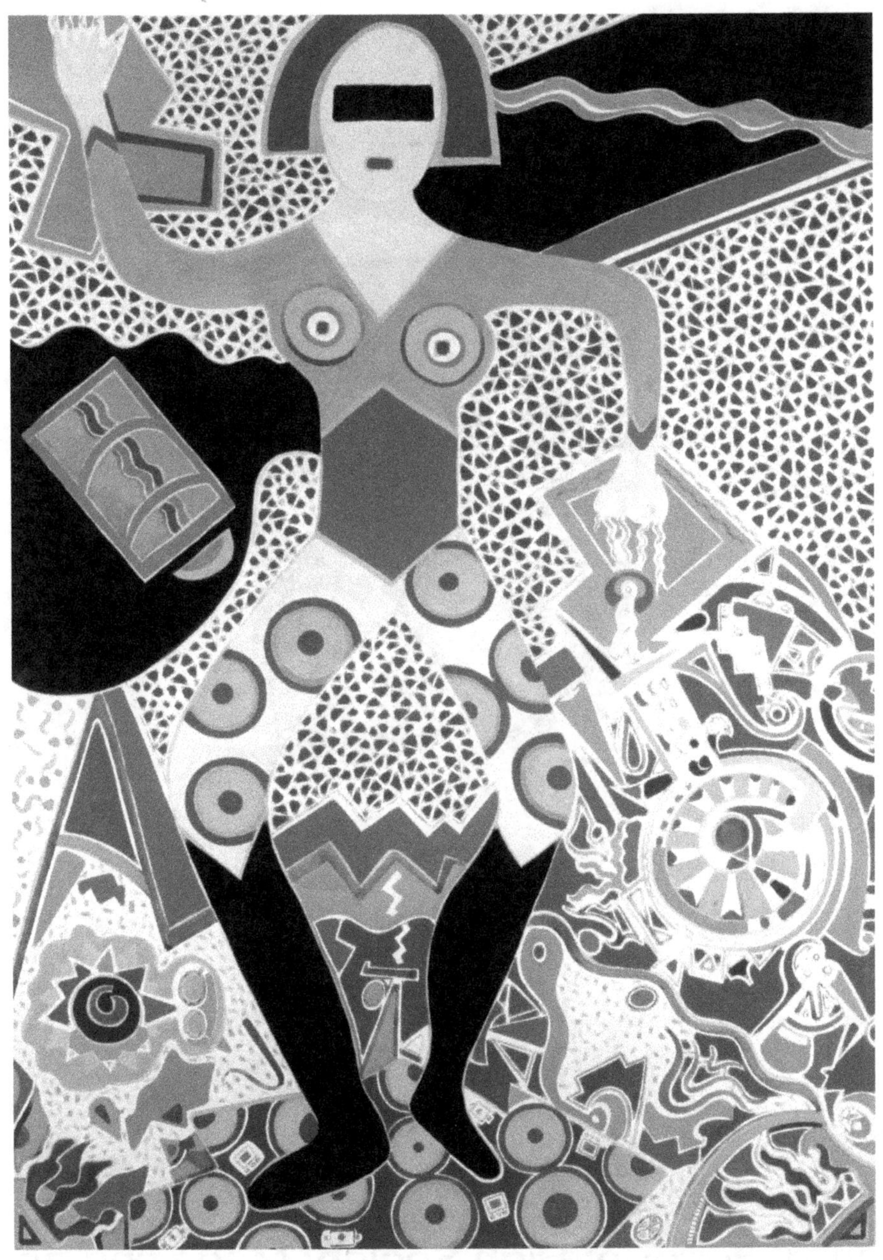

Adnan Khashoggi, Arms Dealer

I learned how really small the world can be.
The son he sorrows for is my connection to Lady Diana, a woman
I very much admire. (Lady Gaga says Diana is dancing in the dark.)

Painting by Serena Czarnecki

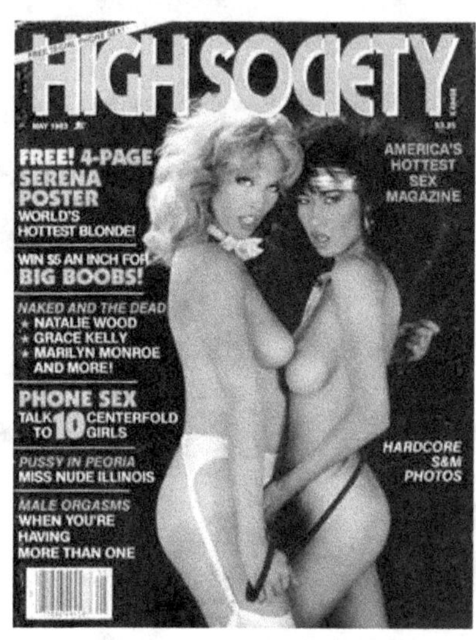

Gloria Leonard, Editor of High Society Magazine and XXX Star

I was a big Fan of Gloria's. She was fun, sexy, tall, and extremely capable. And she put me in the magazine she Edited many times. Sometimes we modeled with each other!

Here I am on the Cover with Mai Lin.

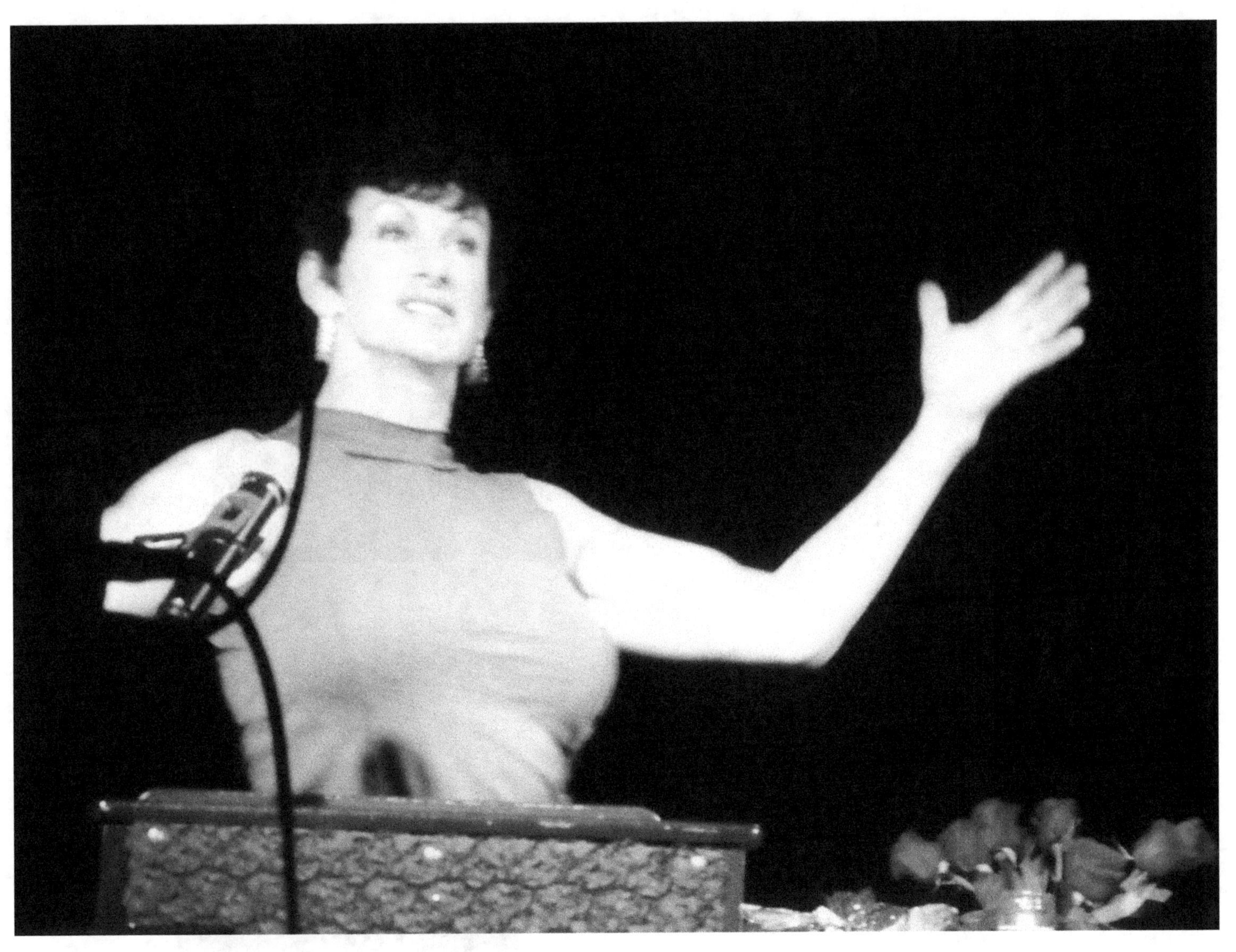

Sharon Mitchell, XXX Star

I met her in NYC and we had lots of fun making movies!

This photo of Sharon was taken by me at Candida Royalle's Memorial. (Candice's ashes were passed out to her friends. You are so loved, Darling, RIP.)

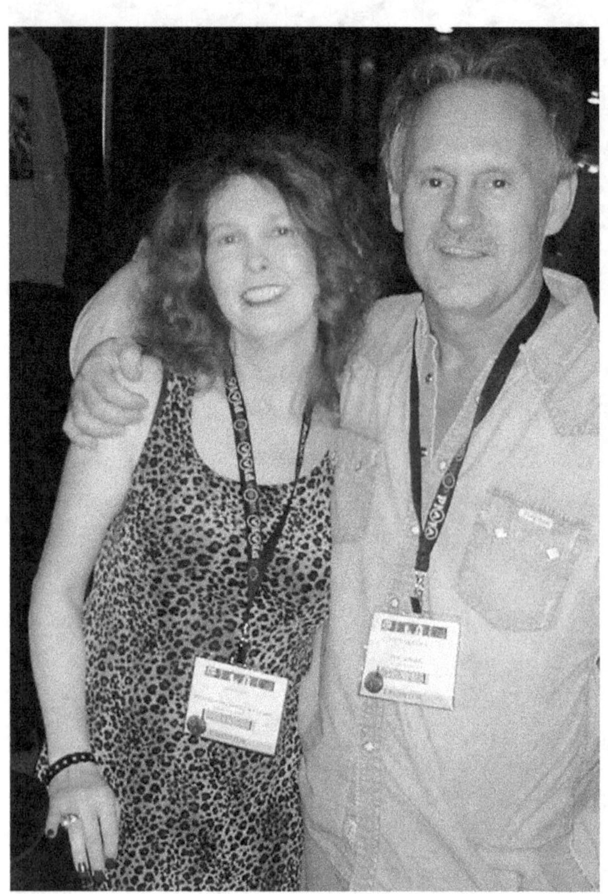

Serena "on TV!"

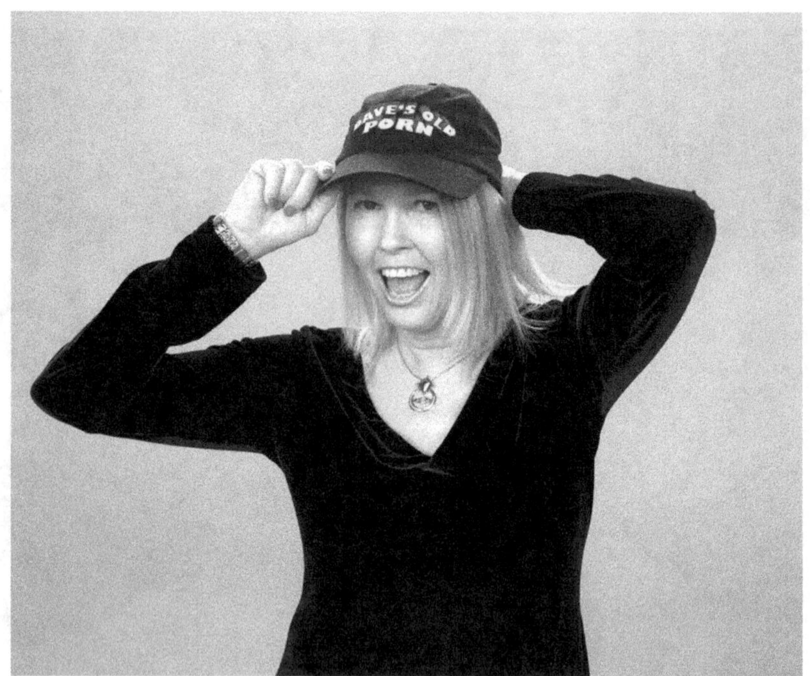

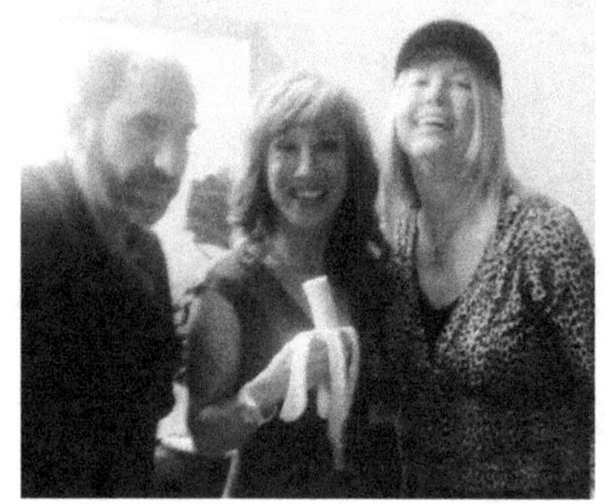

Dave Attell, Kathy Griffin and I.

Joey Silvera, XXX Star

Joey and I made love in the lower level of Show World In NYC. We stayed friends and did movies together. Last time I saw him he was lookin' fine. We were both being interviewed by the comedian Dave Attell for Showtime's "Dave's Old Porn" Show.

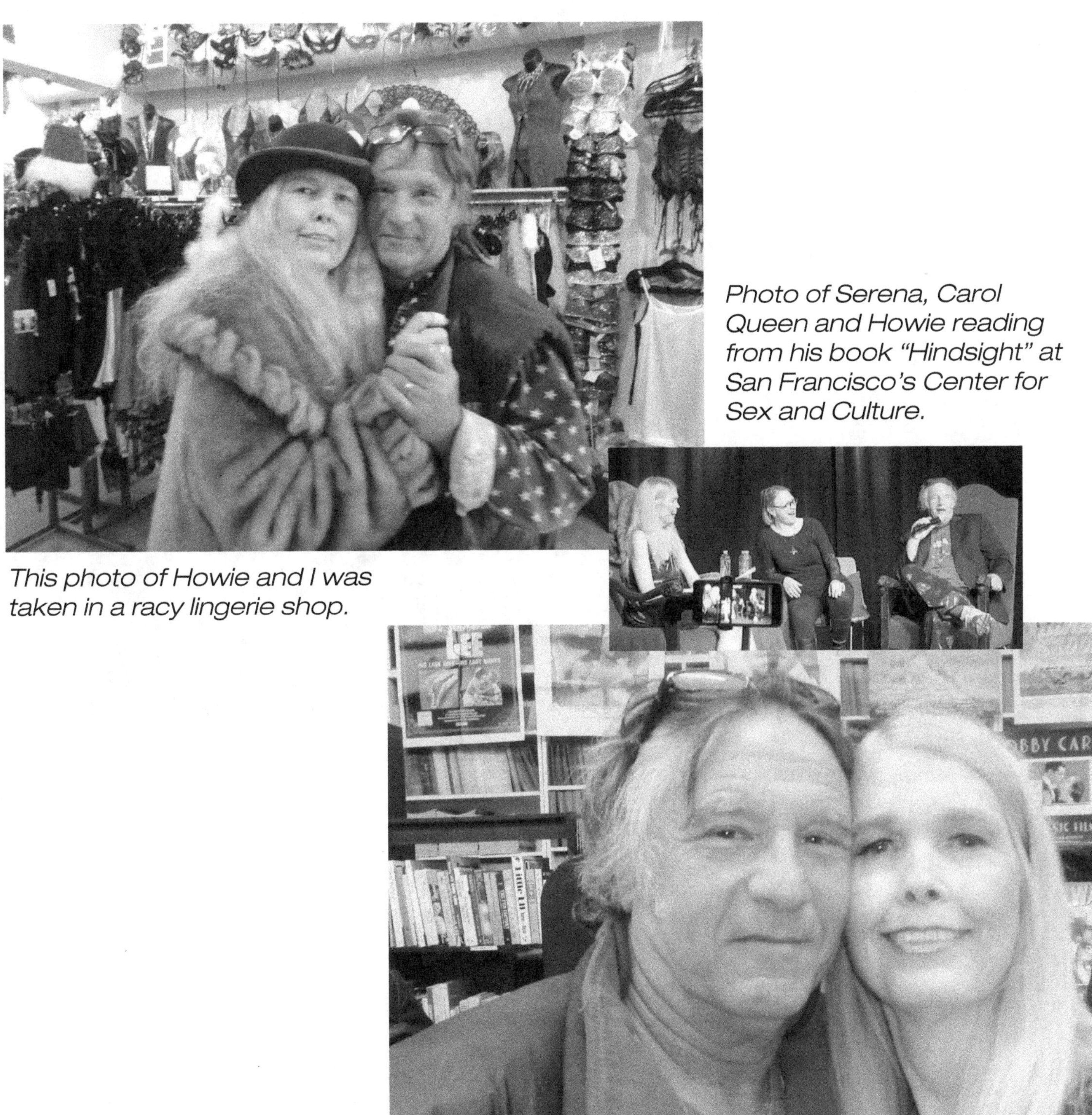

Photo of Serena, Carol Queen and Howie reading from his book "Hindsight" at San Francisco's Center for Sex and Culture.

This photo of Howie and I was taken in a racy lingerie shop.

Richard Pacheco, XXX Star
(friend, and author Howie Gordon)

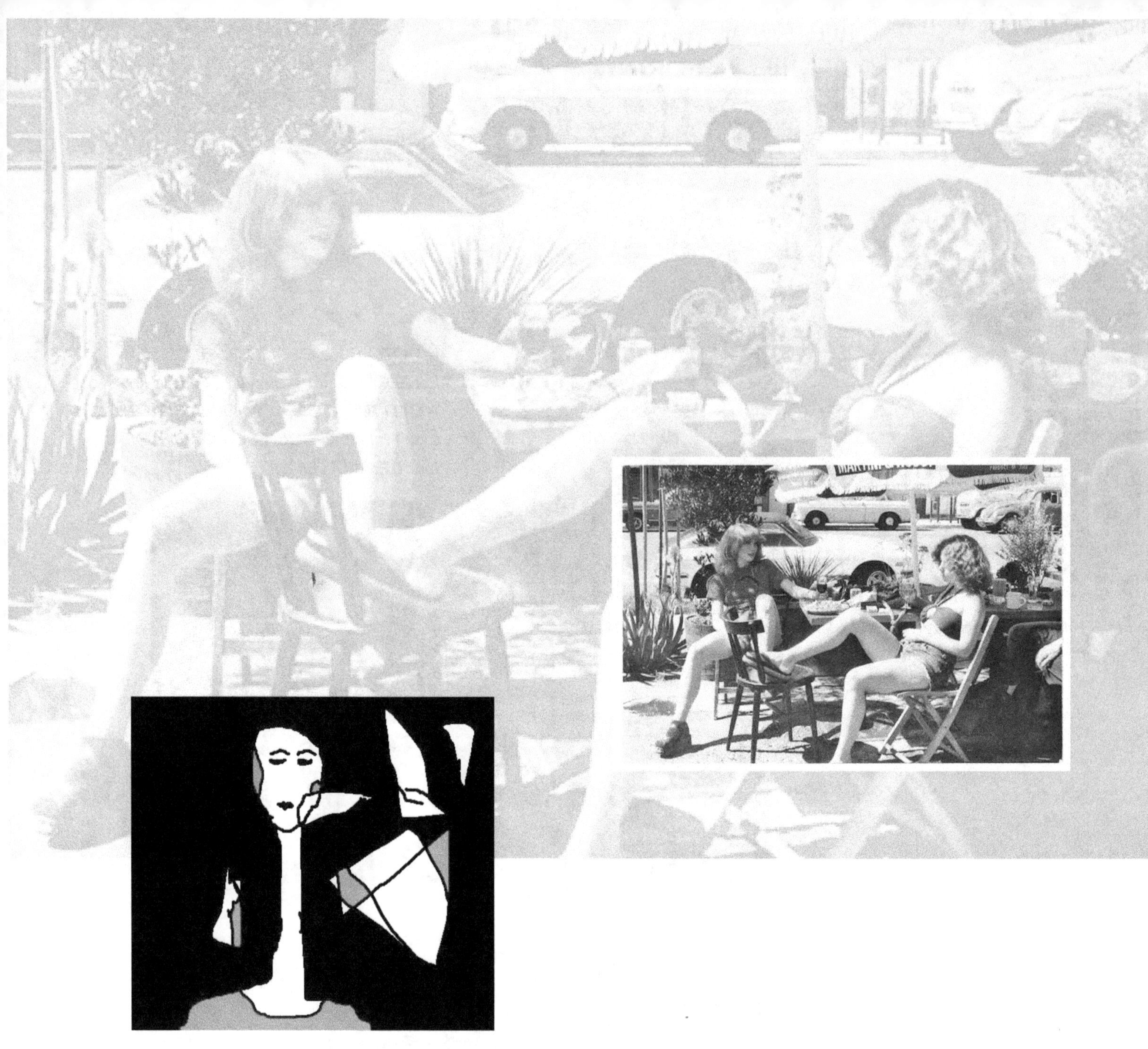

Christine DeSchaffer, XXX Star

We made films together, including my all-time favorite, "Teenage Cruisers." We hung out on Hollywood Blvd.

I had bangs and wore little socks with my wedgies! We drank wine together. But she ultimately taught me what drinking too much alcohol means.

Computer Art by Serena Czarnecki

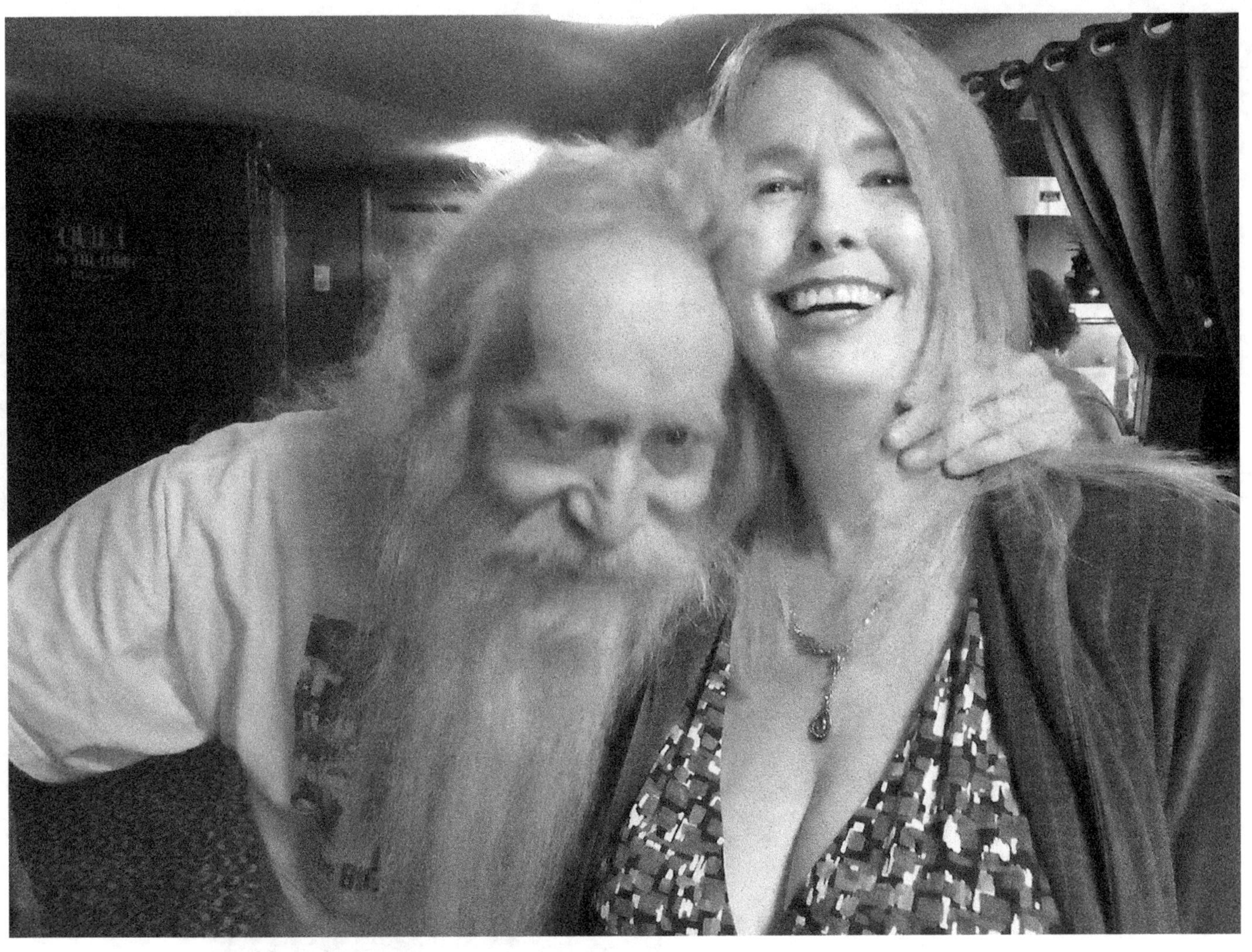

This is me with the Director of "Teenage Cruisers".
Men just seem to cuddle up to me.
This was an appearance Johnny Legend and I made
at the Roxie Theater in San Francisco.

Photo by Paul Johnston

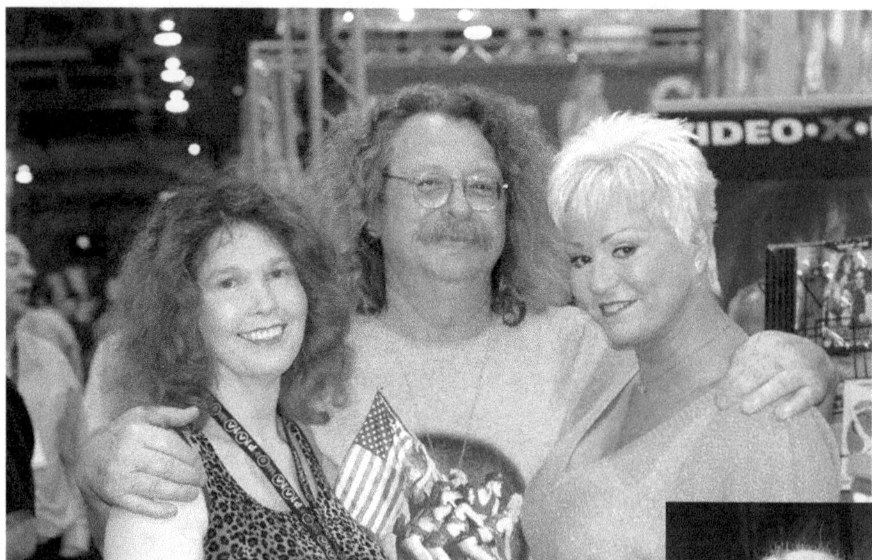

This is me, Big-Brother-of-Porn Bill Margold with gorgeous Seka. We all met up that year at a Convention.

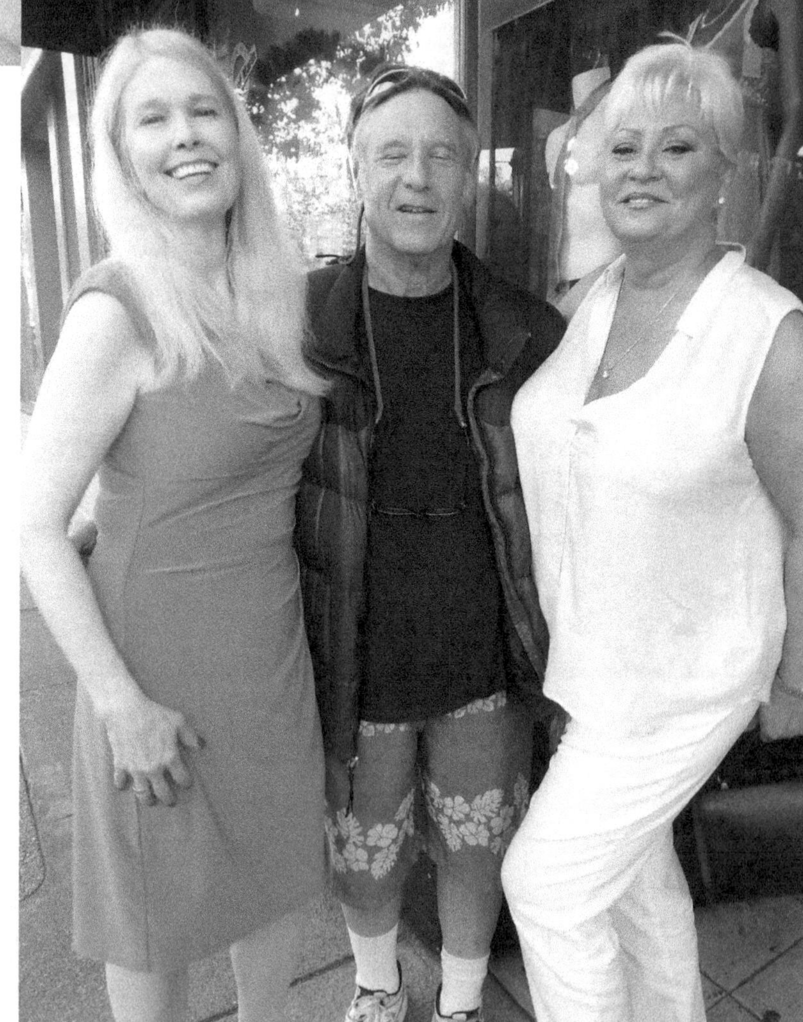

We're on our way to eat Thai food! Howie's in a swoon, being between such beauties!

Photos of the three of us by Paul Johnston

Seka, XXX SuperStar

Seka taught me to never sell myself short.

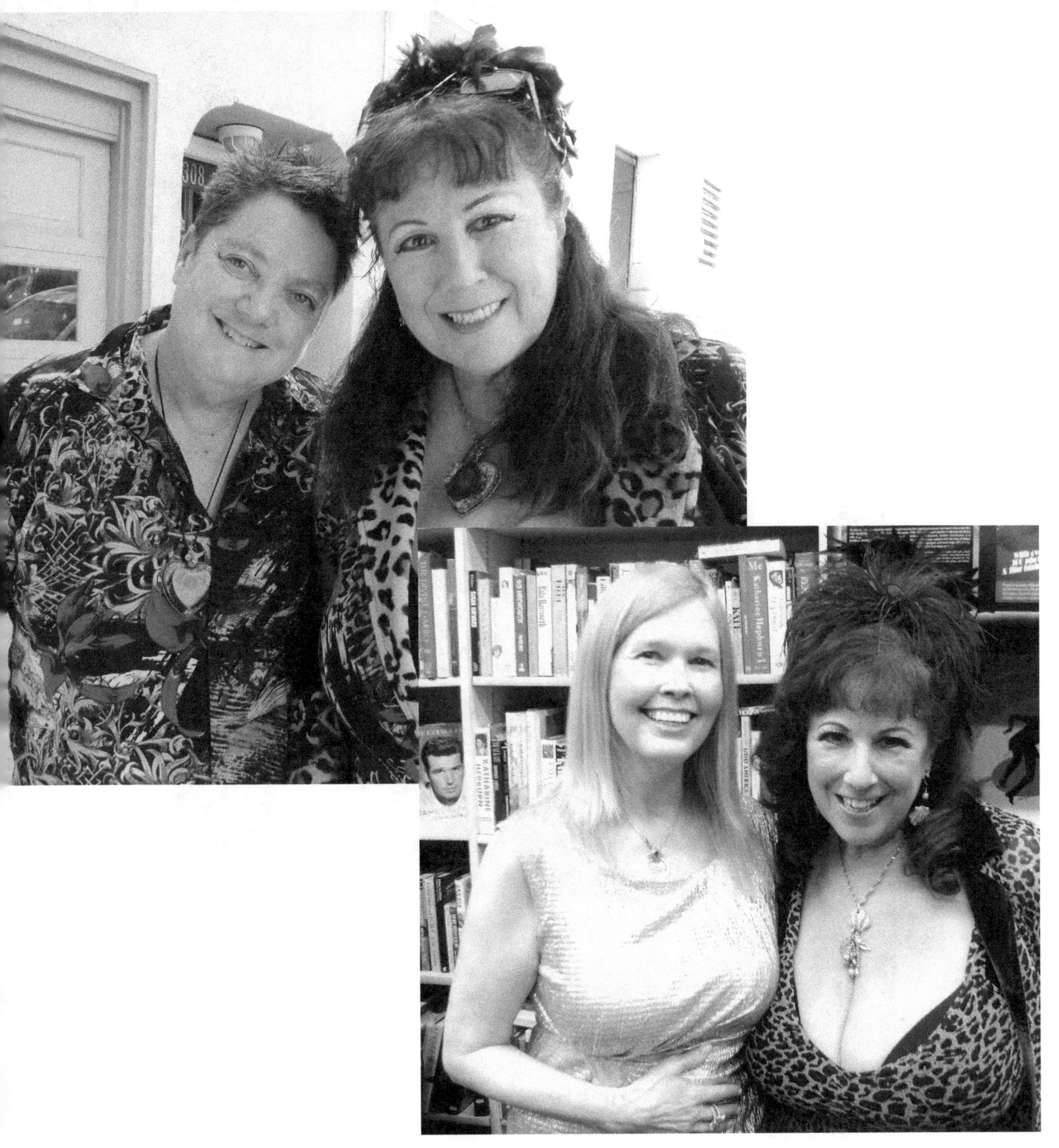

Annie Sprinkle, author, women's advocate, eco-sexual, filmmaker, XXX SuperStar

Love has no gender.

Photo of Beth and Annie by Serena Czarnecki

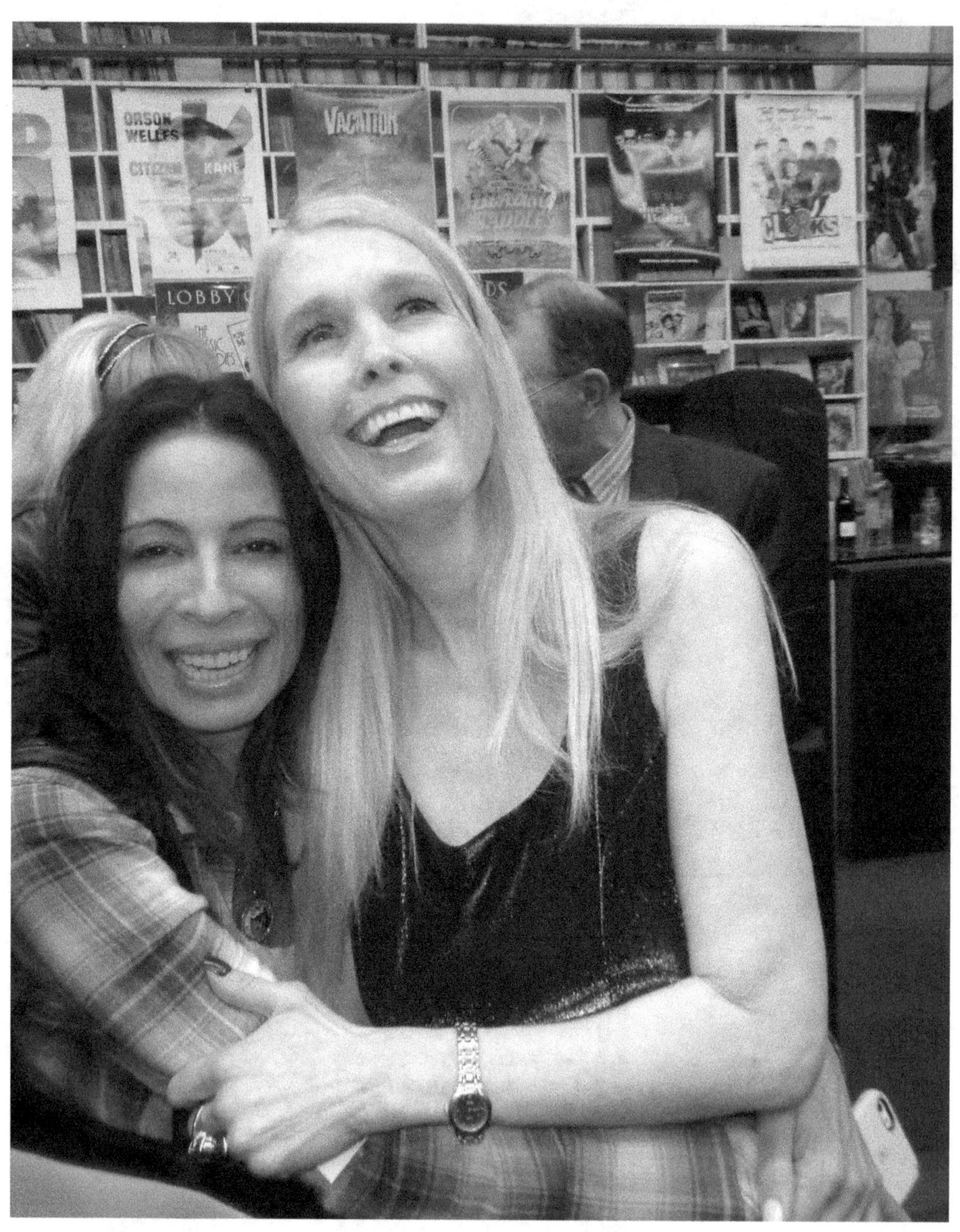

Christy Canyon

Photo taken at my book signing at Larry Edmunds Bookstore on Hollywood Blvd. Christy came and gave me lots of hugs and support. And bought two of my books! Thanks for your friendship, Darling!

I learned that you can be a mother and a good friend. I learned to have an interest in what Fans are needing, what they think counts!

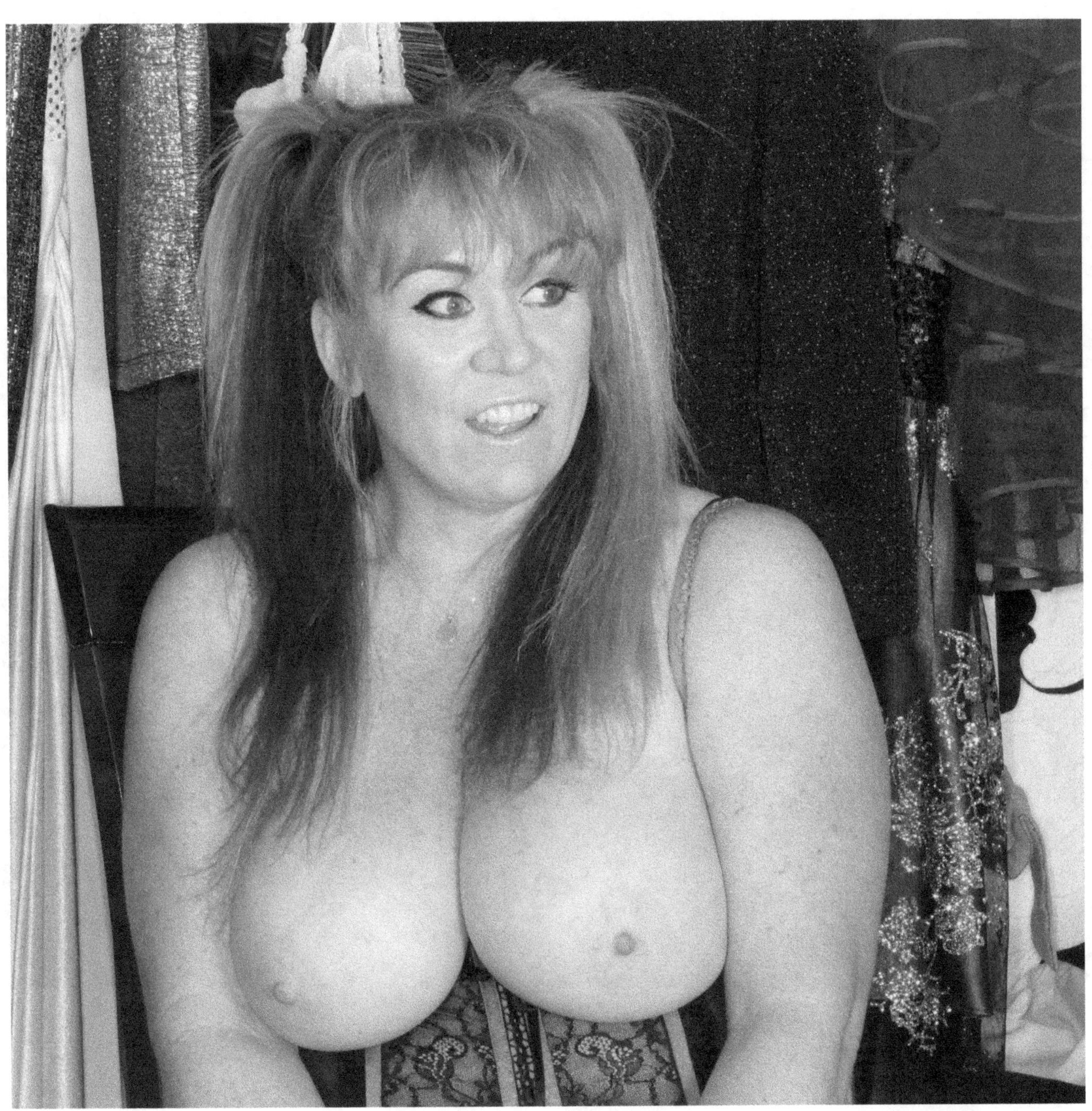

Cannibal, XXX Star

Margold said if he and I would have a child, she would be Cannibal. She is studying law while showing her tits.

Photo of Cannibal by Steve Zambrano

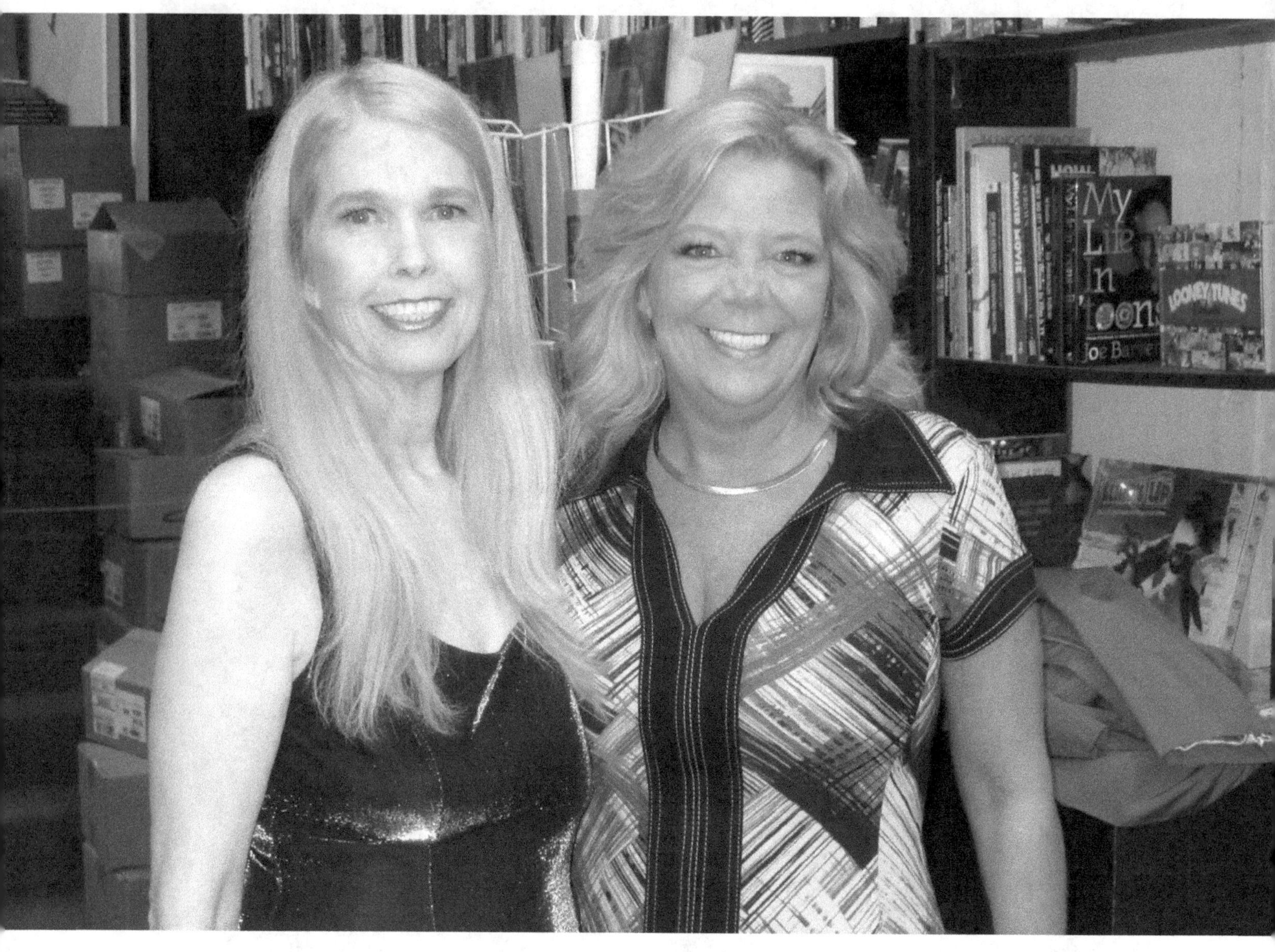

Karen Summer, XXX Star

Karen helped me by posing as a "Backstage Girl." Thanks, Babe!

Photo of Serena and Karen Summer by Kenji

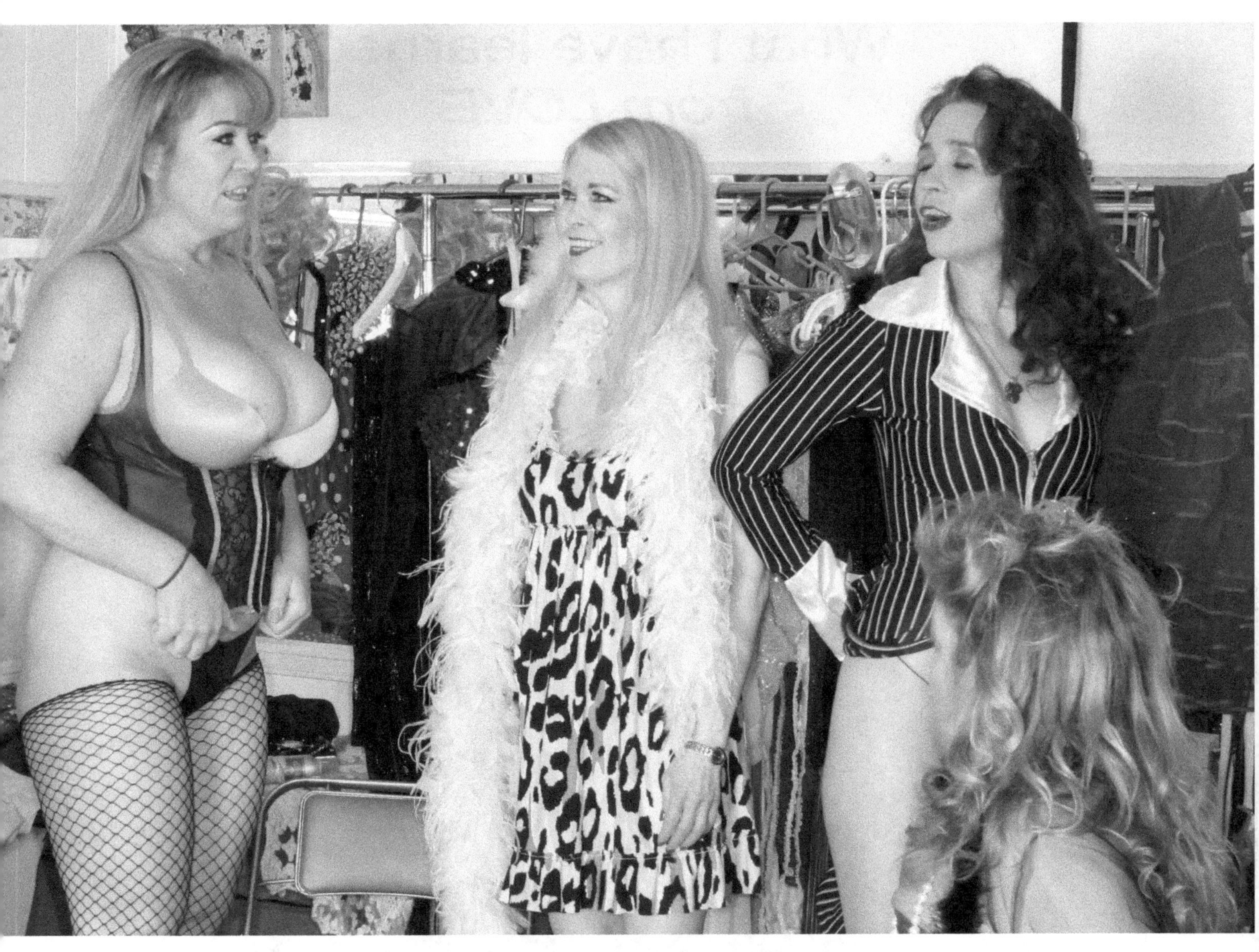

Sultry Sable, XXX Star

An intelligent and sweet person.
This is the Sultry one of "Backstage Girls."

Backstage Girls: Cannibal, Serena, Sultry Sable and Karen Summer

Photo by Steve Zambrano

What I have learned *from LOVE*

That Love is, indeed, all there is.

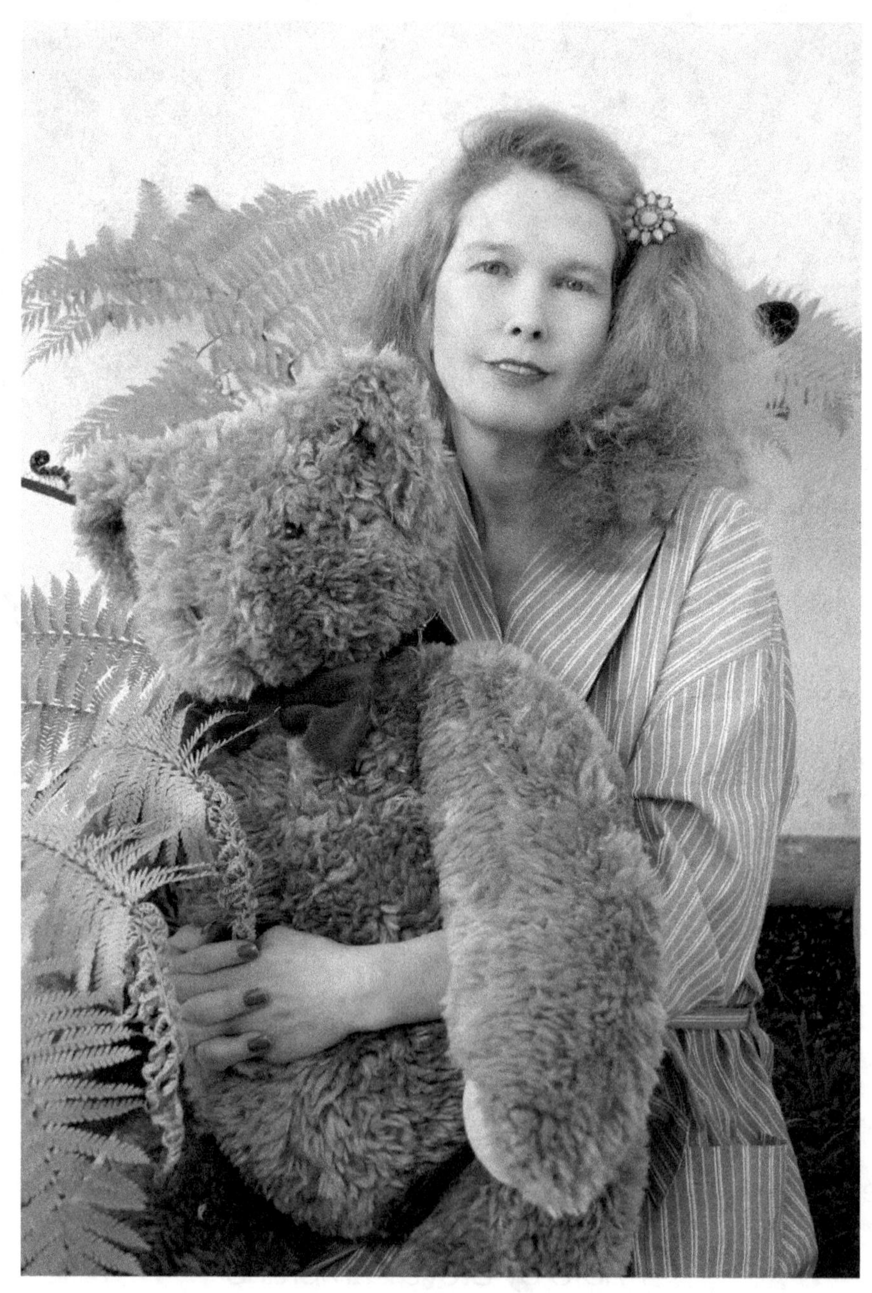

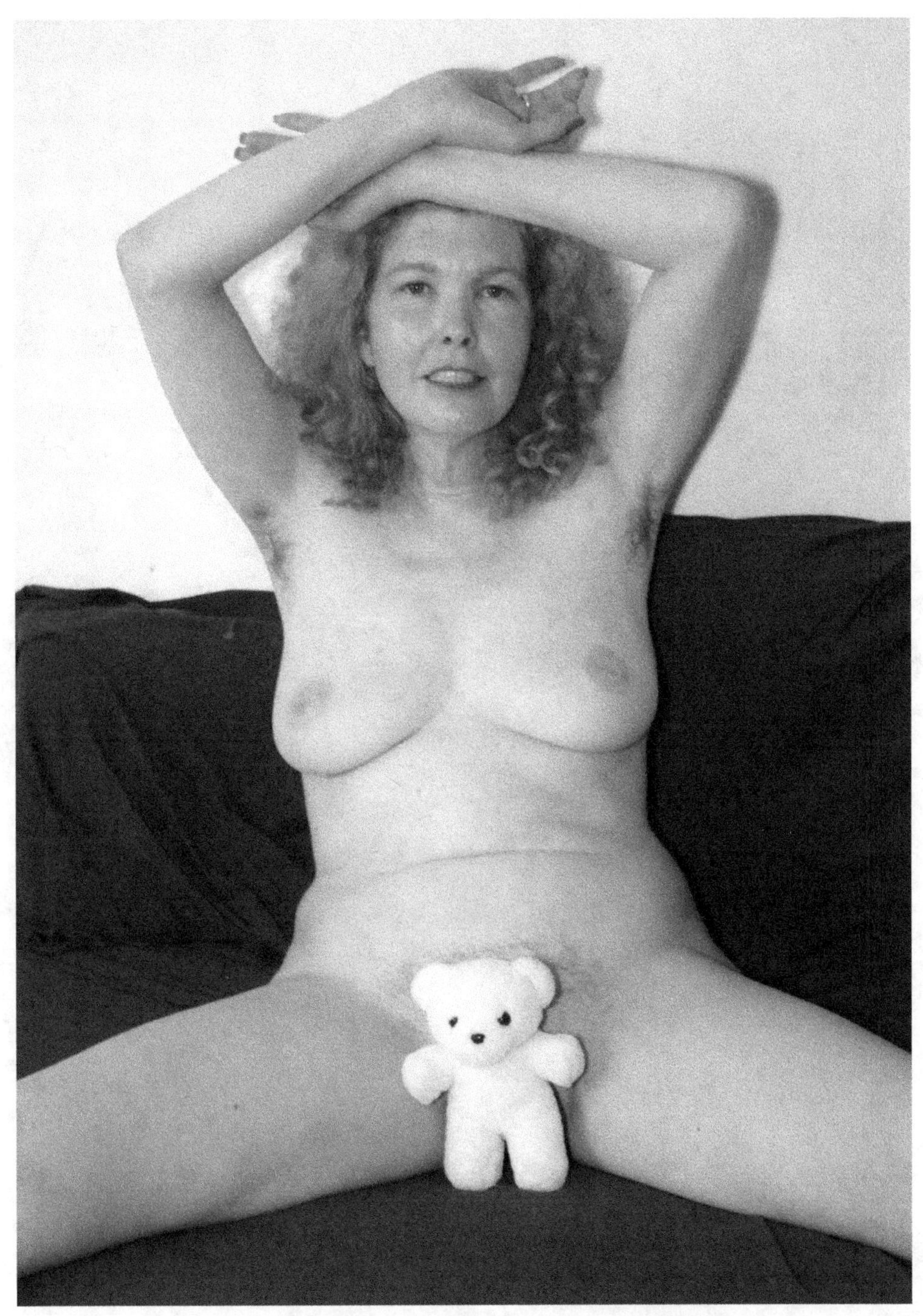

"Henri", my far-away Love

That Love can flow between two people, even across the earth.

I've never met "Henri", yet we've been long-distance Lovers for many years. He's helped me with money when I needed it, and I've sent him tokens of appreciation in the form of autographed photographs, magazines and movies.

Photo by Steve Zambrano

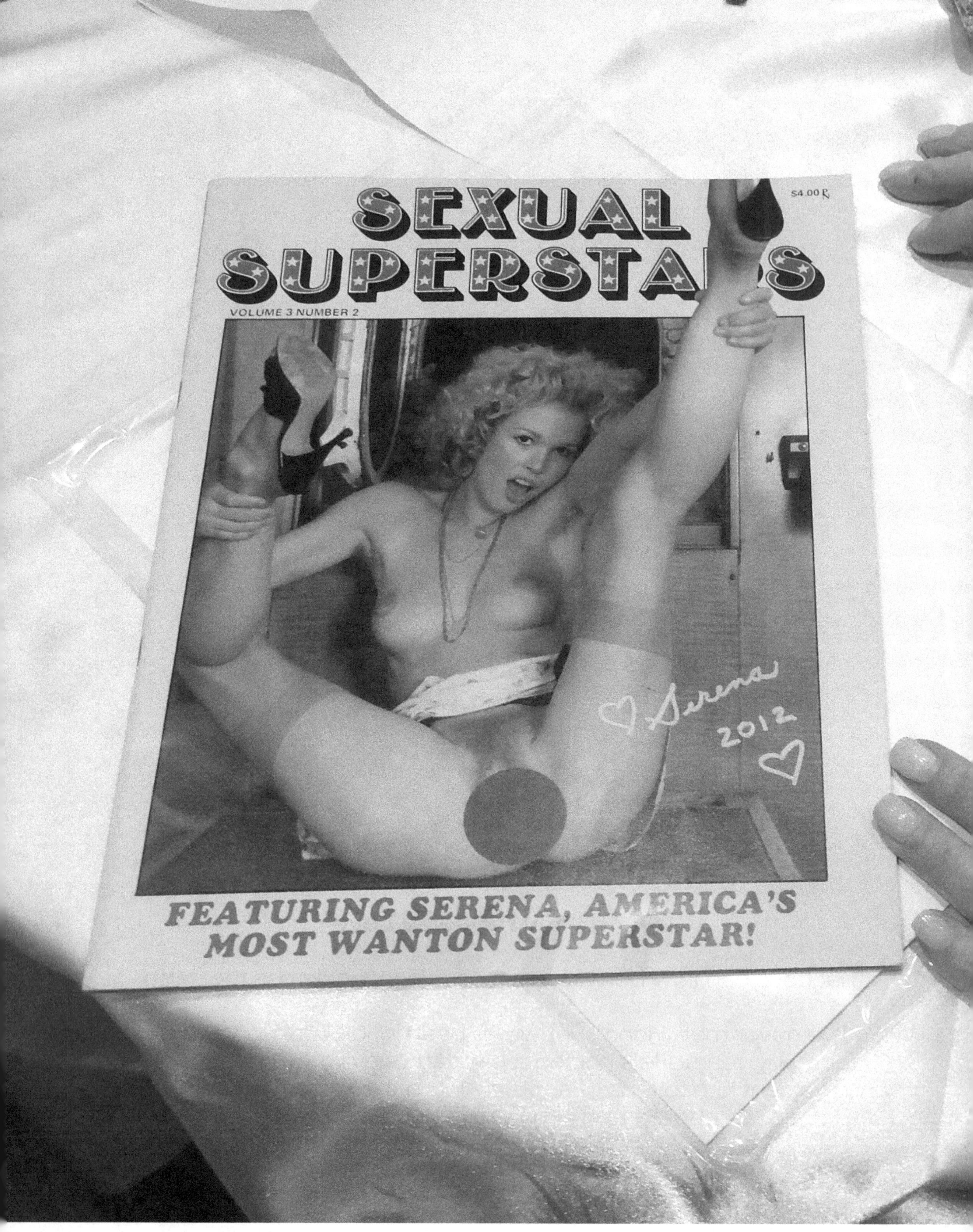
SEXUAL
SUPERSTA S
$4.00
VOLUME 3 NUMBER 2
Serena
2012
FEATURING SERENA, AMERICA'S
MOST WANTON SUPERSTAR!

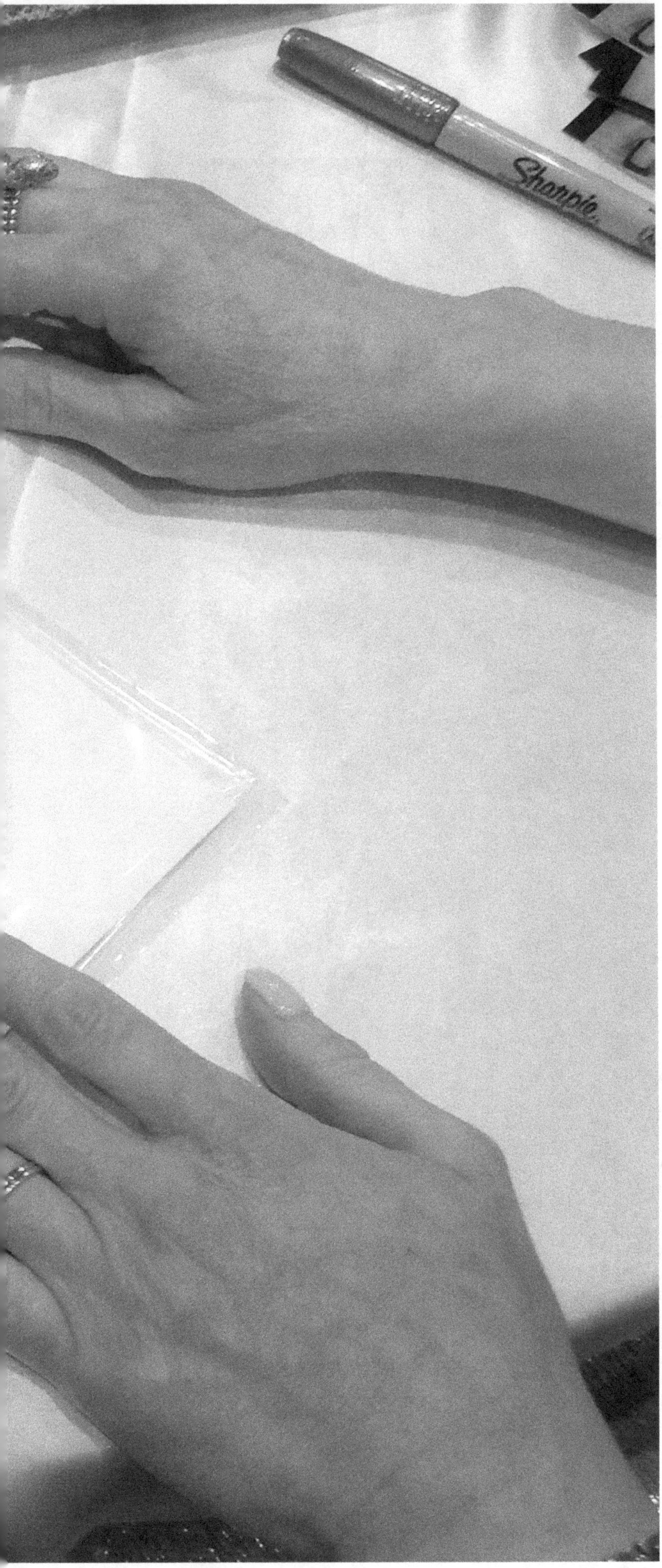

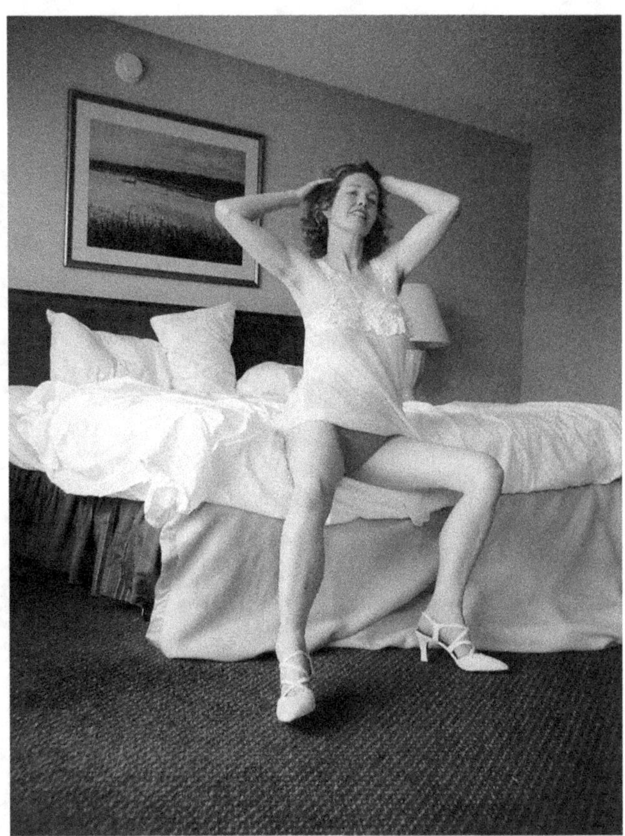

Our friendship has grown through our emails as he travels the planet with his job. We send one another kisses across the miles. He goes into the deserts of Africa.

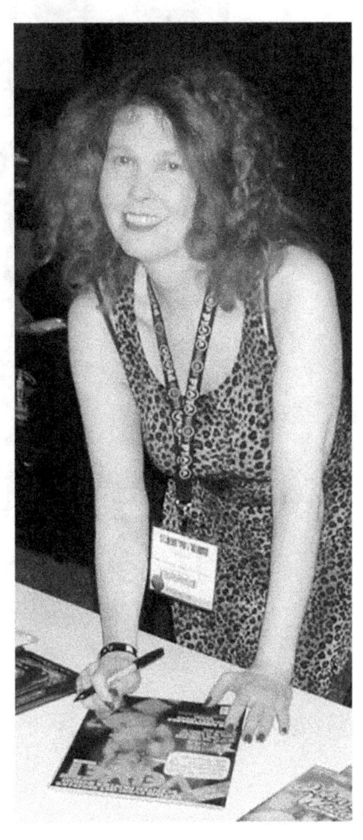

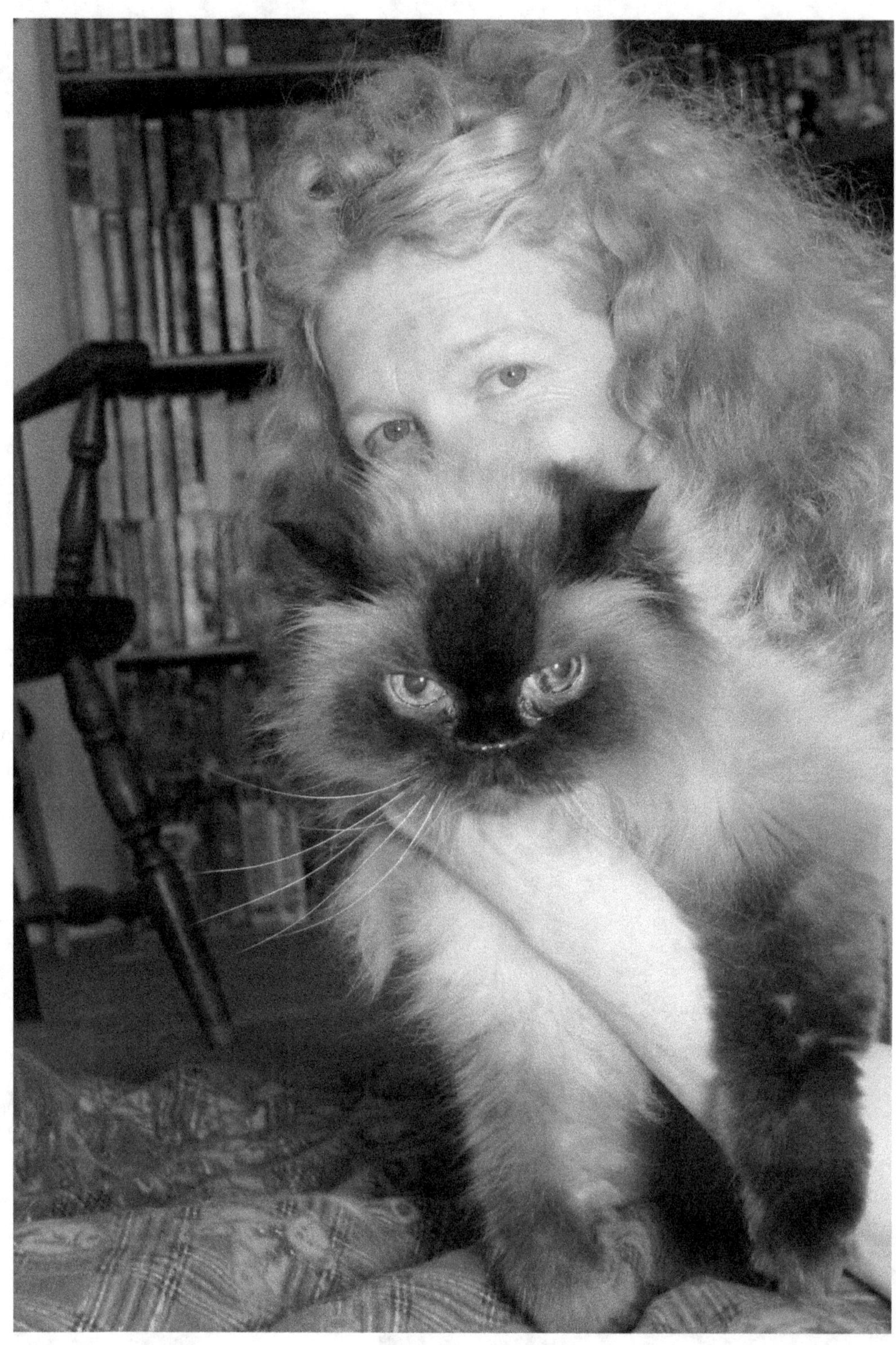

I know him to be a kind man. He has adopted cats, even a three-legged one he calls "Tripod."

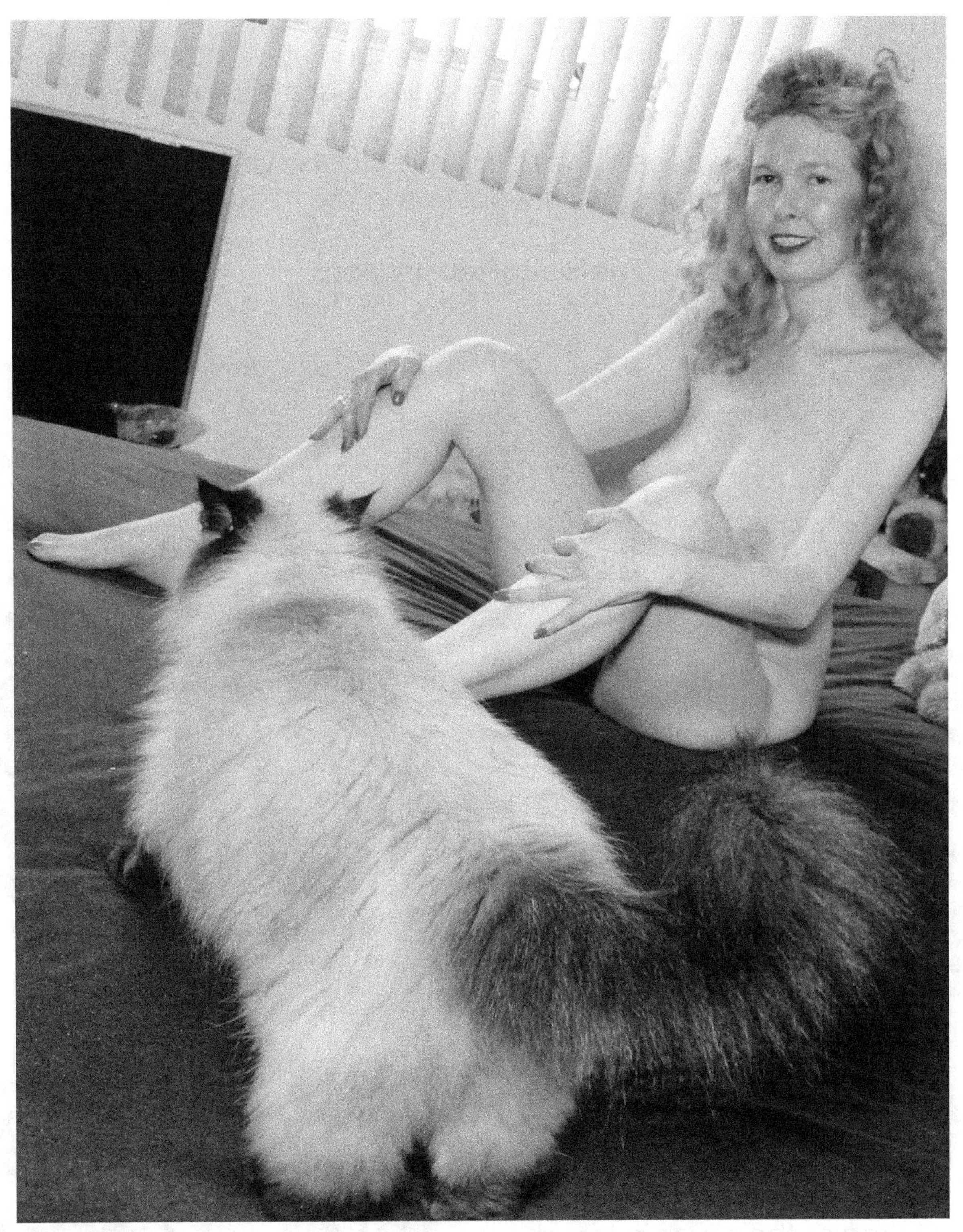

With the cat that owned Bill Margold

Henri speaks Italian, but his English is good enough to write to me.

Out of the blue I found out that he communicates with my New York friend Ashley, who speaks fluent Italian.

Ashley has a British accent and is married to the delightful April Spicer. They create the best of all websites in the history of erotica...

TheRialtoReport.com

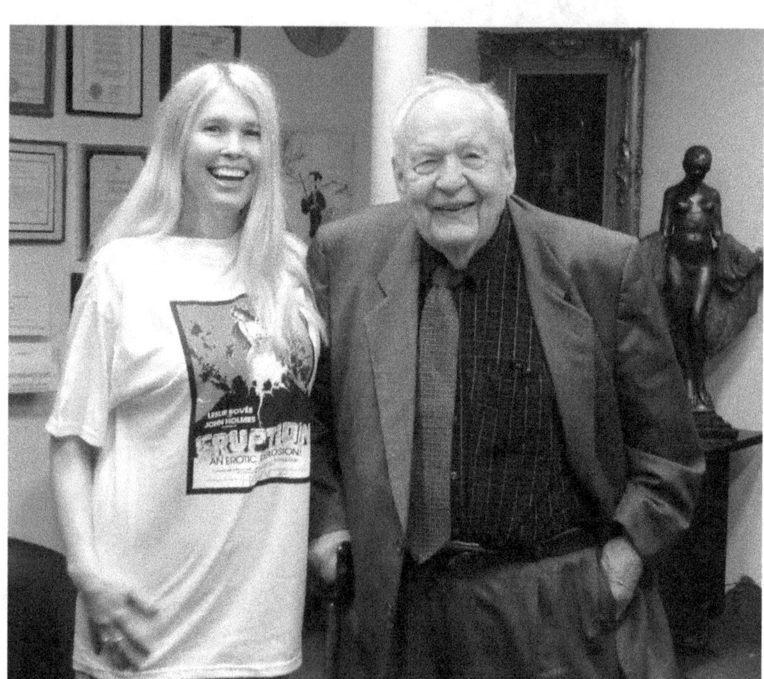

With the amazing Dr. Ted at his School/Library.

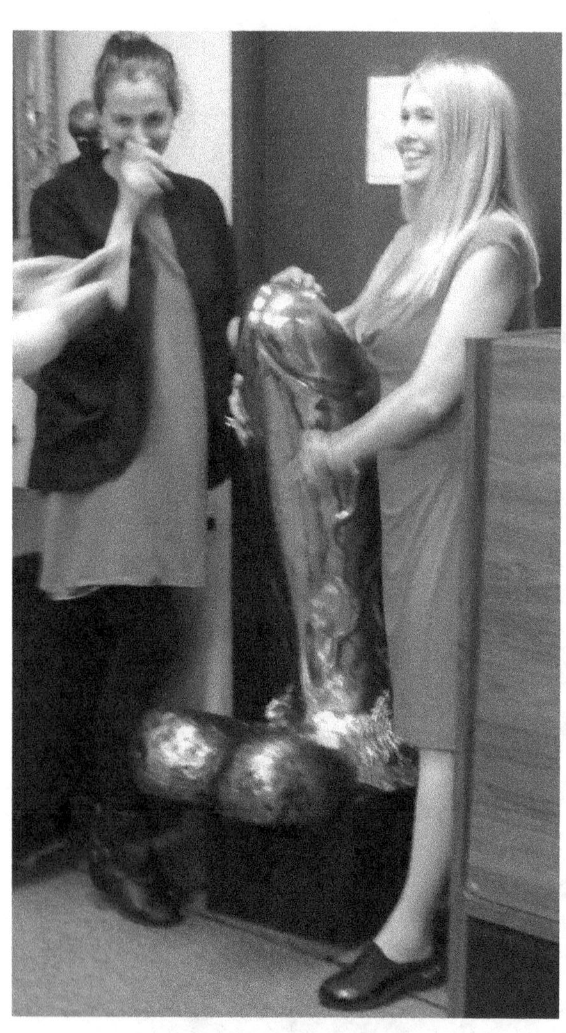

This was taken at the much missed (RIP) Dr. Ted's place. It is a photo of April, Dick, and myself.

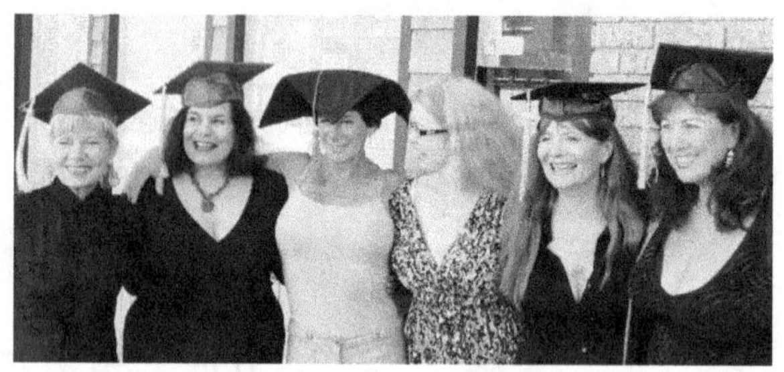

I visit the Graduates of Dr. Ted's school.

Photos by P. Johnston

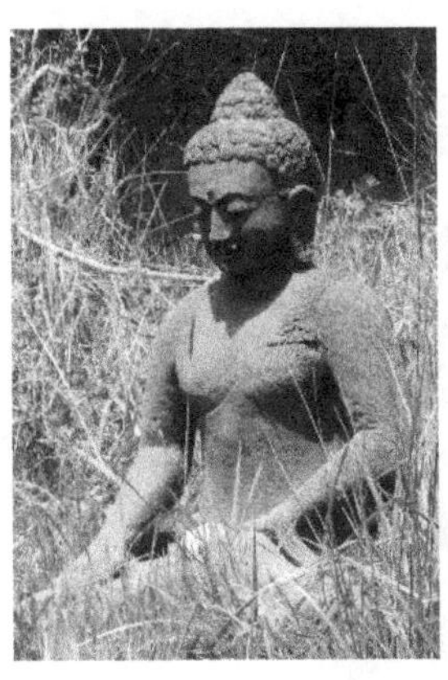

Marc and the lovely Ati

You can cross the world to find your soul-mate.

Catherine Gigante-Brown, Author

Cathy is my sister "Cathy spelled with a 'C.'"

I see great tenacity in her, still keeps on writing, keeps on ticking!
I've read and love her books.

She sent me this photo of herself. I think she looks like Lady Gaga in it!

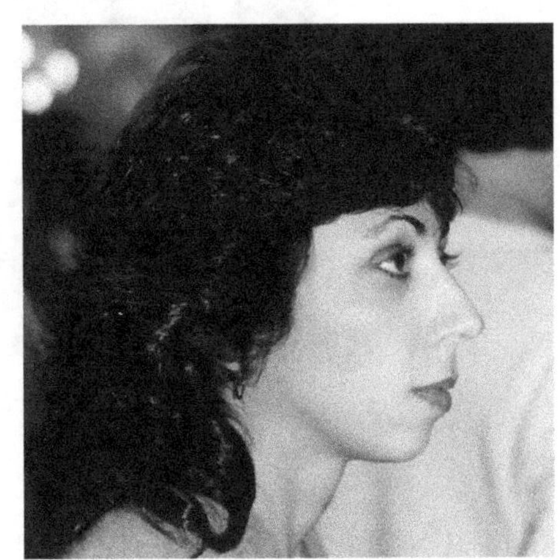

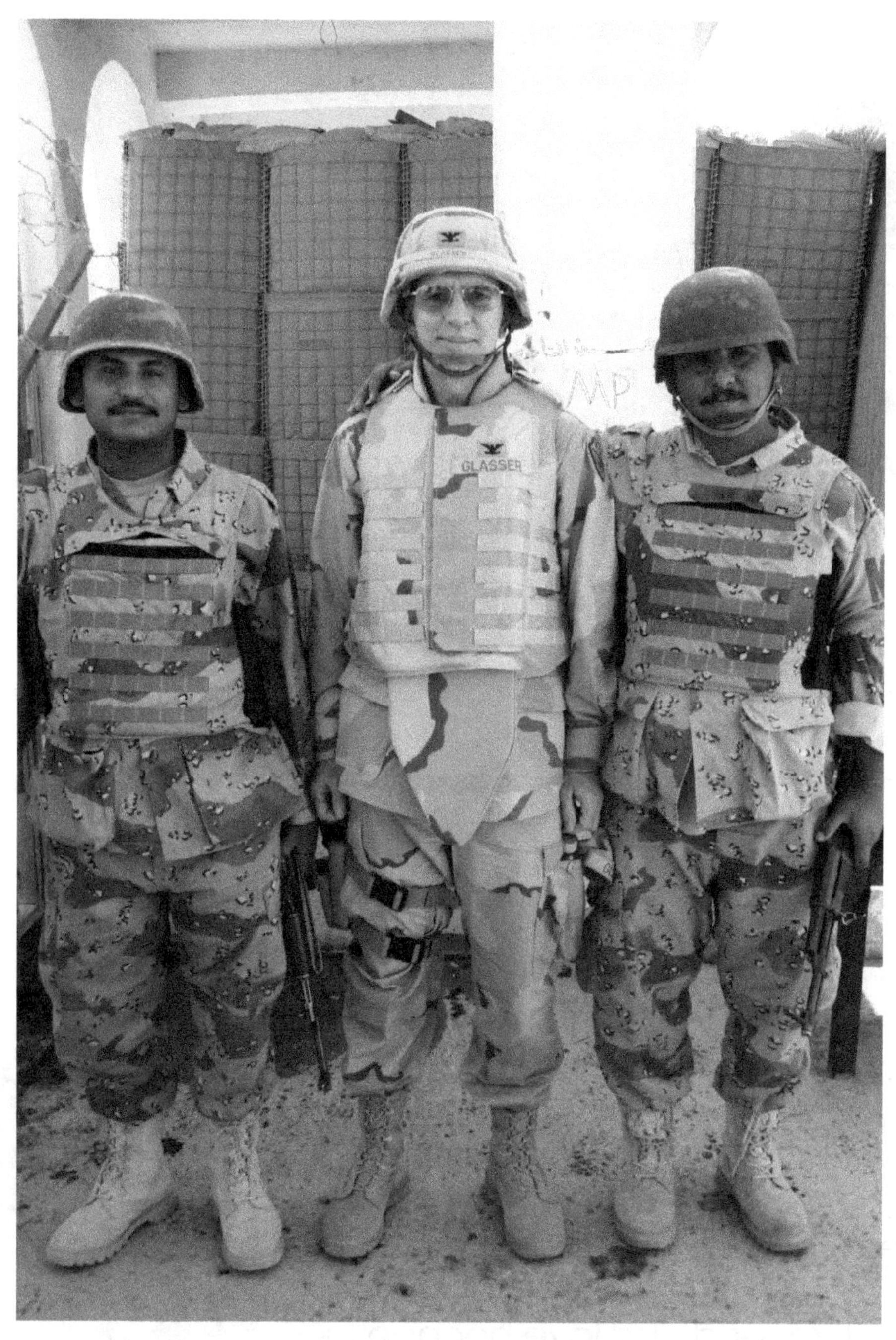

"Bill from Iraq"

That you can be high-ranking with a healthy interest in sex and love.

He has been my "New Bill," taking over from Bill Margold.
He has been a really good friend to me.

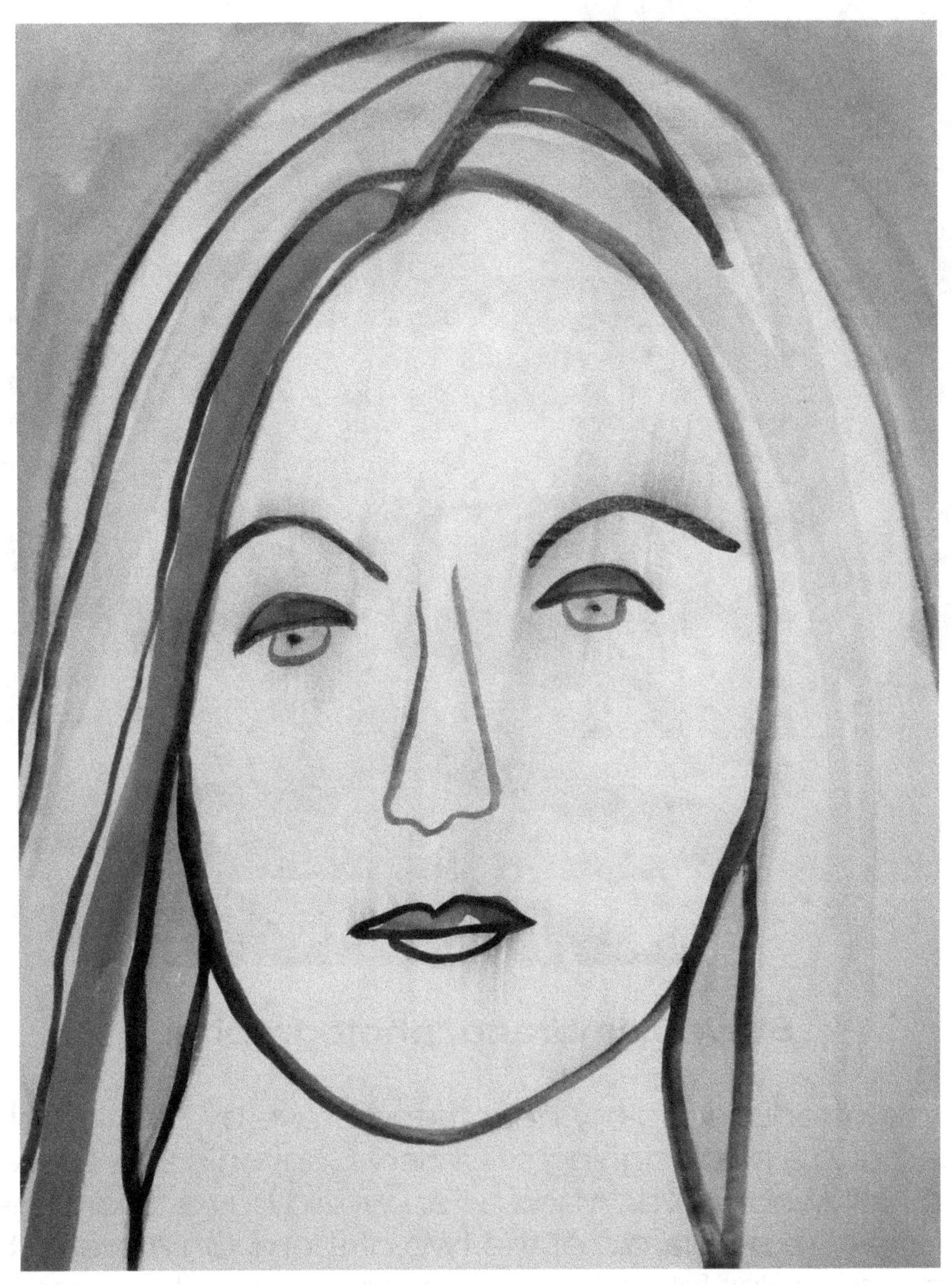

Bo in Denmark, my email friend

I learned that it's possible to connect deeply through words, through the computer.

Watercolor by Serena Czarnecki

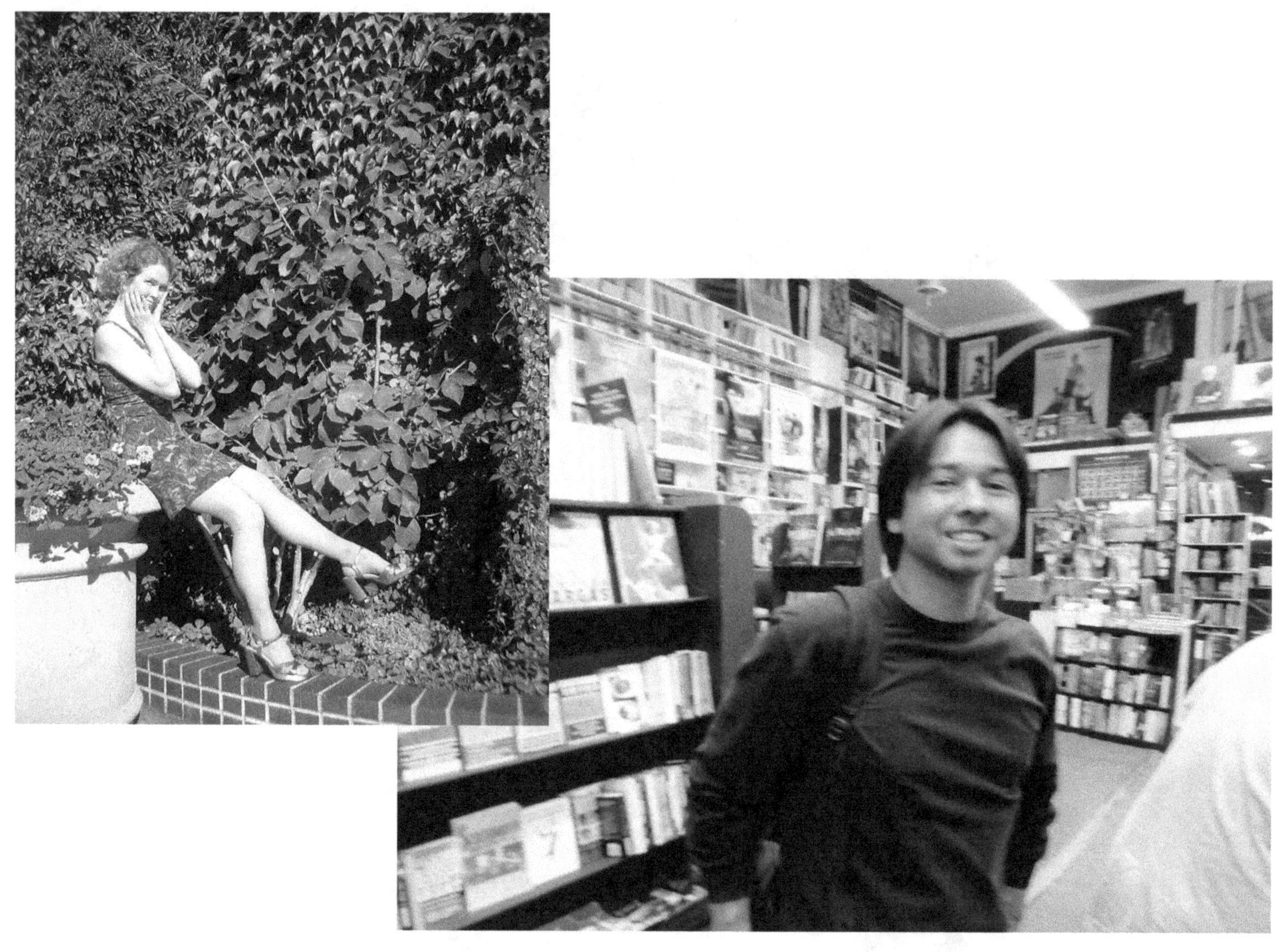

Steve Zambrano, photographer

I was introduced to my dear friend Steve by Bill Margold. We'd come to a book signing of Christy Canyon's at a poster shop on Hollywood Blvd. When a Fan would buy a book, she'd have Steve take a Polaroid of the two of them. On a break, Steve showed me his Portfolio and boy was I impressed! Images in photography that clearly showed that he was an Artist.

I was staying at Bill's, as I'd do when in LA. Steve came over and we became fast friends taking photographs. He'd eventually do the majority of pictures in "Backstage Girls." We stay in touch through postcards. I began collecting postcards because my Dad did. I've been adding to the Czarnecki Collection of Post Cards for years. My Grandkids remember to send me postcards when they travel, and my friend Steve always uses postcards when he writes to me.

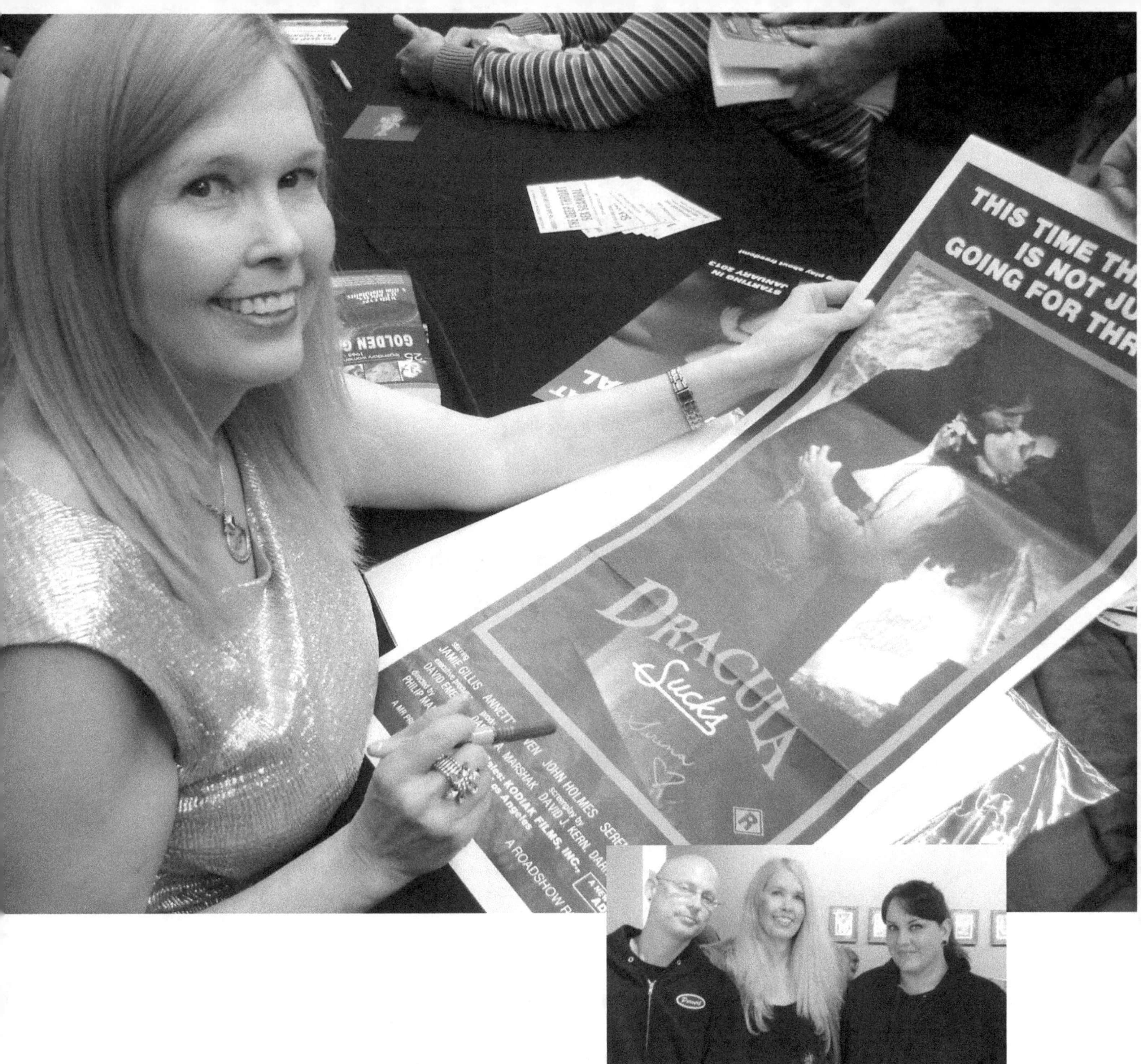

Mark and the lovely Miranda

I learned that you can start as a Fan,
become a Friend, and develop into Family.

I love them as a couple because they really Love each other.

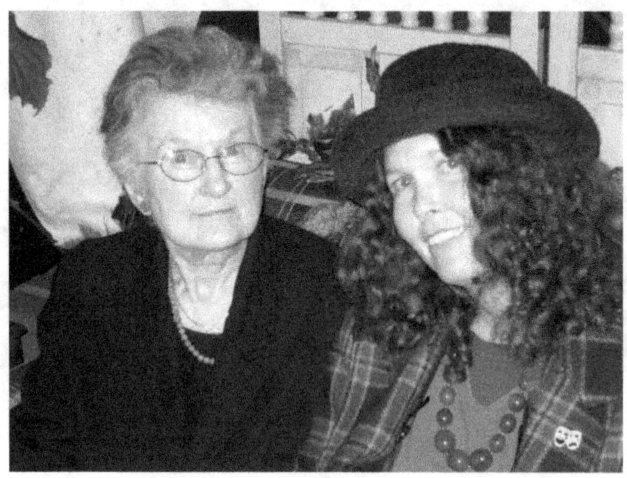

Photo of Mom and me. She kept her cool in all my mania-madness.

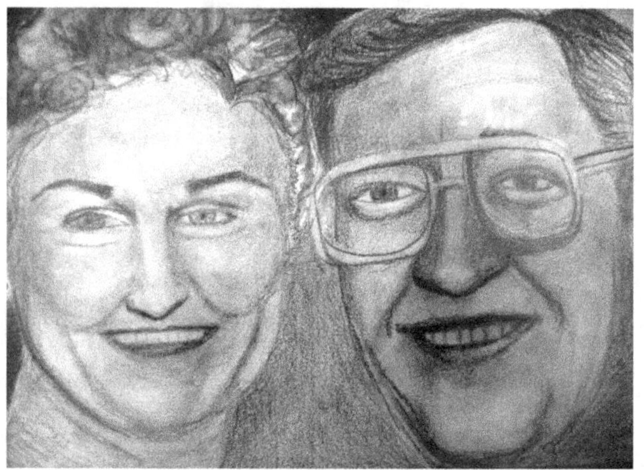

Pencil sketch by me of my folks.

Mom and Dad

I learned from my folks that real love can be rocky
and have ups and downs.
But if it is true love it will survive all slings and arrows.

I dream about them all the time.
Mom and Dad wore a Mizpah necklace at all times,
never taking the broken heart off. Put together, the necklace reads
"Grow Old Along With Me, the Best is Yet to Be."
They admired Robert Browning's love of Elizabeth, enjoyed their Poems.

I wear Mom's wedding ring to Dad as my wedding ring to Paul.

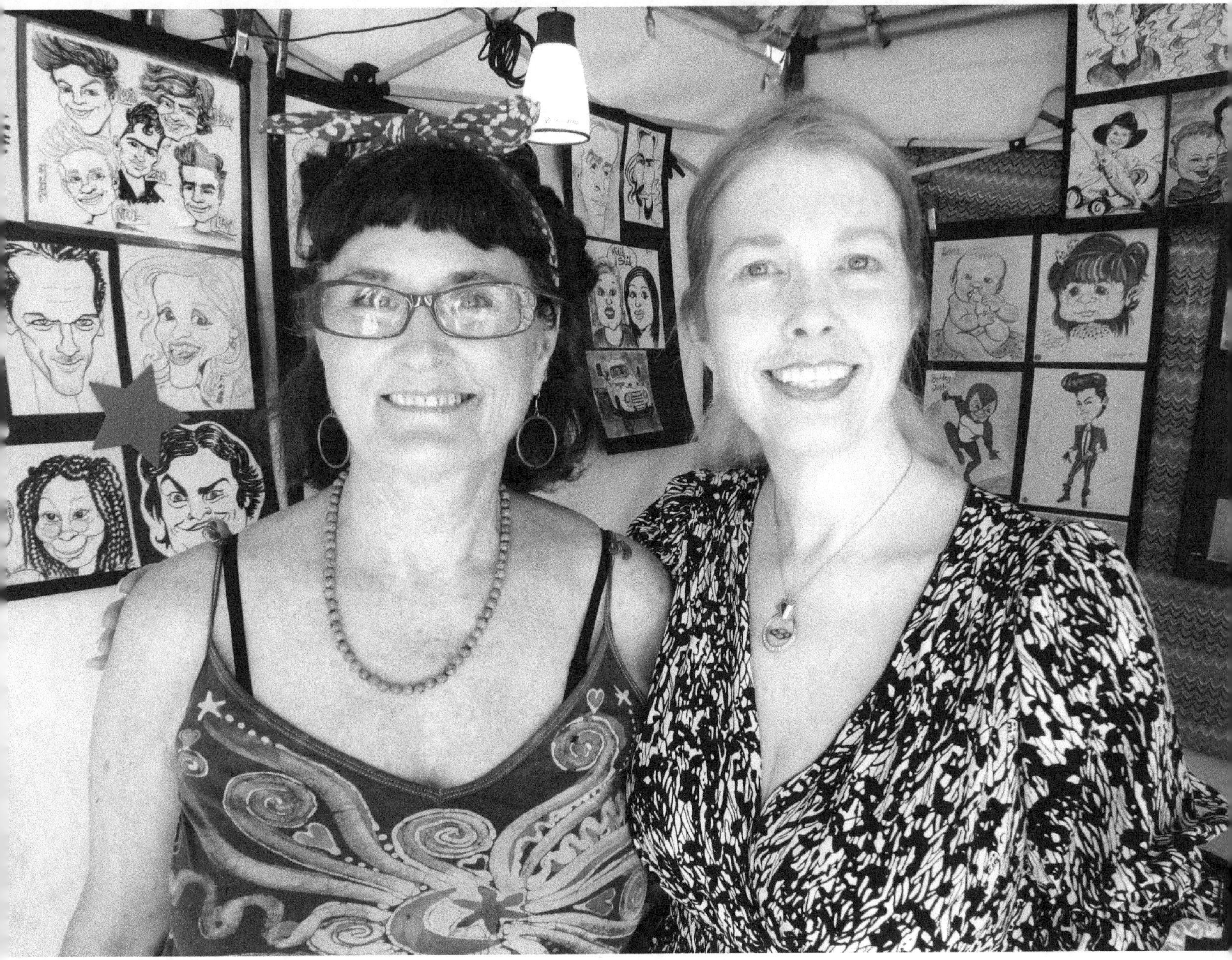

K my sister

I will always return to my best Friend.

This picture is of us at the Alameda State Fair in her Caricature Booth.
She's an Artist, and can make her living this way.

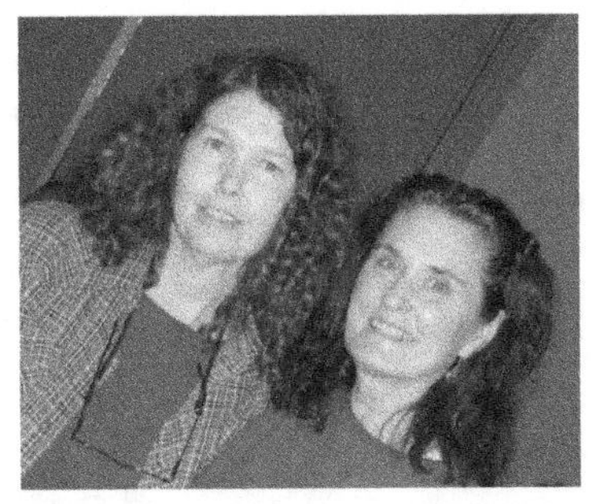

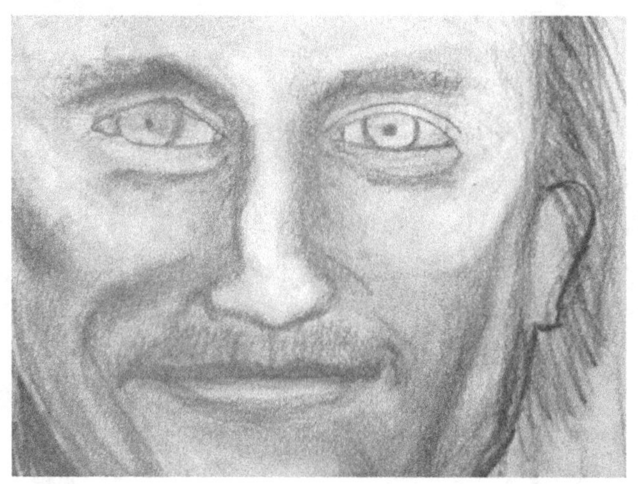

Pencil drawing by SC.

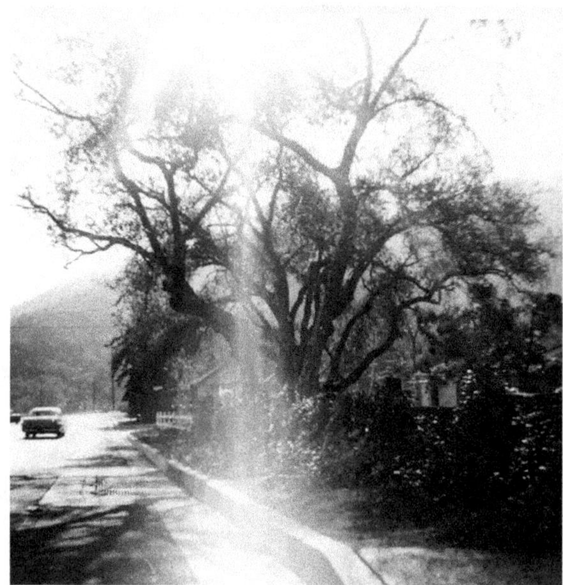

Photo of oak tree under which I was born.

D, my brother

He helped deliver me into this world.
Thanks, Honey!

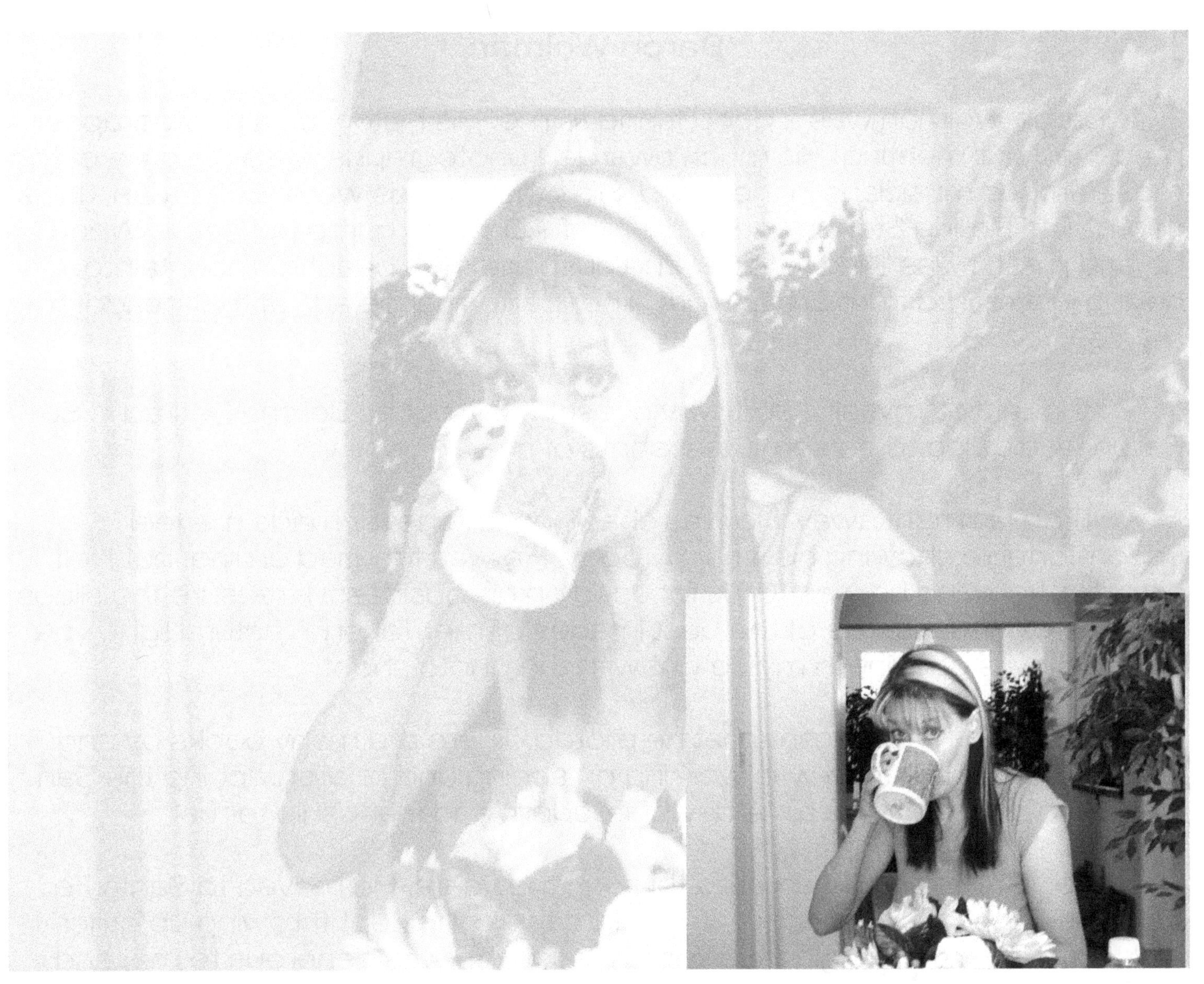

CC, my sister

CC and I learned to drink coffee from our sweet mother.
I took this photo at CC's fabulous house,
where Mom had her own wing.

I've learned from this sister that blood is, indeed, thicker than water.
No matter how we may argue, we always have each other's back.

Baron Wolman

Baron Wolman was a good friend to me. His history as a photographer preceded our meeting. His much awarded photographs were of some of the most famous musicians in the world. His other friends were: Bob Dylan, Janis Joplin, The Rolling Stones and The Grateful Dead to name but a few. When he and I met, I was living with my 2nd husband on a beautiful mountaintop, having just retired from Erotic work. The "performance art" of that period of my life.

I thought to myself, "Self, why not sell a lay-out as Serena Retired?" So Baron was called to do some test shots of me.

I liked him right away. He was charming and never made me feel uncomfortable showing his lens my body. He was focused on me, but I felt assured, knowing he was 100% focused on his business. I treasure the slides he gave to me as some of the best images of me. Taken in natural light, you can see I was genuine in my delight with the photo shoot.

I went up in his Cessna that he piloted. There are many books by and about his work. He then was working on seeing and photographing the San Francisco area from the air. A day of freedom and friendship for us!

We've spoken and emailed through the years. He moved to Santa Fe from the Bay Area. I never got to visit him there, life kept throwing up other trails to wander. I'm so glad we kept in touch, he was generous to me, and always a lot of fun. He sent me PIC of himself:

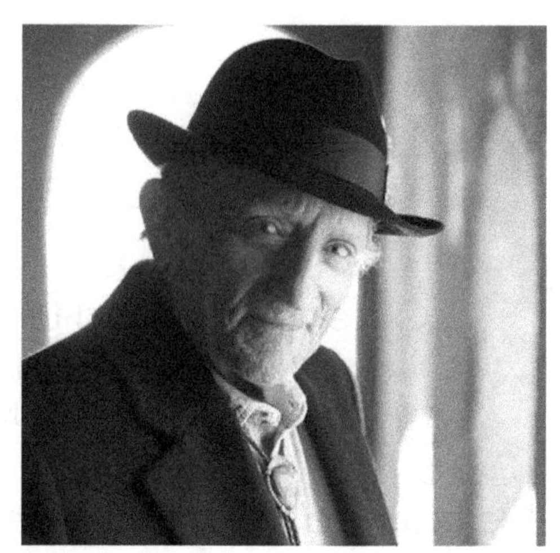

The photos he took of me in the 1980s have graced all of my books. We discussed my books and he seemed glad to be part of them. I will always remember him with love.

A Fan of mine on Social Media told me when Baron passed away. Take some images in your Hereafter. I know they will be peaceful, restful; RIP.

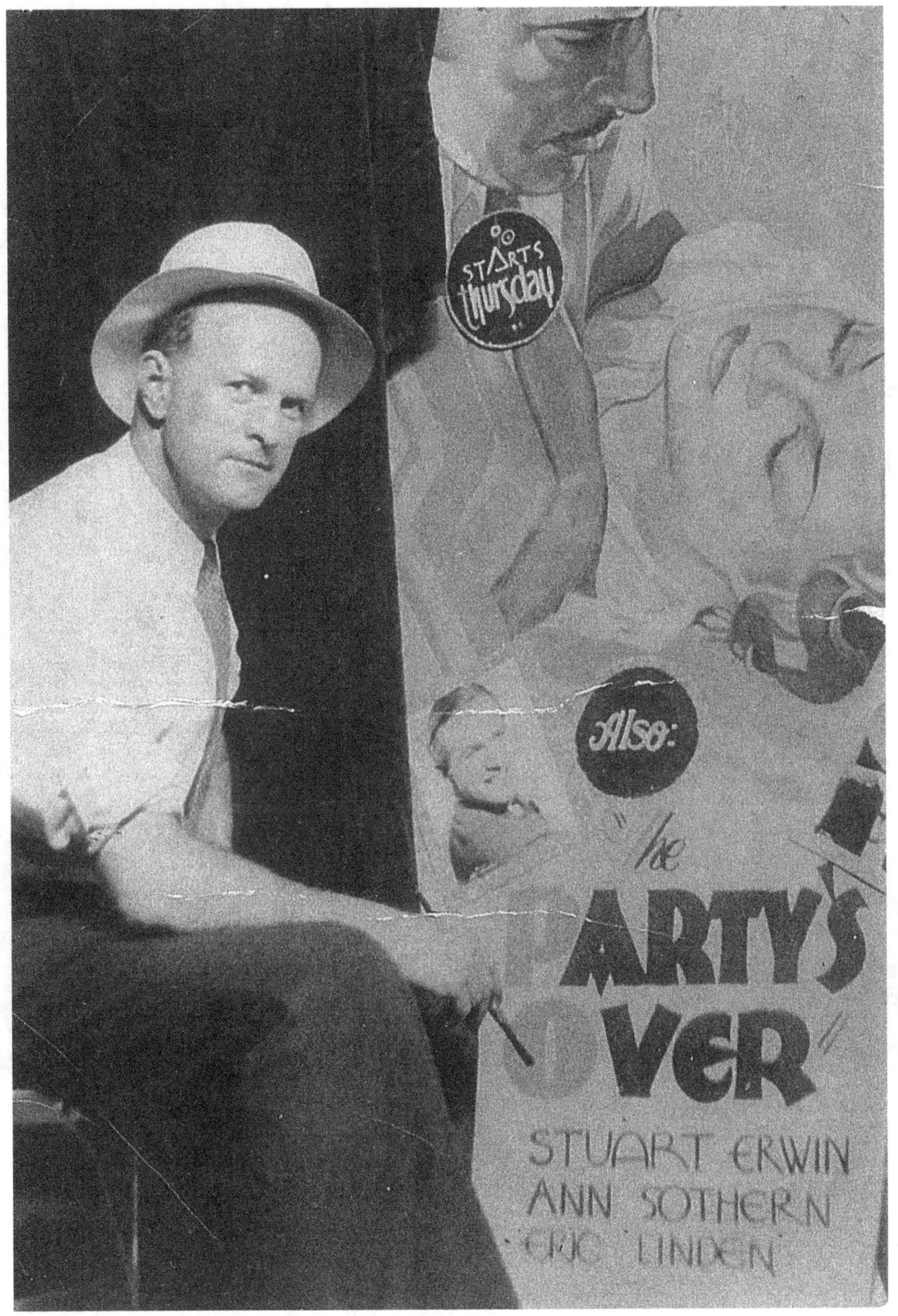

Carlos, Leberman my Grandfather

That it is possible to be a Poet and an Artist and make a living.

Photo of Carlos at his easel.

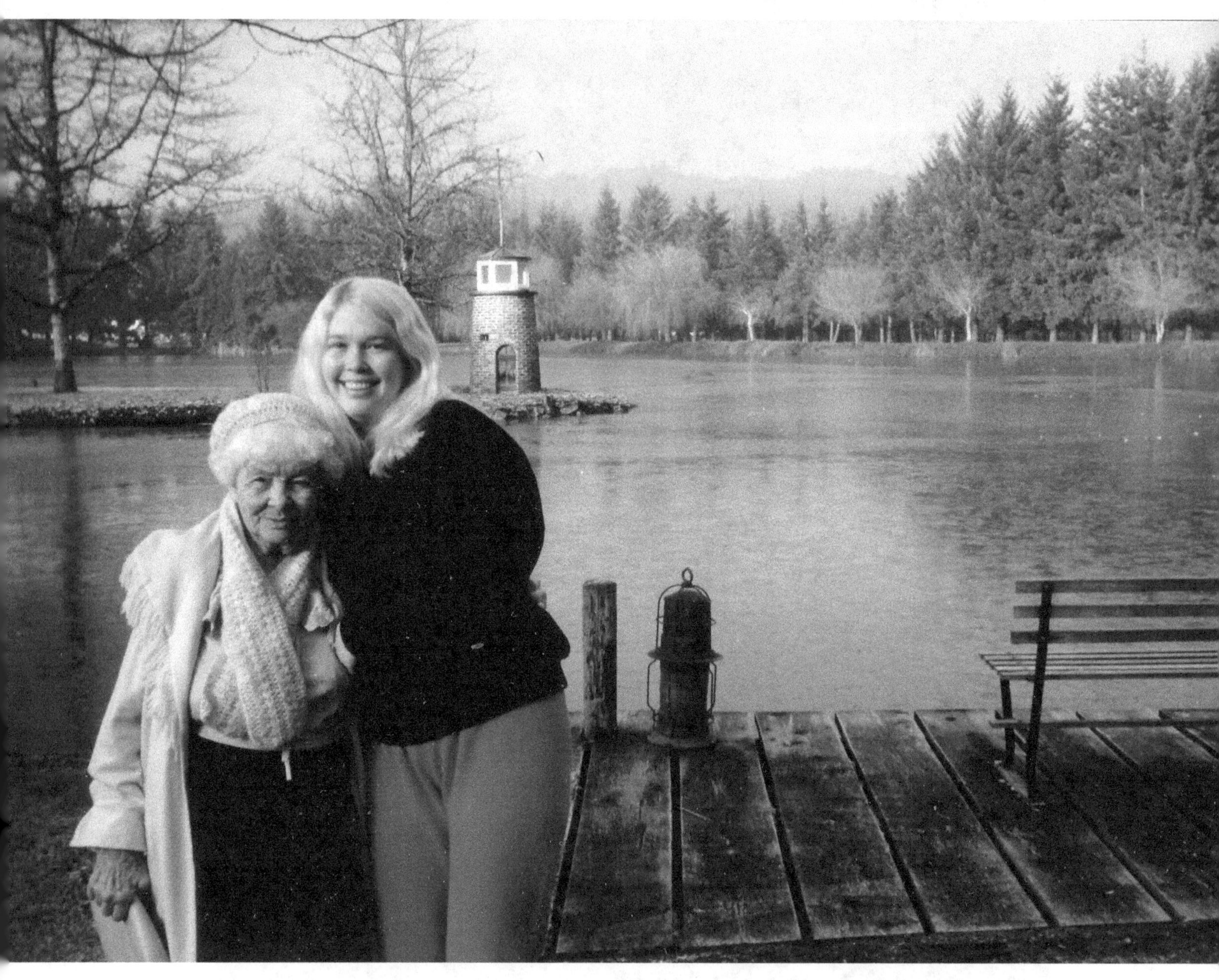

Busha, my Grandmama

I learned what love is, manifested. She was a bundle of pure Love.
She was my personal Yoda!

Serena and her Busha in Oregon.

Section Two

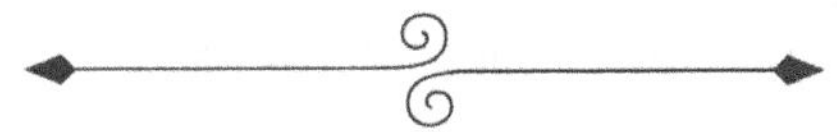

Work Play

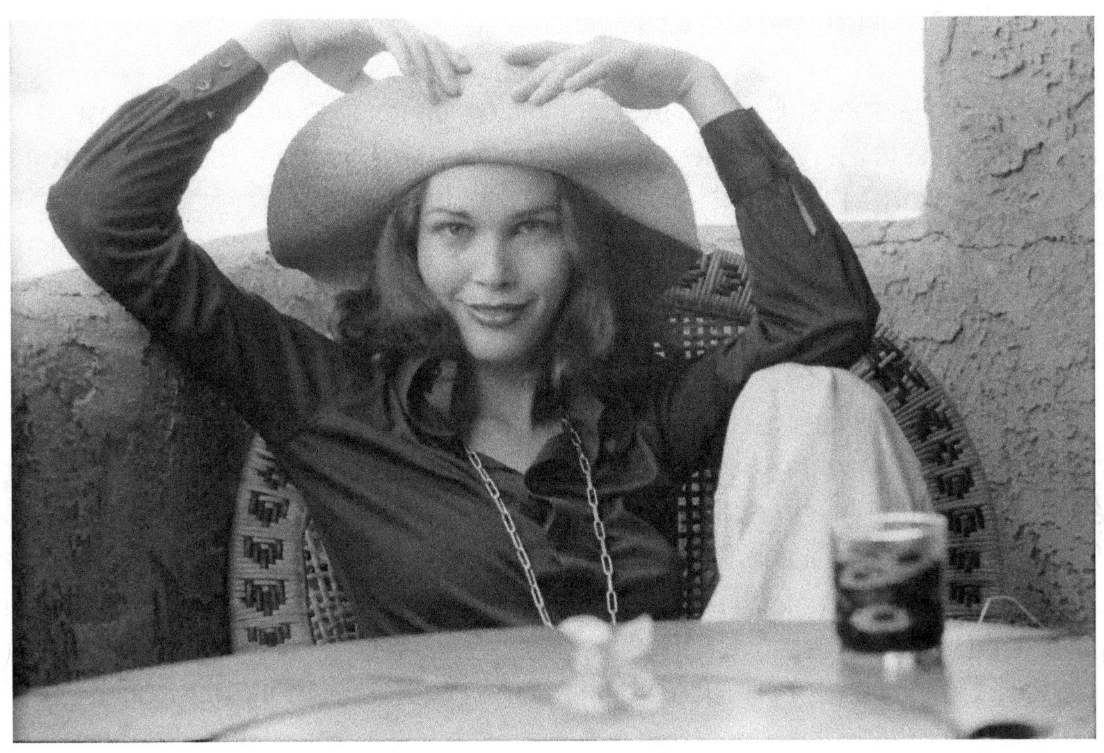

Photo by Titus Moody

Work is Play. Work is satisfying, gratifying when work is playtime. When work is play, there is ease and discoveries and fulfillment. When channeling your energy to explore what you are passionate about, you are able to create mental images that are highly focused. When you pretend hard enough, you can become that which is, at first, mere illusion. Albert Einstein said, "Imagination is more important than knowledge." It is from imagining things that knowledge comes. Indeed, some talk about a Super Conscious Mind that contains unlimited Creativity.

The "high" you get from exercise or meditation can clear your normally chattering mind and tune in to a larger insight. The great man, Rabindranath Tagore said that Art is "the expression of the universal through the individual."

I work in series. One take is never enough, I need to see an image from many angles. This book itself is the third book in a series of books I've written. The third in a set. When painting, I have several series I work, then leave. Series may resurface later, sometimes years later, seemingly out of the blue. For instance, the "Faces" series I've done in oils, watercolor, ceramics and pastels.

I've made "Masks" in various media. Anything that's at hand I will incorporate into my work, artwork. I see the world as something to have fun with, everything is a tool in my workshop paintbox. Art is my special communication with ideas that want to be actualized. When play/working my mind is free of restraint, and I am more in the present. Time itself seems to bend, and can become a place of "no-time." Seconds, minutes or hours may pass in this "no-time."

Before moving into a large studio I took college classes to have a place to paint. I learned from my professors, and took Art History to learn my place. At first, I had lots of money to buy supplies. There was a paint store in San Francisco that would mix up gallons of oil paint in colors I'd want. I hired people to build stretcher bars and to stretch canvas, although I loved applying gesso as a ground. I bought a van and hired a driver just to transport my large pieces to exhibits. I flung myself into the very idea of Art. I collaborated with an Art Curator, Michael S. Bell; he guided my early career. I sold my work at exhibitions, and was represented by a Gallery in Florida and in New York City. I really hustled to get my work to the public. When my finances changed, I began to work only for my own enjoyment. Of course I still enjoy selling my work!

I acted up as a bipolar kid, I acted in movies, I acted like an Artist until the role consumed me. Thoroughly, completely, until I could be nothing else. I'd never wanted to be anything else!

Art is my Song from the Silence. From the void comes inspiration and Art can follow. To paraphrase the Grateful Dead, "It is a ripple in a pool where no stone has been tossed." The Source, the Fountainhead is unseen and is yet all there is. The vastness, the subconscious, god, everything is a loud silence. When calm, we can dip into the Silence and hear it's Songs. We can bring a reflection of them back to our reality.

Art in each of its forms: music, architecture, sculpture, literature, theatre, and painting is to dance to the Silence Songs. To open yourself up to the Universe is to "tune in." Your soul is the conduit to the radio of bliss. The Songs play through your body/radio, and can be interpreted as harsh or mellow, black, white or full of color.

I may leave one series of work to percolate in my subconscious. The series may pop up at any time when I'm busy doing other things. If the passion bursts forth, I must follow. I follow my passions in sex, words, paint, whatever is at hand. I live for these moments of inspiration/passion. I am a willing slave to where they take me.

I entertain myself by working. Art is play. My mental movement guides my fingertips and I engage with a continuous flow of spontaneous creativity. I love to solve the problems that Art gives me. I believe there are no accidents in Art, there are intriguing puzzles to solve. Art uses me as it's tool. Art is the task I am summoned to do; Art is my work/play.

Within my happy work there is struggle. I may see the reflection of greatness, but it's a fight to reproduce it on paper. The artwork is an adaptation of what I sense.

As Picasso said, "Art is the elimination of the unnecessary." I think this may apply to Life itself. Each moment is a new you! Use your life as a blank canvas! Paint your true, unfiltered, self upon your days. Let your subconscious steer you and reveal to you what is most important. Think about who you truly are, and become that every day. If you imagine yourself to be a good, productive person, you will be one.

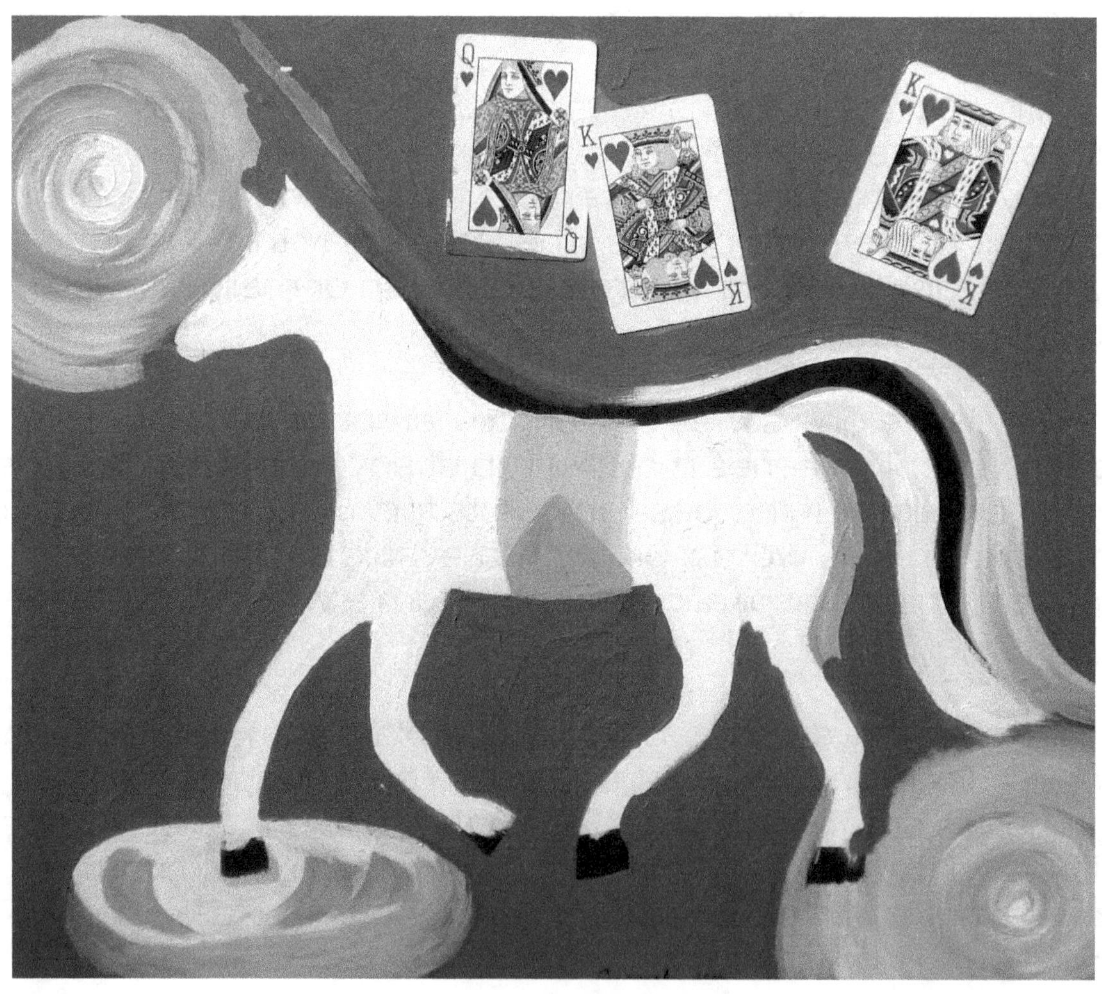

Section Three

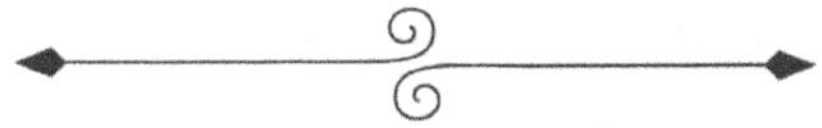

Art and Sex

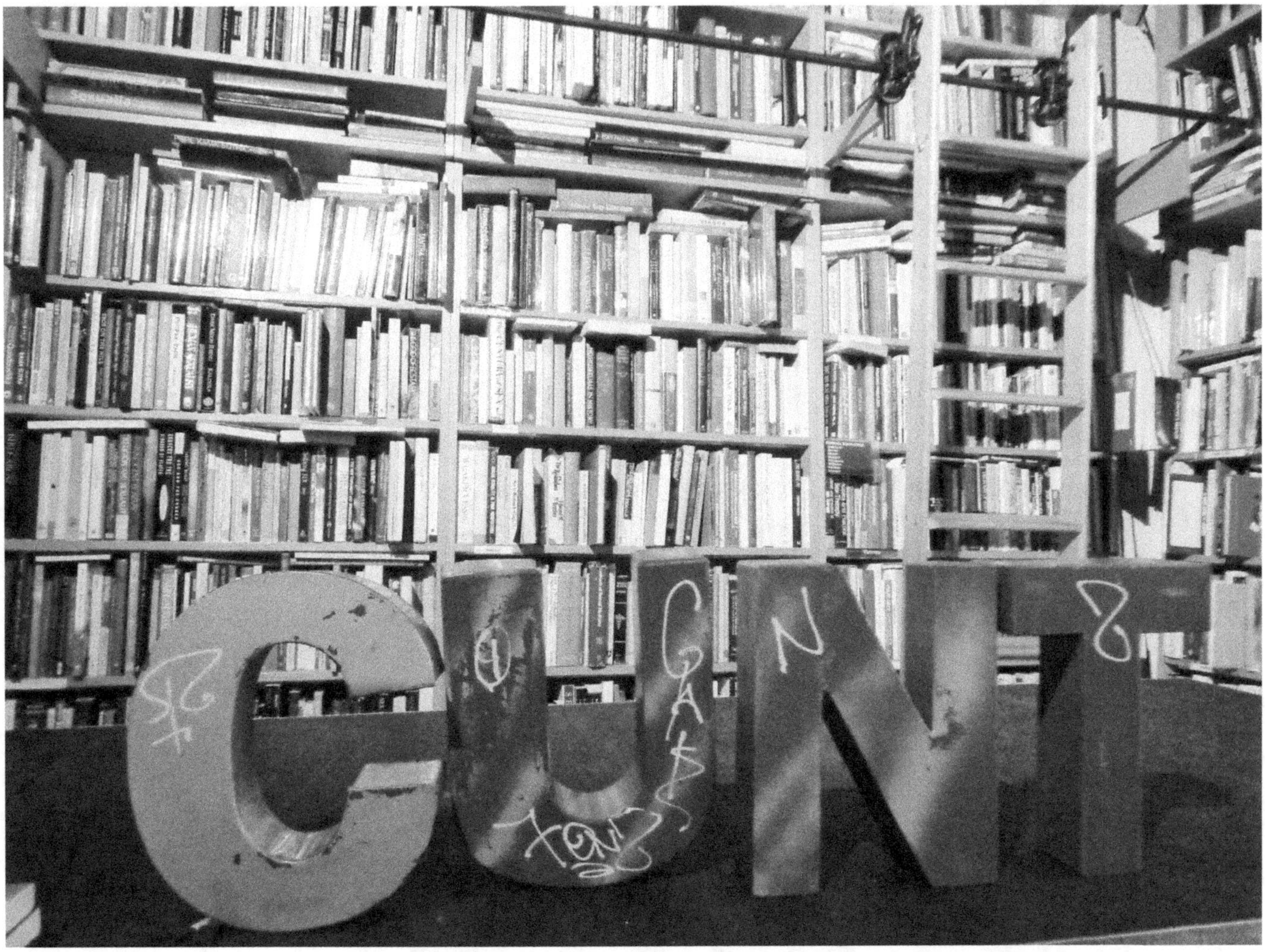

An email from my friend in Denmark, Bo:

Hi Serena,

I have been doing a lot of thinking about that text that you sent me. I have sort of a follow-up question. I remember a Danish poet once writing about this, how messy his surroundings would get whenever he entered the creative phase.

It's the same with painters, obviously. It certainly is with me. Suddenly I have stuff everywhere and I don't care, and it's not until I come out of it and look around I see what one might describe as the 'destructive' aspect of creation.

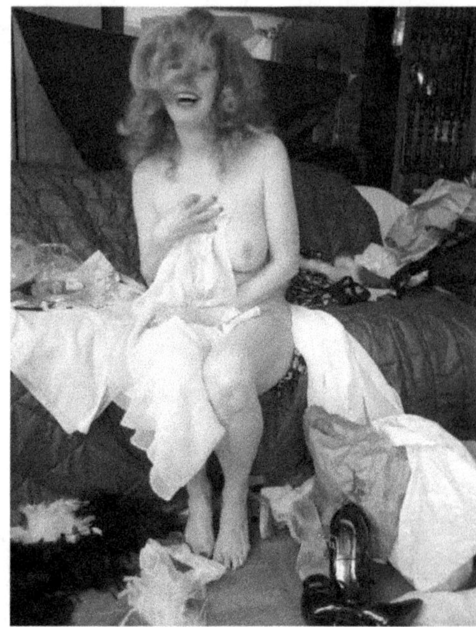

Serena creates. Serena creates a mess.

Maybe it's simply a question of focus.

You focus so intensely on just one thing that you neglect all of the others -- or maybe there really is a more profound and 'cosmic' aspect to it all, that you can't create without some amount of destruction. I would love to hear your thoughts on this, and I would be especially interested in hearing your thoughts on whether this applies to sex and porn as well. Or to eroticism in general. If creation can be said to be somehow - also - inherently destructive, and it can't be helped because it's part of some 'cosmic' rule, does the same apply to eroticism?

And I have a follow-up-follow-up question to that as well. If that is so, is this why sex is often considered to be dangerous? Or perhaps even more to the point:

Is this why sex HAS to be a bit dangerous and transgressive in order to arouse us? Completely safe and totally non-dangerous sex might sound lovely but I have a suspicion that most people would find it somewhat boring. Is it like with a work of art, I wonder. If you sense that the artist had no difficulties doing it, that there was no resistance whatsoever, with no destruction involved, chances are that the work will feel hollow and fake.

Is it the same with sex?

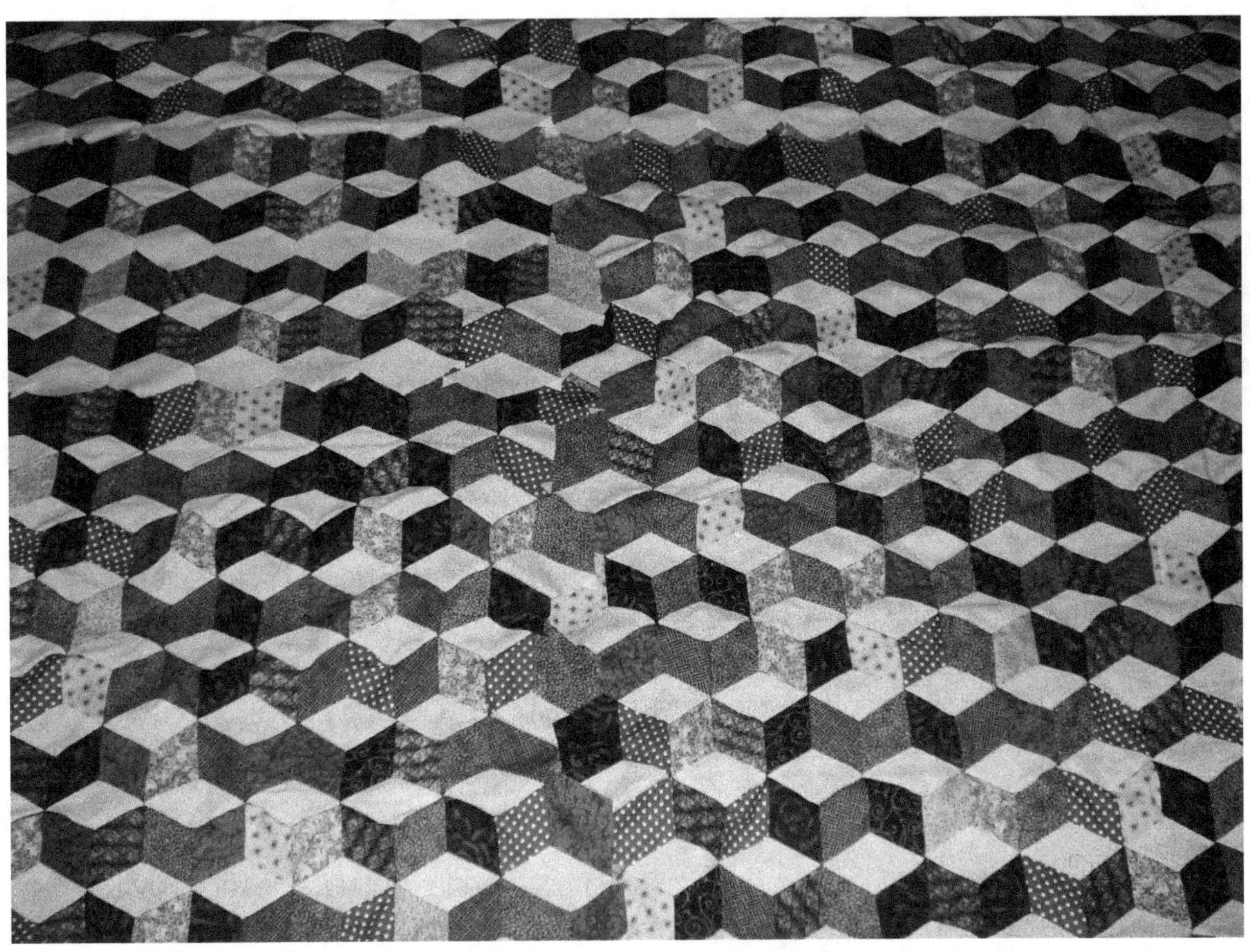

Quilt by Serena Czarnecki

Art and Sex
with Pain

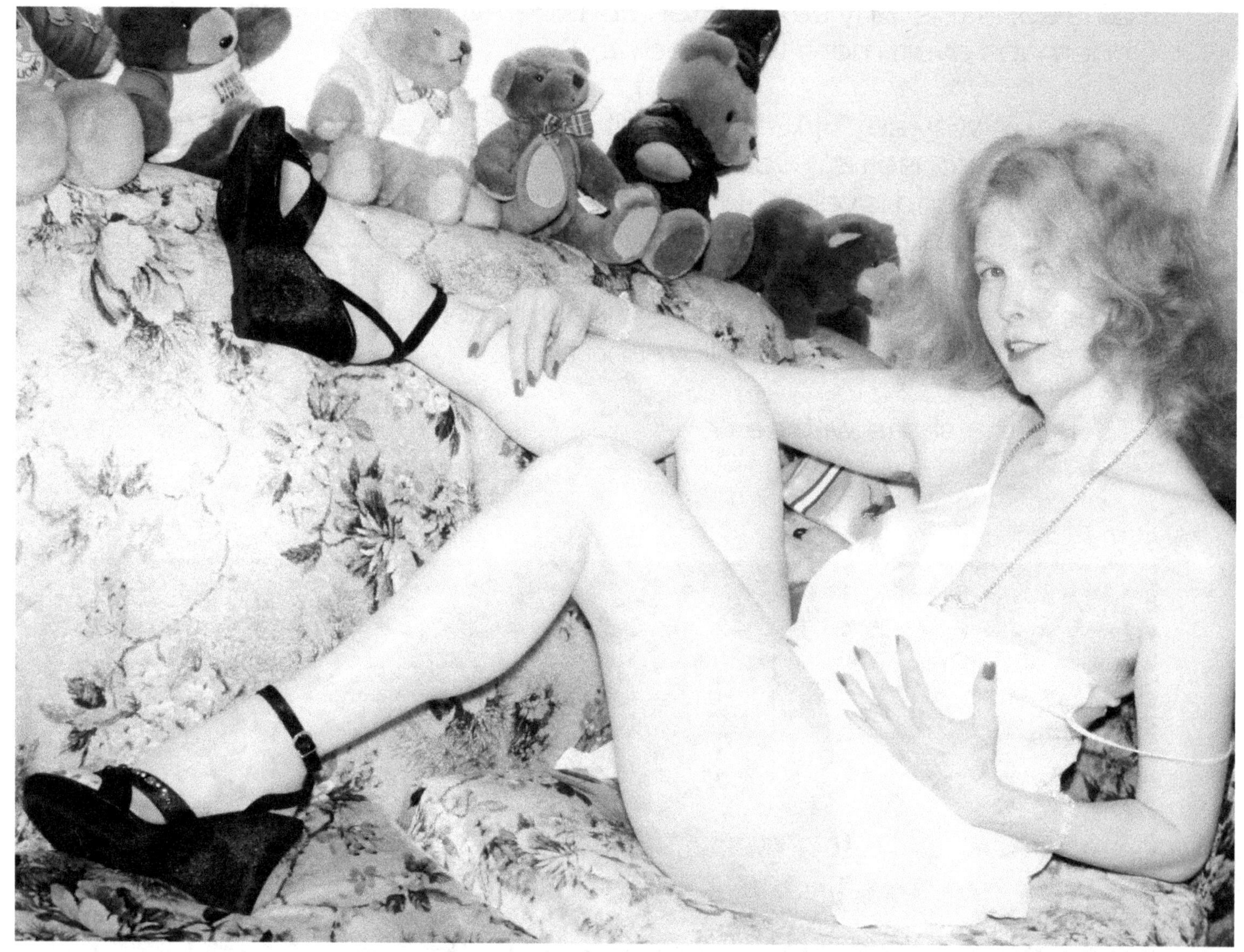

Photo of Serena at Bill Margold's house by Steve Zambrano

I have been in pain and on my back since the middle of September. It is Day of the Dead today. I Tweeted many pictures of Halloween black cats, owls and pumpkins and witches yesterday. This week I've begun to walk, although there is still soreness. For weeks I haven't been able to bathe -- yuk! I'm sweaty and stinky.

I'd been doing great -- walking everyday and sticking with a diet of salads in preparation for attending next April's Cleveland Convention.

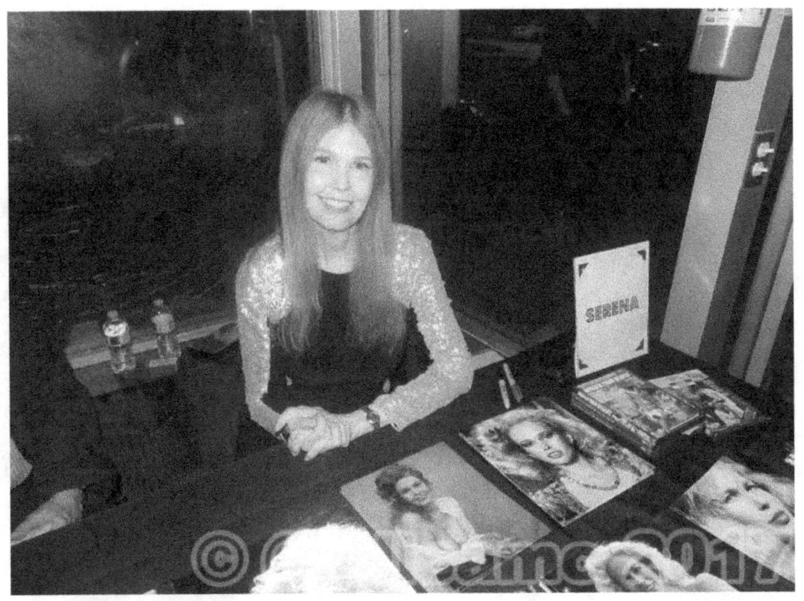

Serena signing at the Cupcake Theater in North Hollywood

I hope to sell autographed 8x10's and other goodies having to do with my X-rated movie career.

It is a Horror Convention, actually, but because erotic films were also played at Drive-in movie theaters I am known to this crowd.

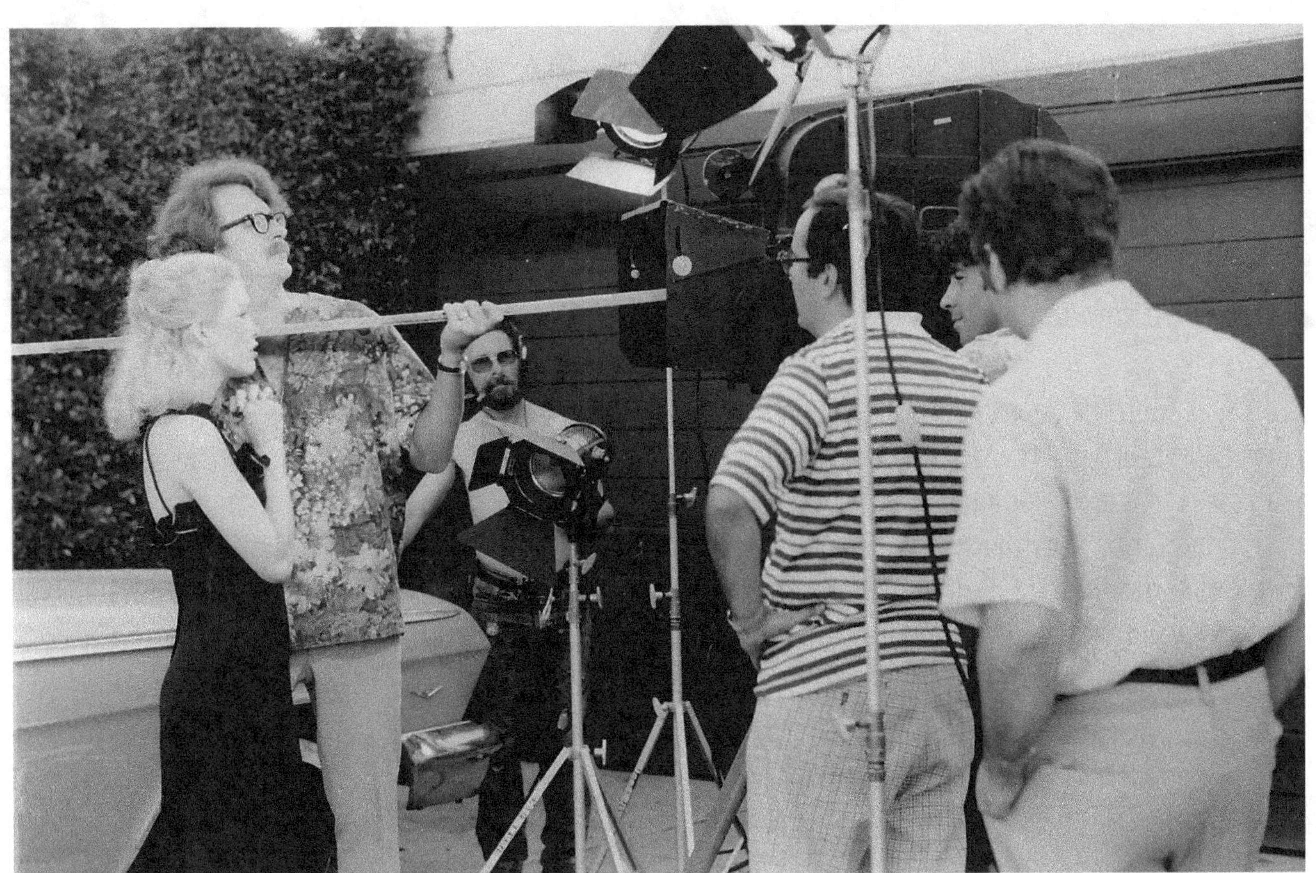

Serena and Bill Margold on set

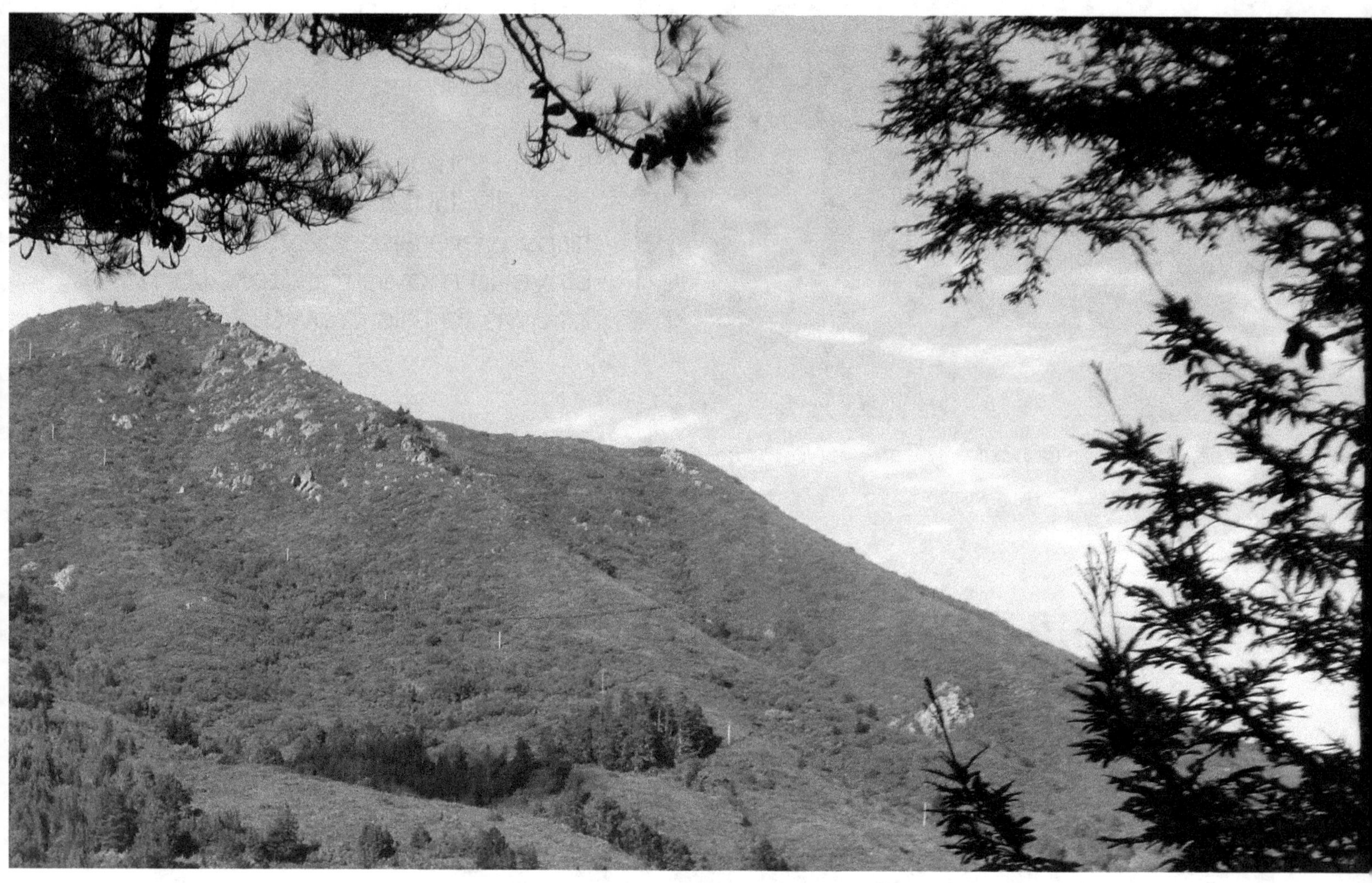

But one day I got home feeling great from a walk over the mountain path, to crumple in pain on the living room floor. Severe pain hit my haunch area and all I could do was scream and cry for hours, waiting for Paul to get home. And I stayed down, taking Ibuprofen and Tylenol and sleeping as much as I could to avoid the pain which was like a toothache in my crotch. HA! Me, the Sex Goddess, done in by a groin-pull!

Photo by Serena Czarnecki

Even being laid-up, in horrible pain, ART came. I need to create as I need to breathe, pain or no. When not sleeping to escape, I found my canvas and latch-hook tool and yarn and started making rugs.

Being busy seemed to distract me from the pain I was in. When I began to feel better, the instinct to create became stronger so I started to design patterns for future rugs. Having completed a design with a marker on the canvass, it then takes me a good three days to contemplate color schemes. On the fourth day I lay out the colors by hooking the colored yarns onto the canvas.

Hooked Rug by Serena Czarnecki

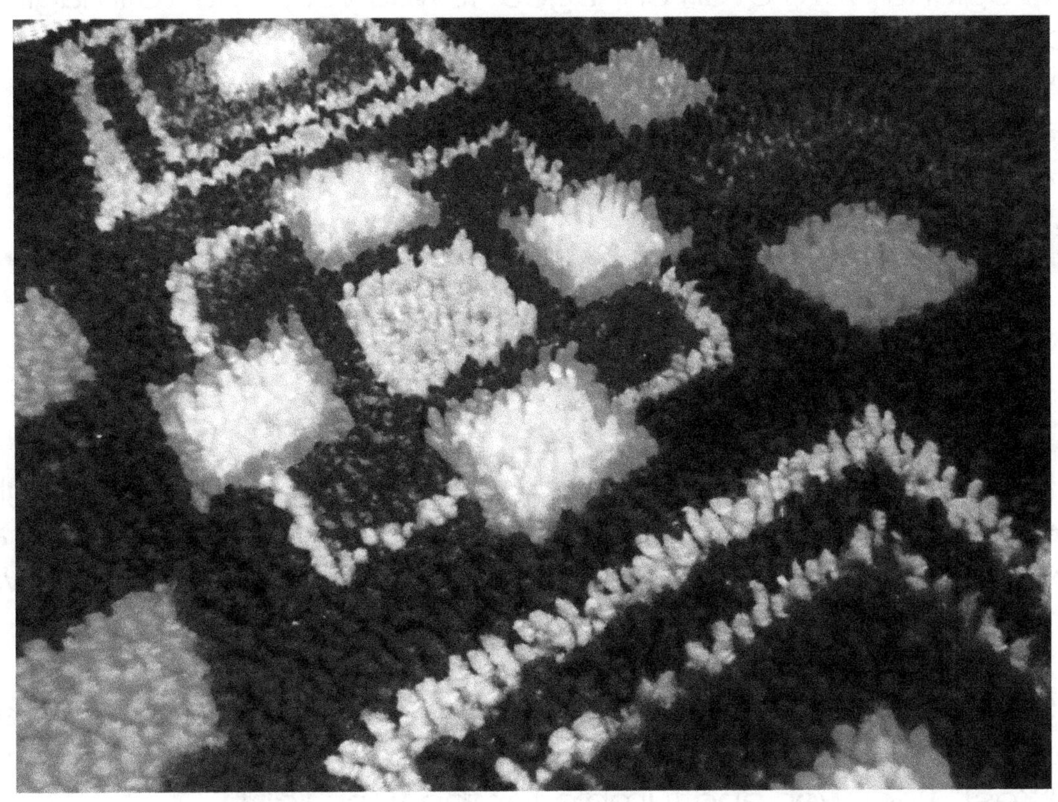

So my day is pain, medicines, sleep, hooking, watching some TV, and Tweeting. Paul feeds me, I stay curled up as much as feasible. As I get a little better (I can stand, crouched) horniness settles upon me. Each awful day my mind turns to sexy visions, with thoughts of masturbation.

I would drift into wet dreams. The bottom half of me was in a cage of pain and strictly off-limits. The pain wasn't throbbing like the heartbeat I heard on my pillow; the pain was constant, steady, never-ending. It felt like the sound of a Dial-up connection with the phone off the hook -- a screeching drone, machine-like.

Eventually, below my waist being cut off with any sensation except pain, my thoughts went to another pleasure place: my mouth, and my imagination. I distracted my focus, even a few seconds was a relief from the pain. I imagined my tongue a prick, and delved into my Lover's face. Brought myself back to the time when french-kissing was long make-out sessions, before the below regions were even engaged. It was very hot! To imagine my tongue exploring the insides of him, to prod and poke and twirl around his tongue.

A satisfying time was had by all.

Now as I'm starting to stand (not crouched, mostly upright) and walking a bit and swaying to the music, I think of him and am shy. Kissing him sweetly, gently; I do not tell him I've had my way with him (in my mind) in waking and sleeping moments.

Sound asleep, I wake up asking myself, "Do you really want to get up to write the words from your dream?"

"Yes!" I answer, and fumble for the flash light.

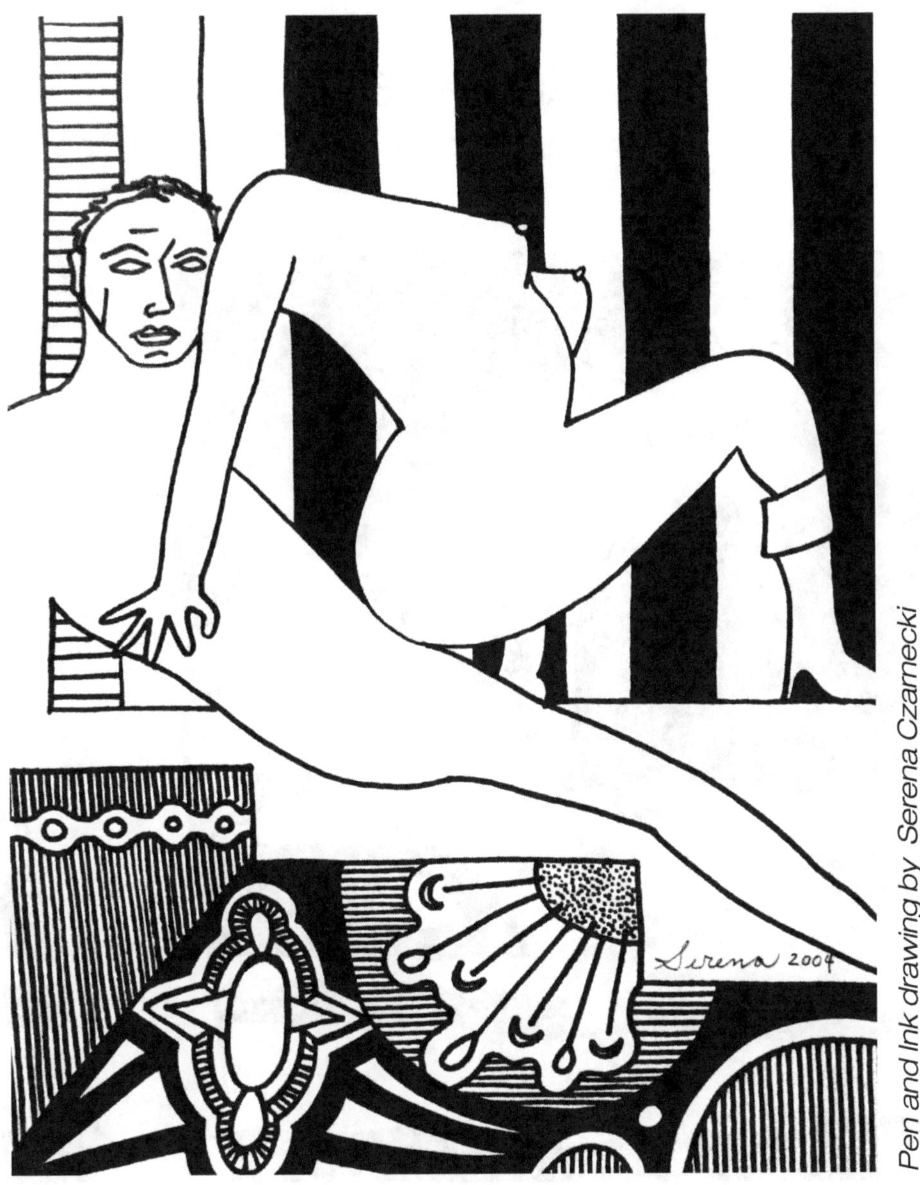

Pen and Ink drawing by Serena Czarnecki

I write:

The Harlot called in a Handyman.
She was struck with awe
over his beauty -- Adonis,
flames of weed in his pipe.
Pan played the pipe and she heard
her heart beat a galloping song.
The Handyman serviced her and
her throat got husky. Her heart
in her throat -- she was
manhandled with kid gloves.
Happiness burst from her eyes
when our two were one.

Art and Sex
and Addiction

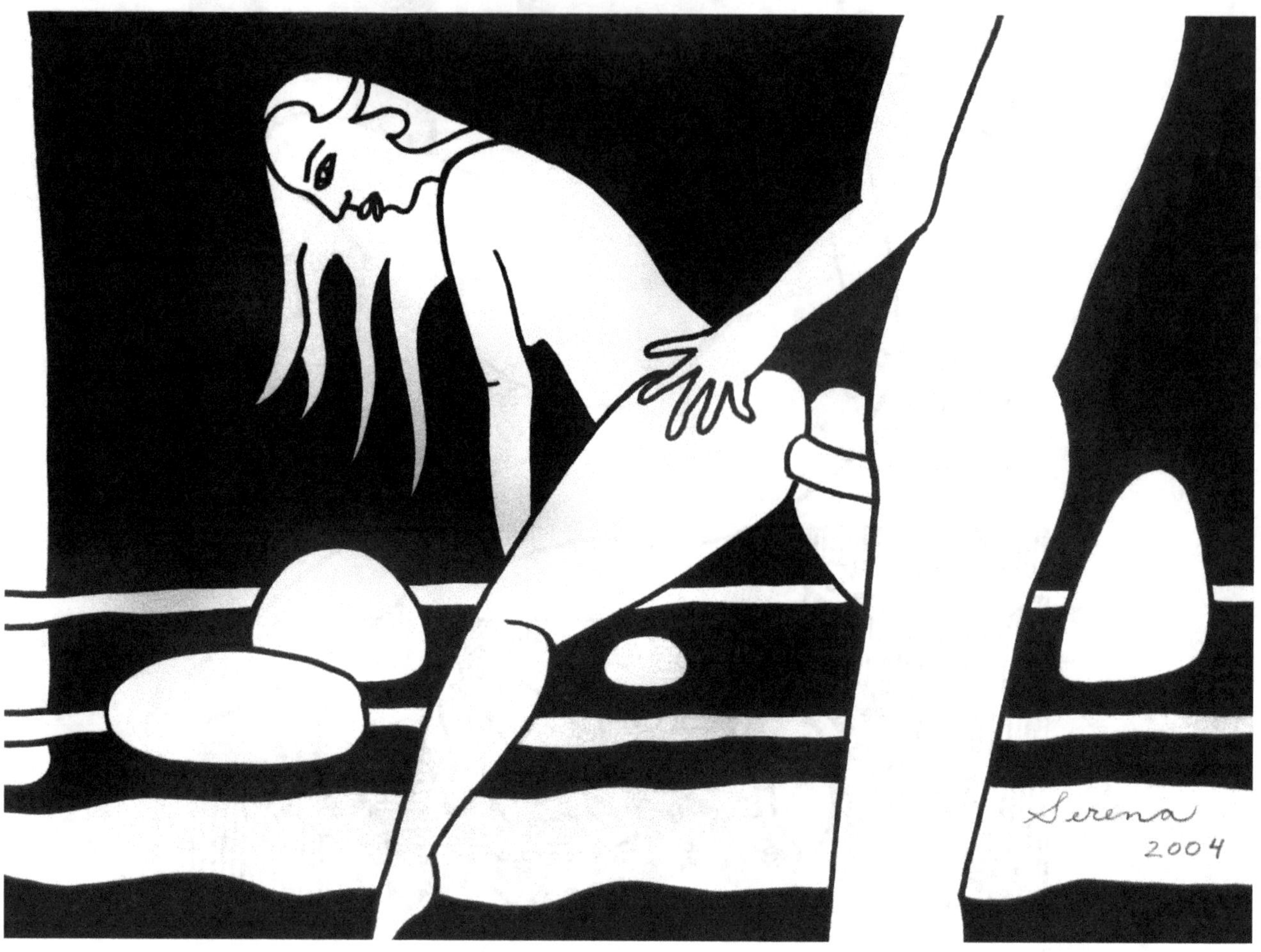

Art and/or Sex can be addictive. Sex can be addictive. There are social groups and doctors to help this. The practice of Art can also become addictive -- it can create such thrills as to become the button you must push to get fed. Sex or Art can be all-consuming of your actions by needing all your time and energy.

Art and Sex can be habit-forming so that you create a hole that only they can fill. Sex or Art (or Drugs) can also be a habit -- something you don't do by choice, but because it's something you've always done, something that is easy to spend time at.

Pen and Ink drawing by Serena Czarnecki

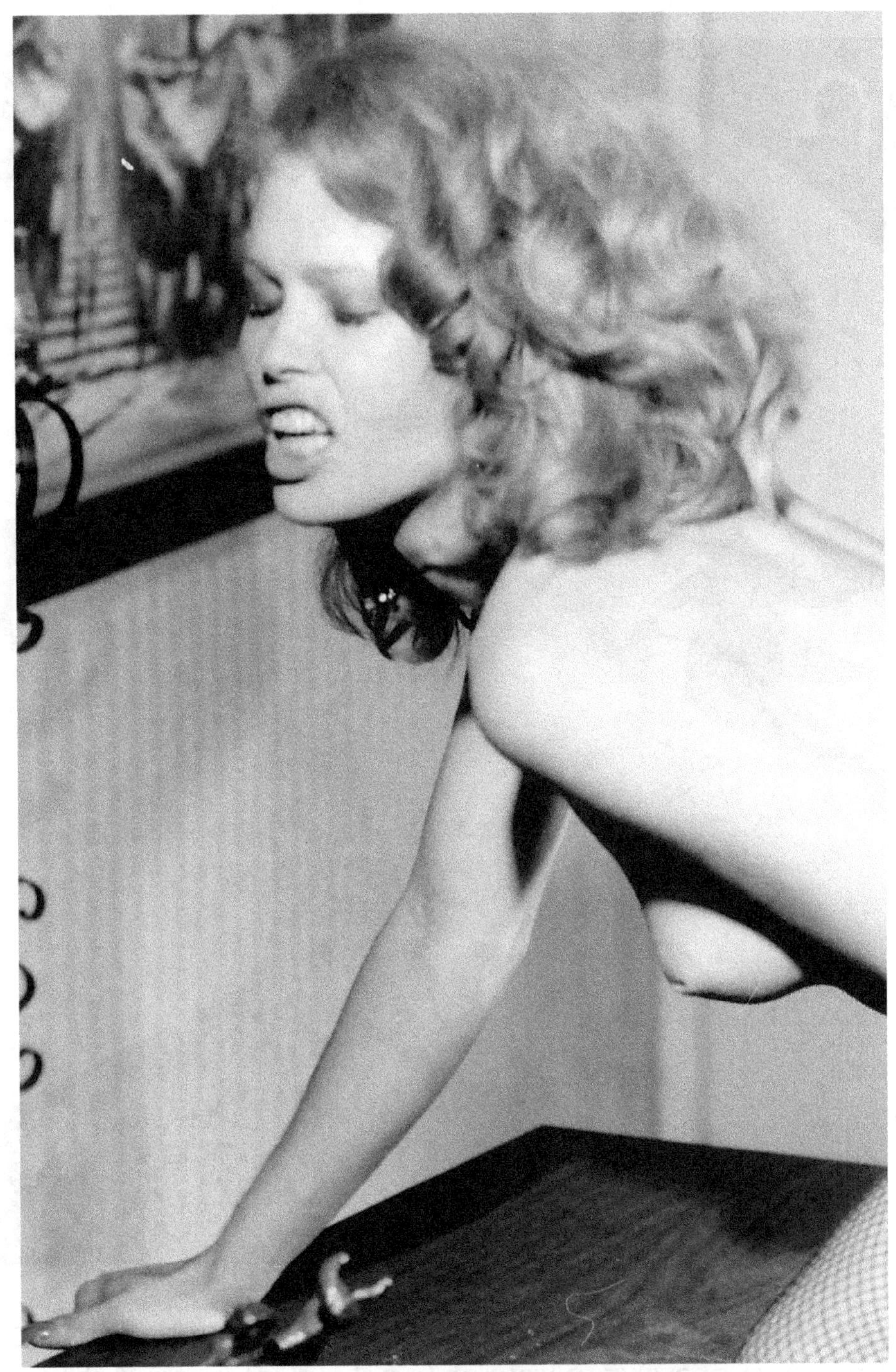

Addiction is more than a frame of mind or even a physical need. Addiction is the root -- the disease itself. The methods of response can be alcohol, drugs, tobacco, sex. Groups are formed to help sex-addition, addiction to porn. I know someone who got help with therapy because he was addicted to porn; yet I know someone else who spends a lot of time on the computer viewing porn who is not addicted. The latter friend spends a lot of time, but it's because she cannot be fulfilled in her relationship with what turns her on -- but can find it online. This ends up being very, very good for her relationship.

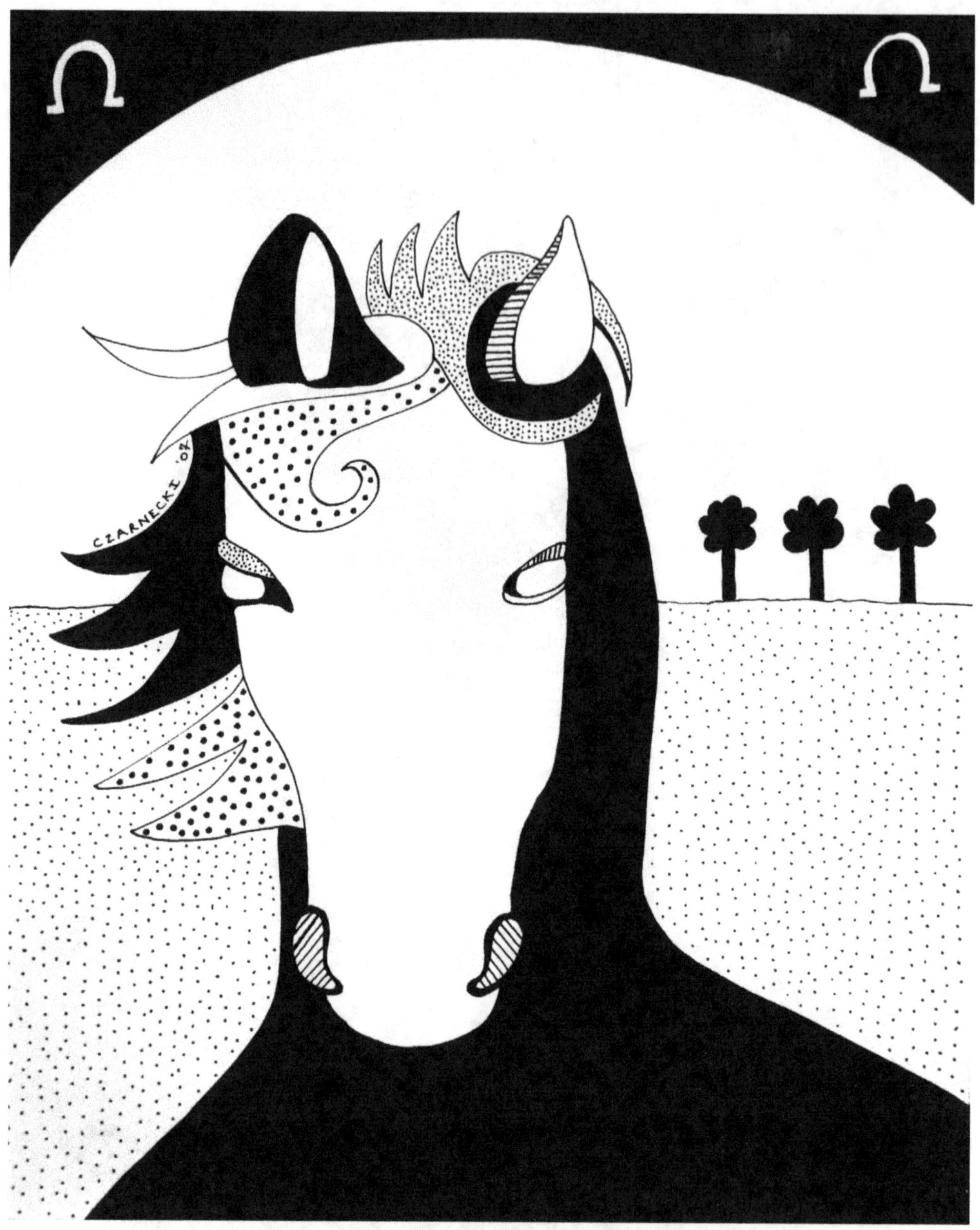

When Manic, I can easily become addicted to the drive of creation. I can stay up all night (and days) in an Art frenzy -- drawing, writing, painting, cutting up scraps of paper or cloth, solving the Big Questions of the Universe! Mania makes an addition of anything you experience.

Addiction hyper-sensitizes anything so it becomes your drug of choice. Addiction is the root disease, there are addictive personality types.

Pen and Ink drawing by Serena Czarnecki

Art and Sex

and Feeling Bad

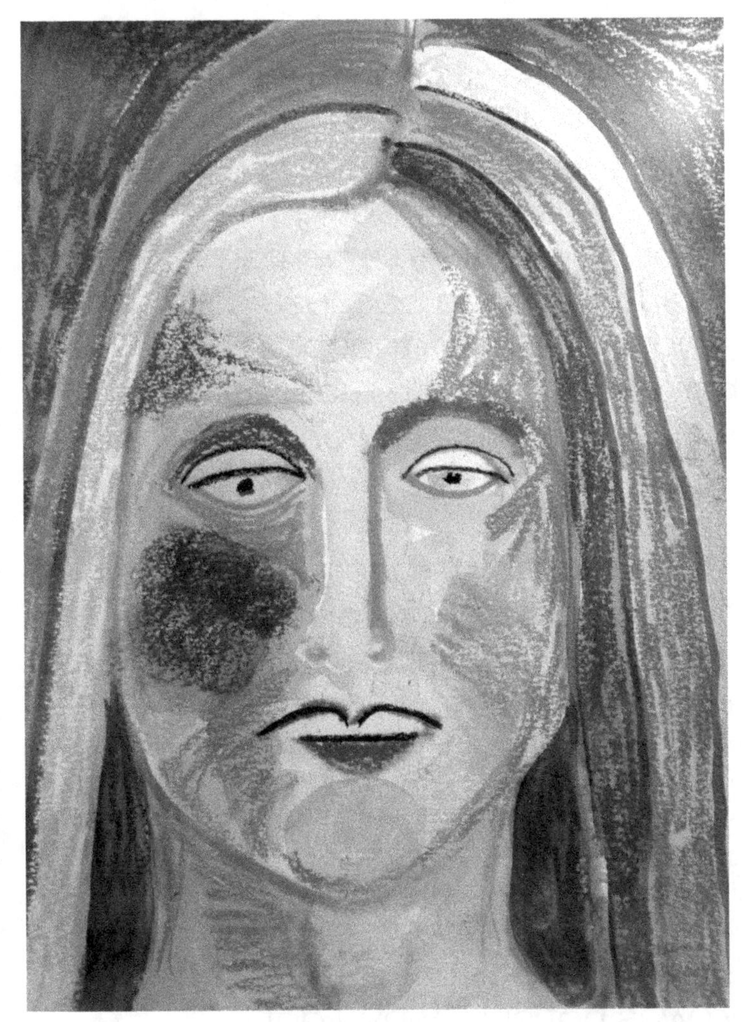

I was made to feel bad by the computer company that I post photos on and chat with far-flung friends. This company has helped me promote the books I've written, but they also put me in what is called by its users "Jail." Last night I reviewed a photograph I'd posted for my fans to see. I saw how truly happy I was in the picture, wondering if I've ever been that happy again -- the face seemed lit from within by the sense of confidence that youth brings.

Just as I was thinking how beautiful and utterly happy the person in the photograph was, my screen said that Big Brother was putting me in Jail for going against their "Standards," that I was Posting explicit sexual content and that I'd be banned from using their Site for a time.

The photo was of me, young, smiling. I was fully clothed, with a cropped top so that my midriff did show my belly-button. But that was all the exposed skin, other than my beaming face. In fact, to see the PIC, I had to click on an icon that stated "Image has one person, smiling, smiling."

So my feelings were hurt. I'm sure by a computer. Any person seeing the picture would delight in my show of happiness. Or would they? Are certain people so dissatisfied with their lives that they aren't rejoicing in others' accomplishments? I love myself and I tend to love other people, always glad when humans achieve. It is a harsh lesson to realize that there are those who are not striving for contentment, but who actually get off hurting and stealing from others.

The computer company has stolen some of my good nature by exposing this harsh fact. And it makes it worse, knowing that it is only a machine making decisions over my life. It's unbearable to think another person would see the happiness in an innocent face and want to stamp it out.

I felt sorry to tell the youthful me that she is still being chastised and discriminated against for being. Being a human being. Being beautiful and healthy. Being set upon because of her happy attitude. It distresses me now, and even though I have bipolar disease, realize that there are legitimate reasons to be depressed! Blocking my image of a happy young woman is definitely one of them!

This is the second time in two weeks that I've been "put in jail" by this company. The first time I posted a photo of myself that a fan had posted years ago. It was the cover of one of the magazines I'd modeled for. The Fan had put stickers over my naked nipples to be able to Post the shot, although nipples were okay to display in magazine racks back then.

I saved it as a memento from a Fan, although I didn't like the stickers covering the skin. Anyway, because it had been posted years ago I went ahead and re-posted it. A split second later I was thrown off the social media Site and was not sure why. I got angry and emailed the stickered PIC to all my friends that this photo got me kicked off. No one could believe it, and some said this is why they hate the Site. I'd only put it on display to show folks that my hair was really red at times in my life. Normally I wouldn't have Posted that PIC because I don't like the censorship of the stickers. Even so, the company's "Standards" put me in jail for that one image.

Today I'm tired, not having got much sleep because this has gotten me depressed. And I remember the feelings of feeling like a Second-Class Citizen The awful fact of being pushed around by "Standards" of being, helpless to do anything on my behalf, of being unable to defend my actions because of the short sighted.

Section Four

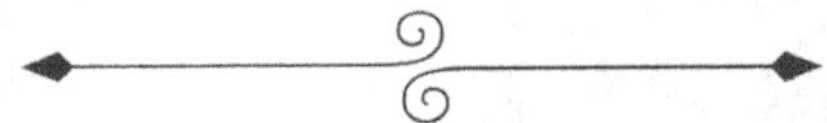

The Big Women

Oil Paintings by Serena Czarnecki

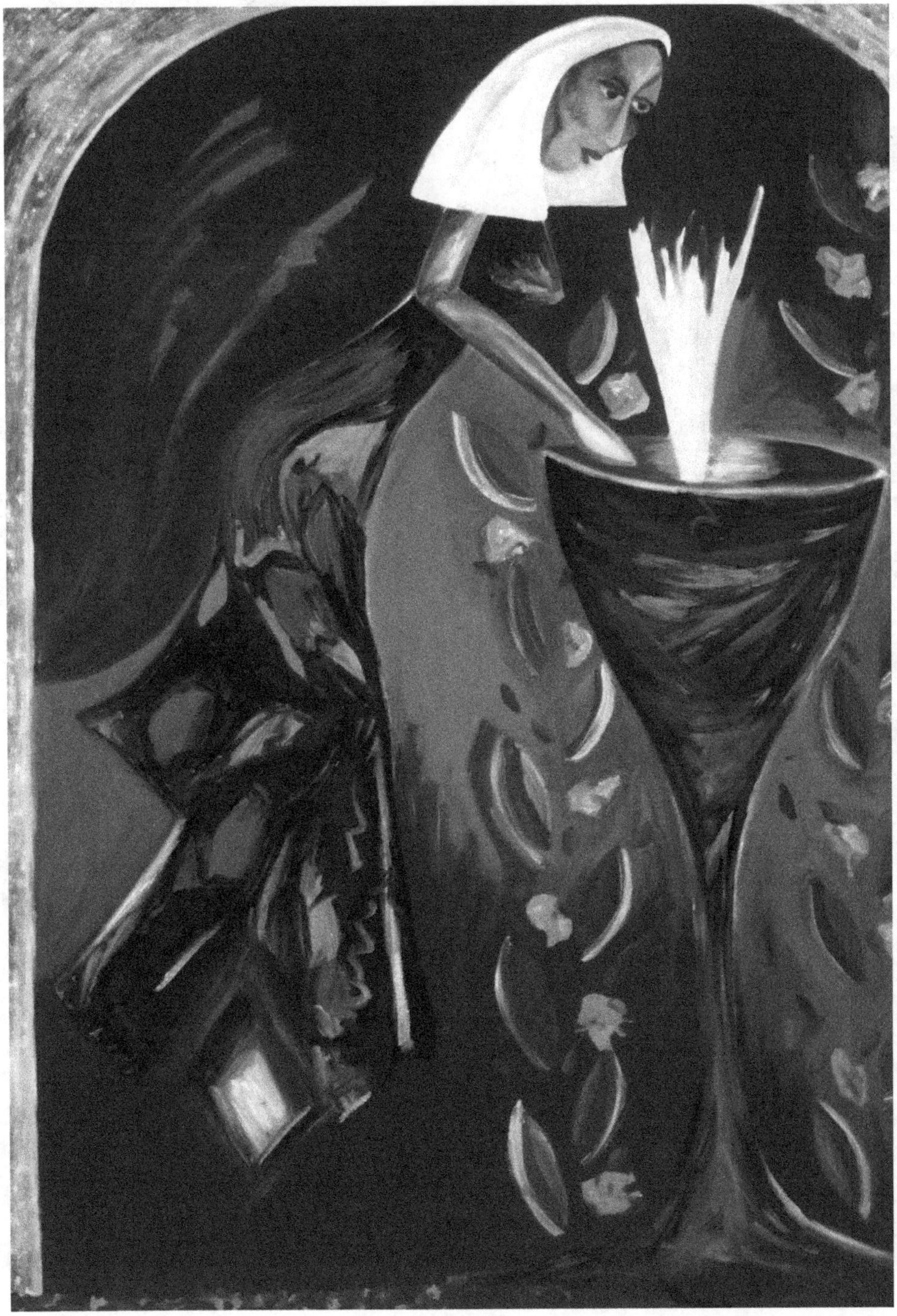

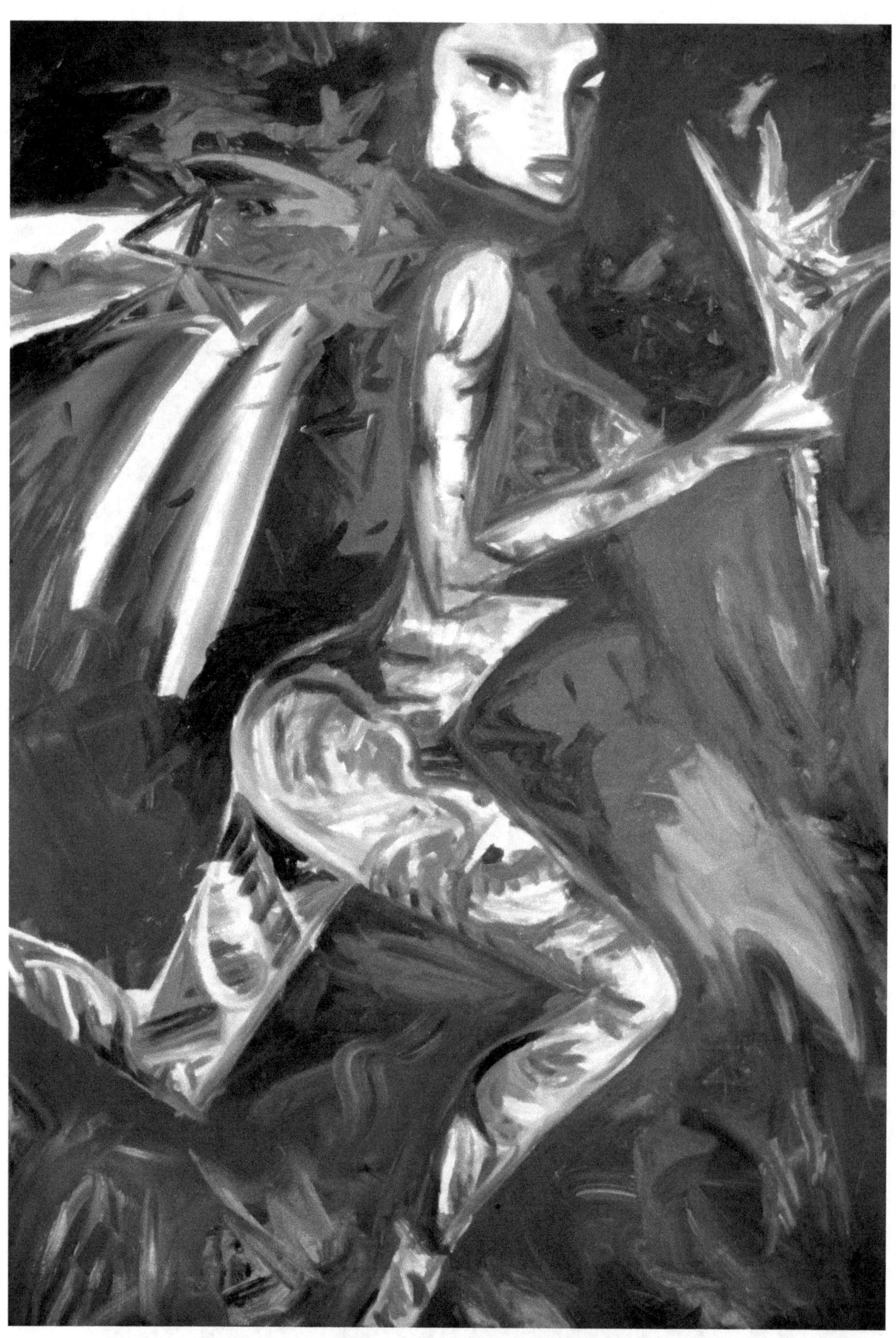

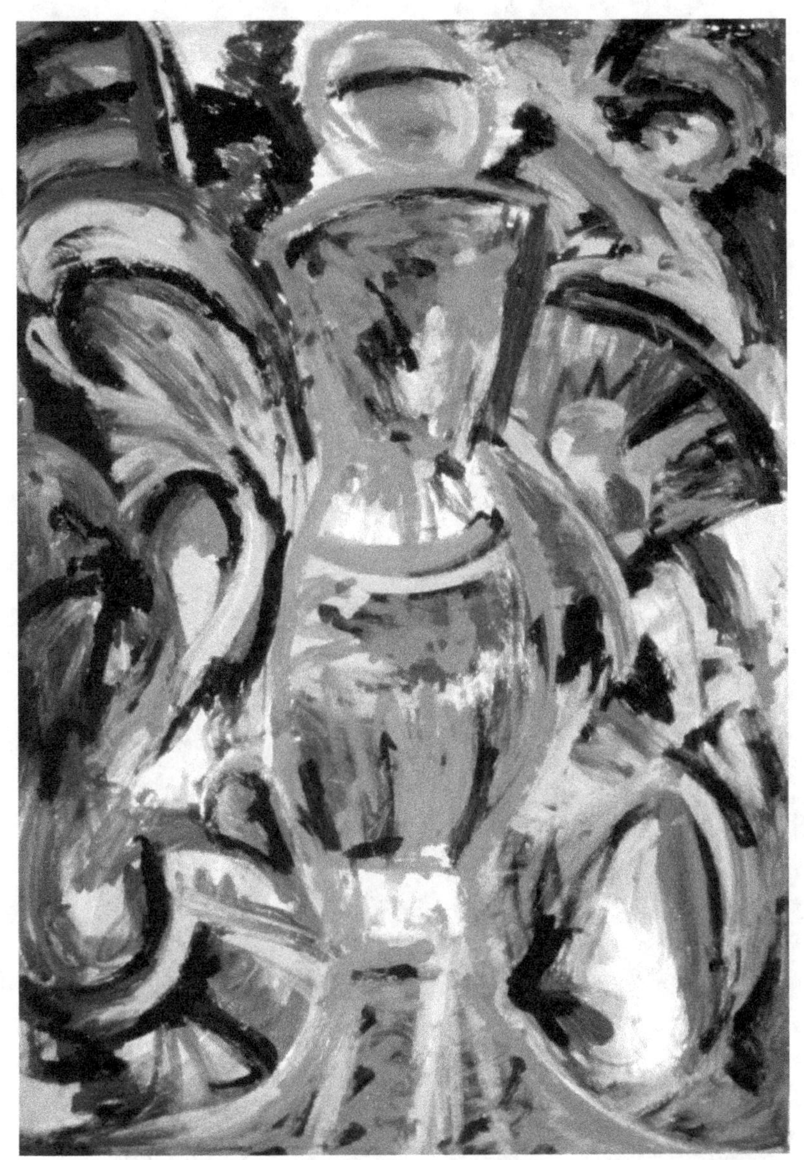

The "Big Women" series is a tribute to Willem daKooning's "Big Woman." I was exposed to this great work in an Art History class I was taking, it's affected me tremendously.

Luckily at the time I had studio space in which to indulge large works of tribute. I see my series as my personal Tarot deck, each big woman an archetype. The reflection of my soul is in there, my art is love made manifest. The "Women" have joined me in my realm to be my band of Guardian Angels. They have given me confidence and Joy.

The Big Women Series

Creation of both Joy and Struggle

They are orgasmic and gestural. When I painted, after years of not painting, my art was bursting forth. Porno had not satisfied my creativity, and I was constipated with ideas. Ideas of Art. What I put on the canvas was a long repressed burst of energy. My relief came as strong women, each an idealized part of me.

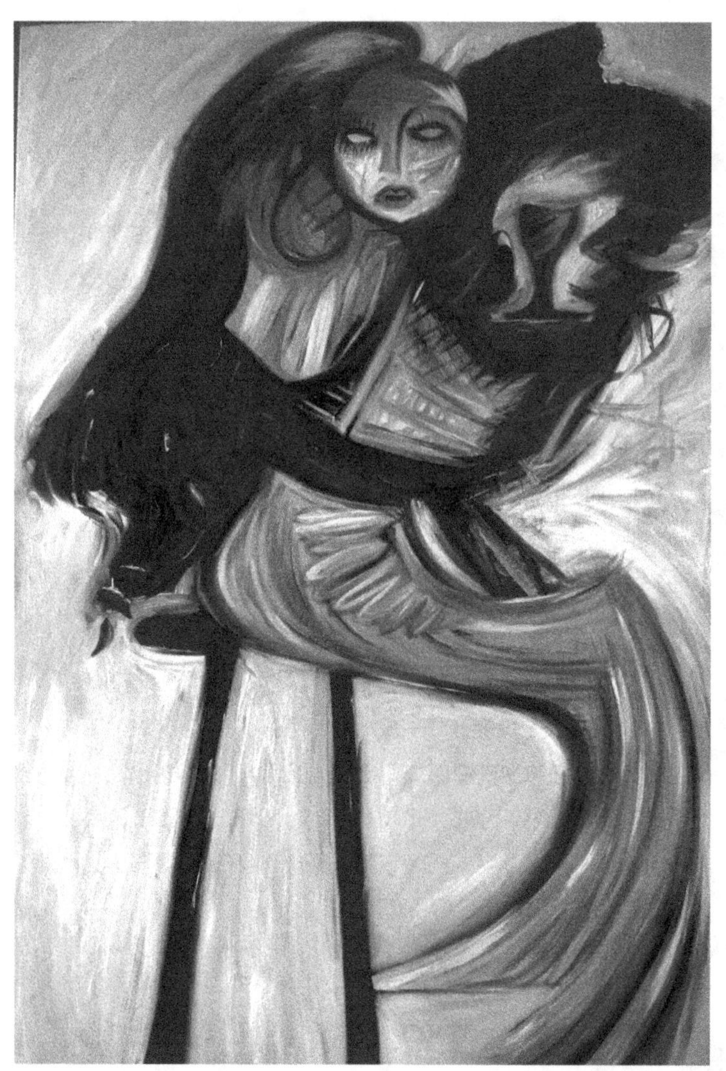

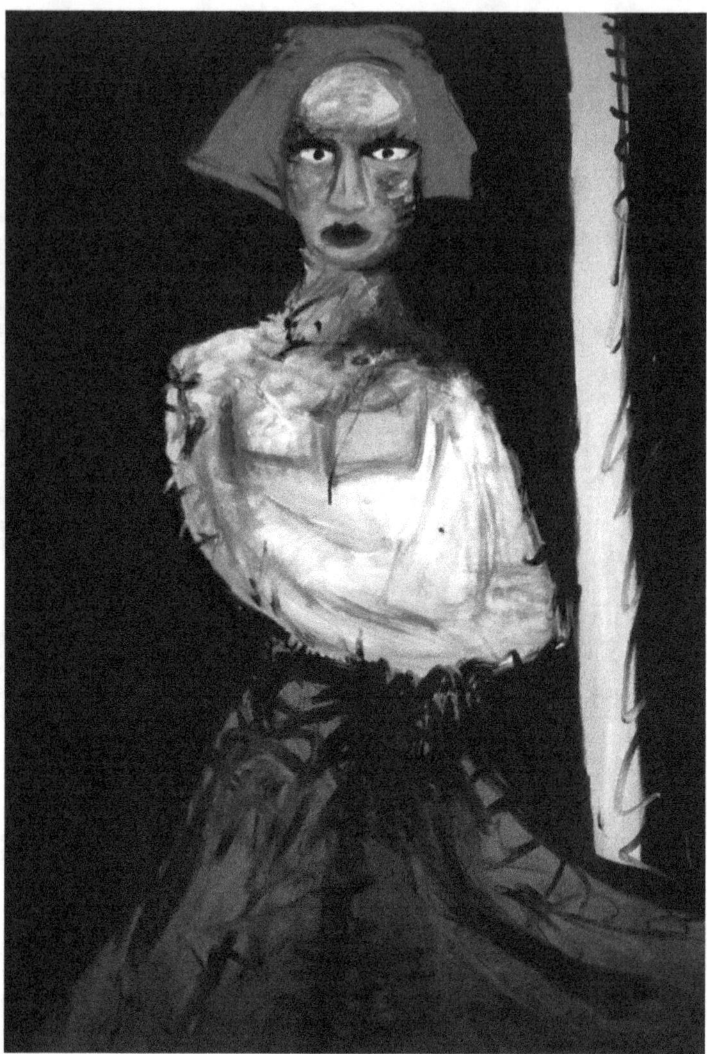

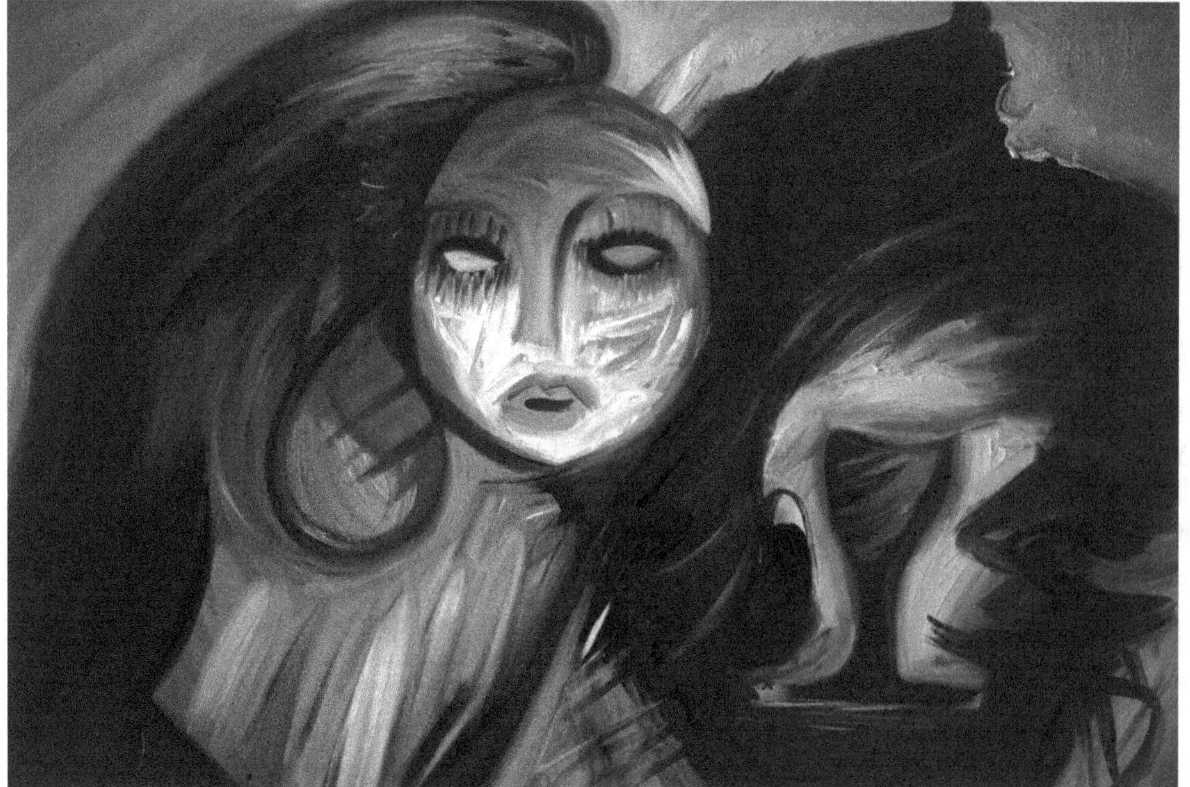

I sold the above Big Woman from my New York apartment on the thirty-fifth floor.

Destruction came by way of my bipolar fits. Hanging from my door is now a bit off the most detailed painting I've ever made. I shredded it with a knife; instead of cutting myself, I suppose. The final hurt I did myself was throwing myself off the mountain into a month-long coma. My friend Cannibal always calls me Coma Girl. An insane manic mood overtook me and my anger turned to fury. I hated that I'd painted such a clue to my thoughts, my soul. I didn't want people to know me. I was hiding from myself. I couldn't bare them a peek. I slashed this beautiful, descriptive painting to bits until I collapsed.

I've given away many of my Big Women. My storage was doubling every couple of years. I've been paying to store my works for forty years now. You see why artists never make money?

I was at one of my storage yards moving things about when a woman approached me to see if I was getting rid of anything. She said she really liked the paintings and I began to pull them out so she could see them. I must have known she was homeless and just wanted the canvas. But I wanted to share my work and figured that tents would be a brilliant solution for the Big Women. They went to this homeless women cheerfully. I hope they provided warm shelter.

I sold most of the Big Women. What I have left are still in storage. I painted one after a painting called "Inmate in the Asylum" that I saw in Art History class. The original painting portrayed a single figure of a woman who I totally related to. Looking at her eyes, I could see she was telling people that she didn't belong locked up.

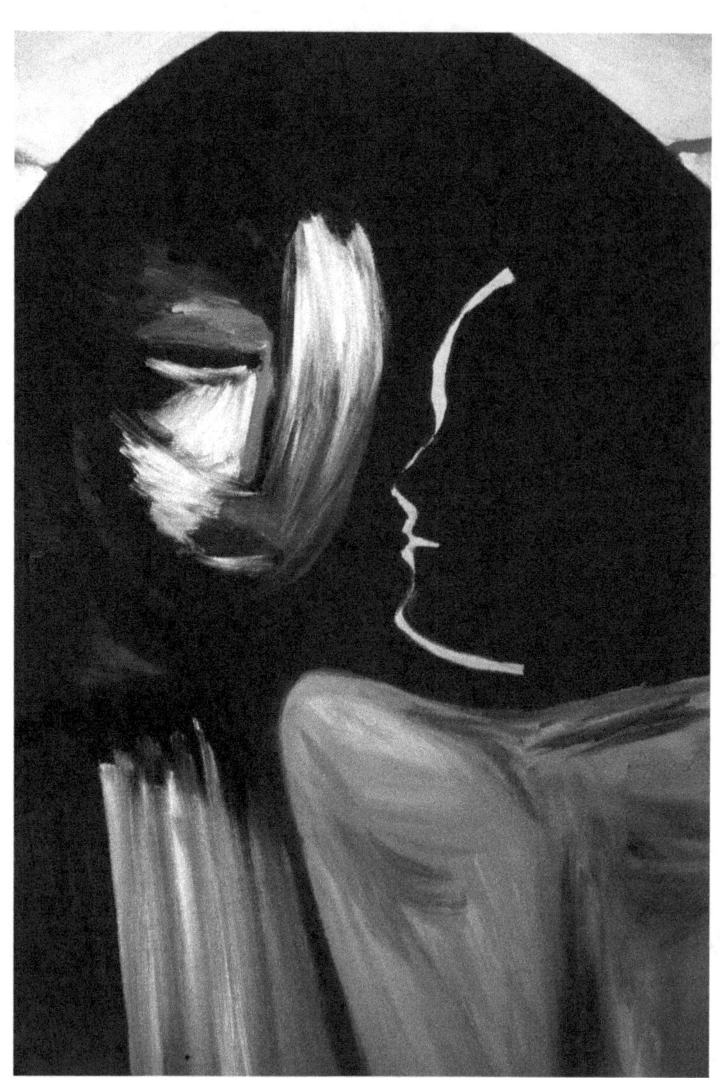

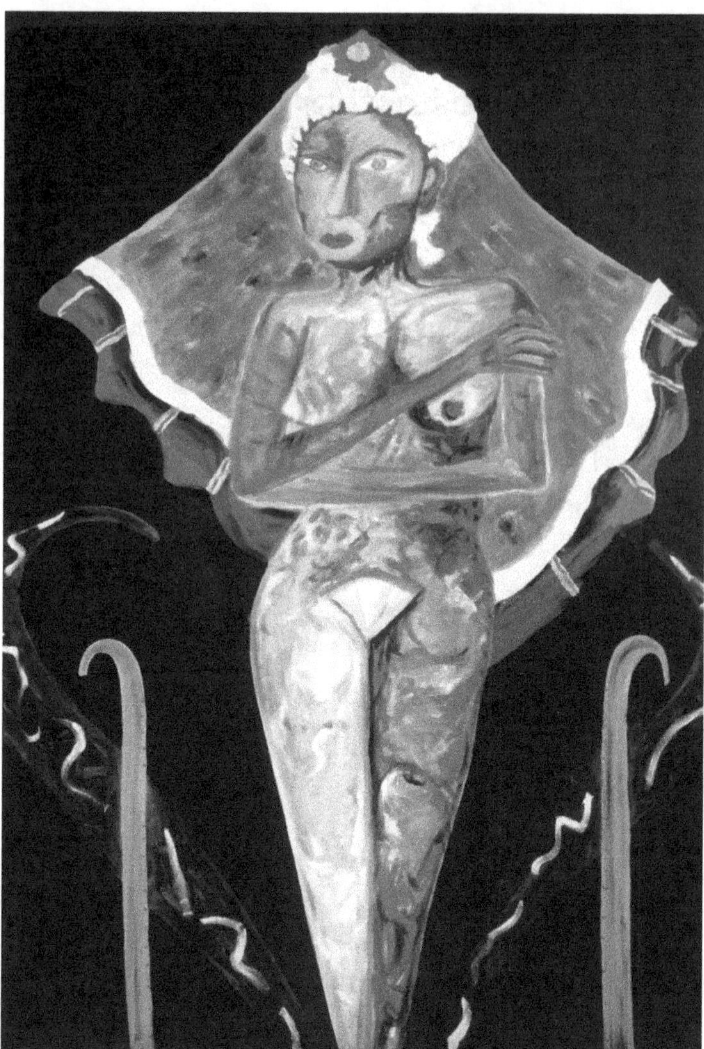

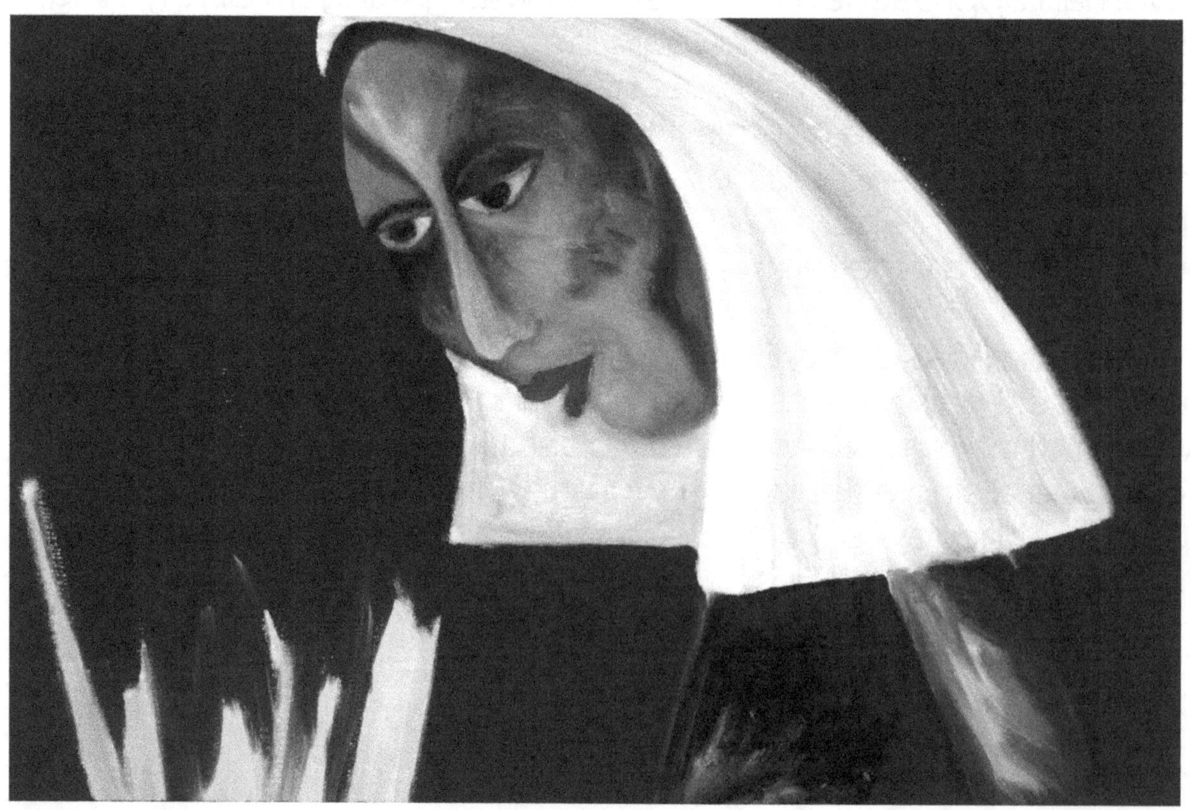

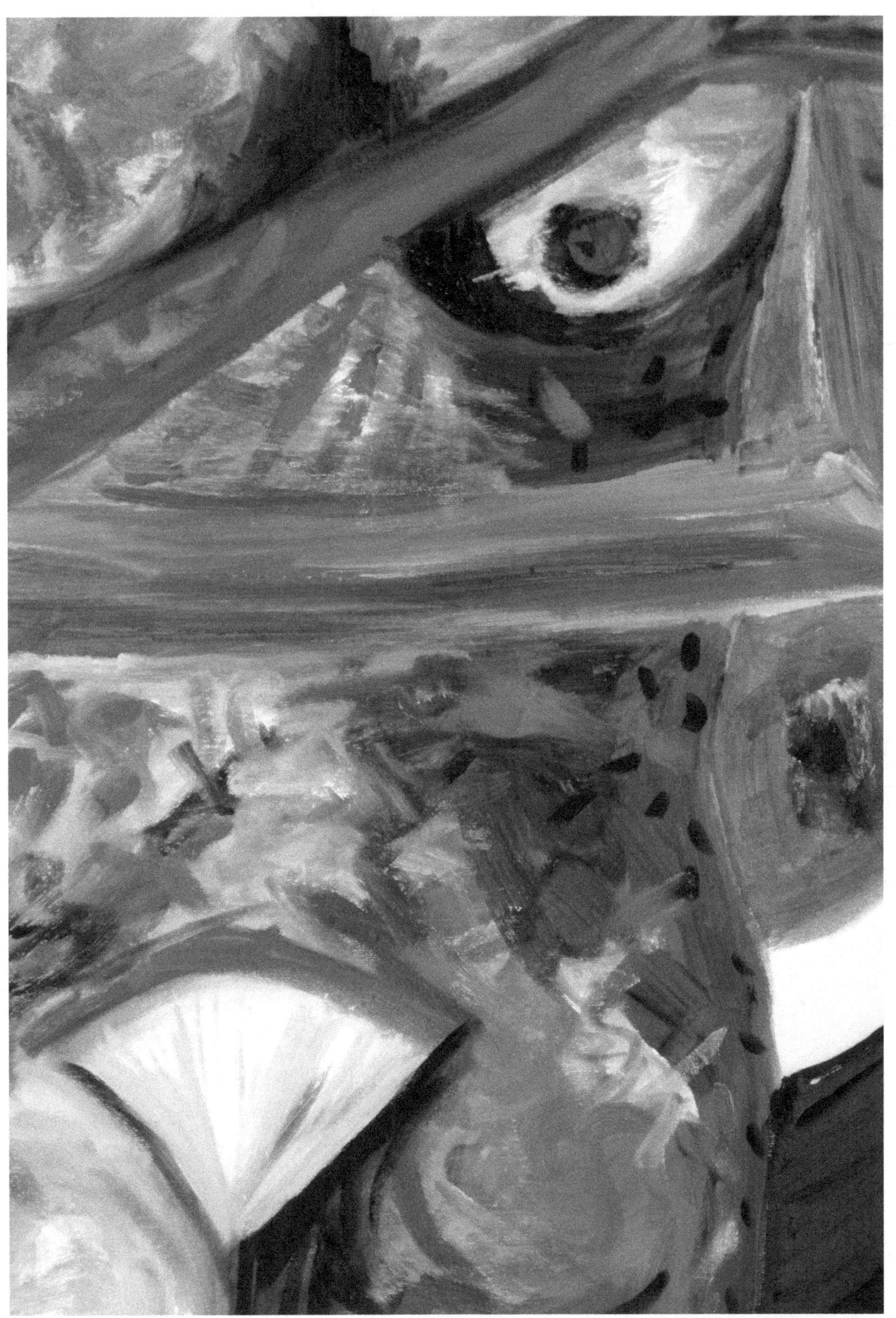

I've been put in straitjackets, chained to hospital beds, kept against my will and misdiagnosed. I was impaired and destructive. Thank the Goddess my Disorder was finally detected. But I was a horror until the time I got onto Lithium.

Many misunderstood people were put away, sometimes for treatable illnesses, sometimes not mental at all. One tragic example of this is Cornelius Jeremiah Vanderbilt. He was seen as weak, put into institutions and never received his father's love or money. He had Epilepsy.

I've learned to grow my life as I would a garden. My garden is the prayer rug of thankfulness. I am thankful to have shelter, to have found my mate, and have great, interesting friends. I am mostly grateful to have creativity flow through my days. My Garden of Life has it's thrillers, it's spillers and it's fillers!

It's Thrillers: I'm able to have a Voice that touches other's hearts.

It's Spillers: What art flows out from me.

My Life is Filled with: thankfulness through the strife.

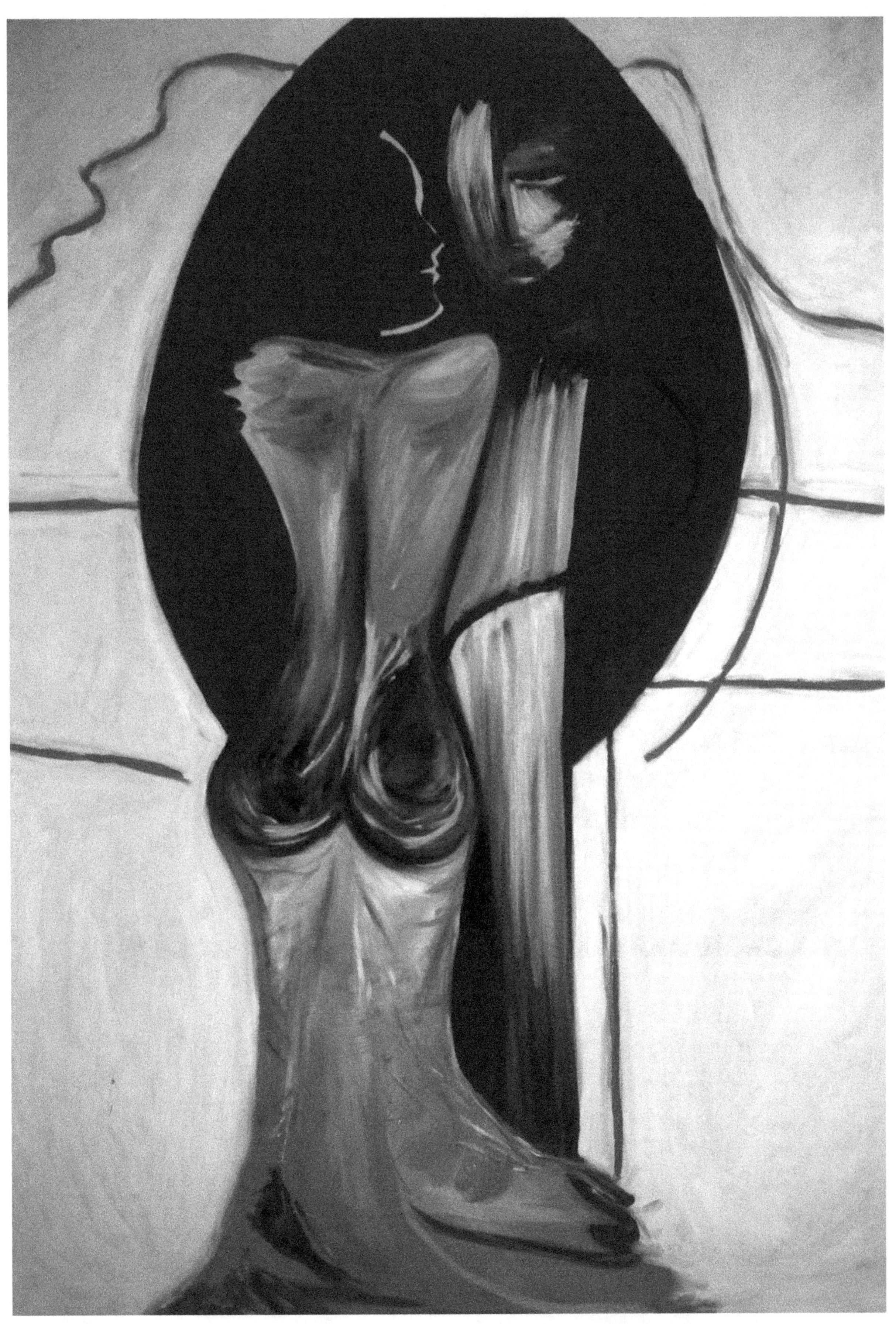

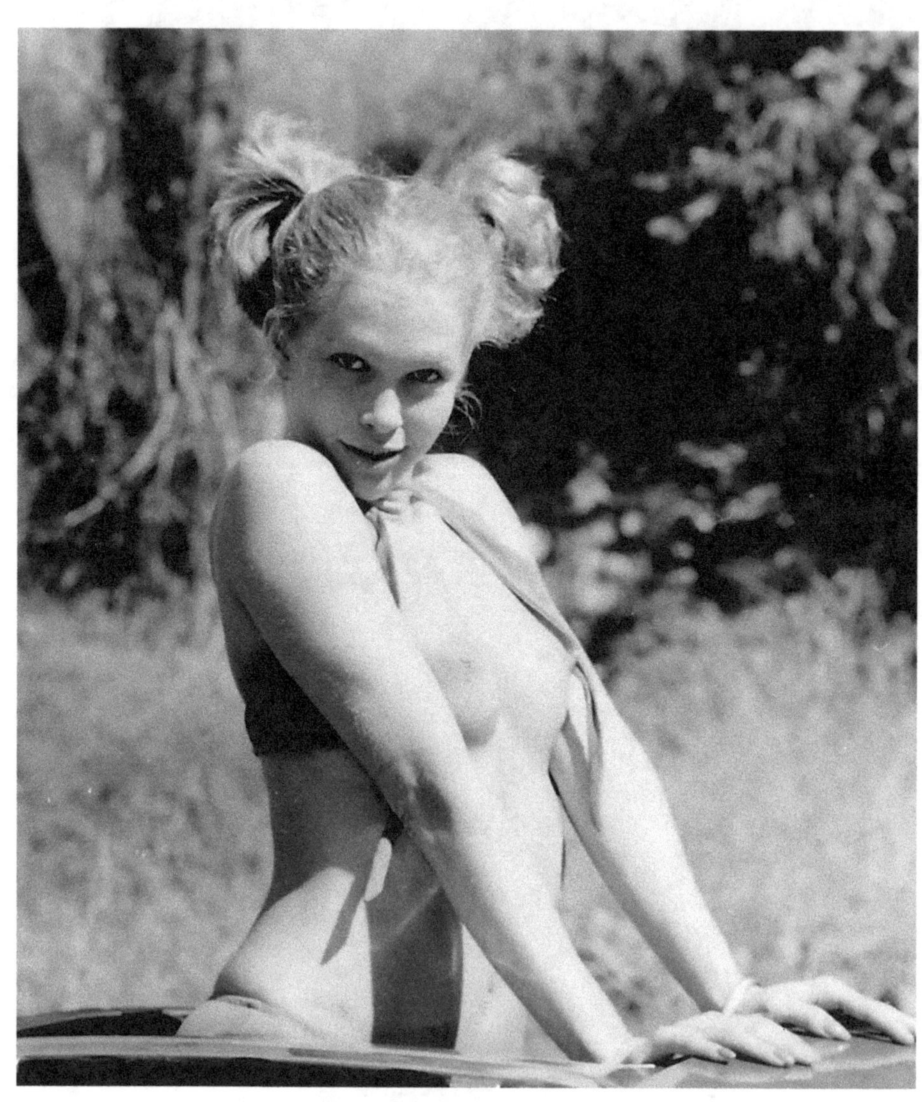

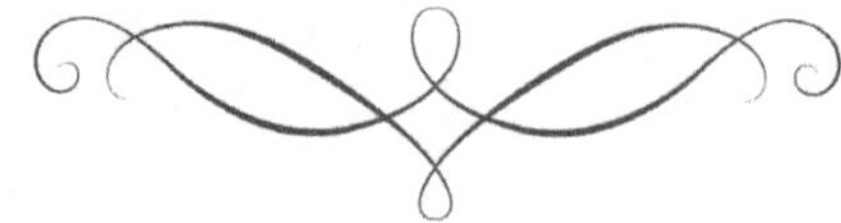

AFTERWORD

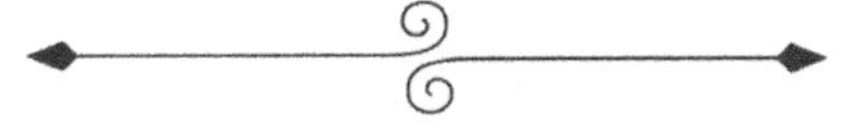

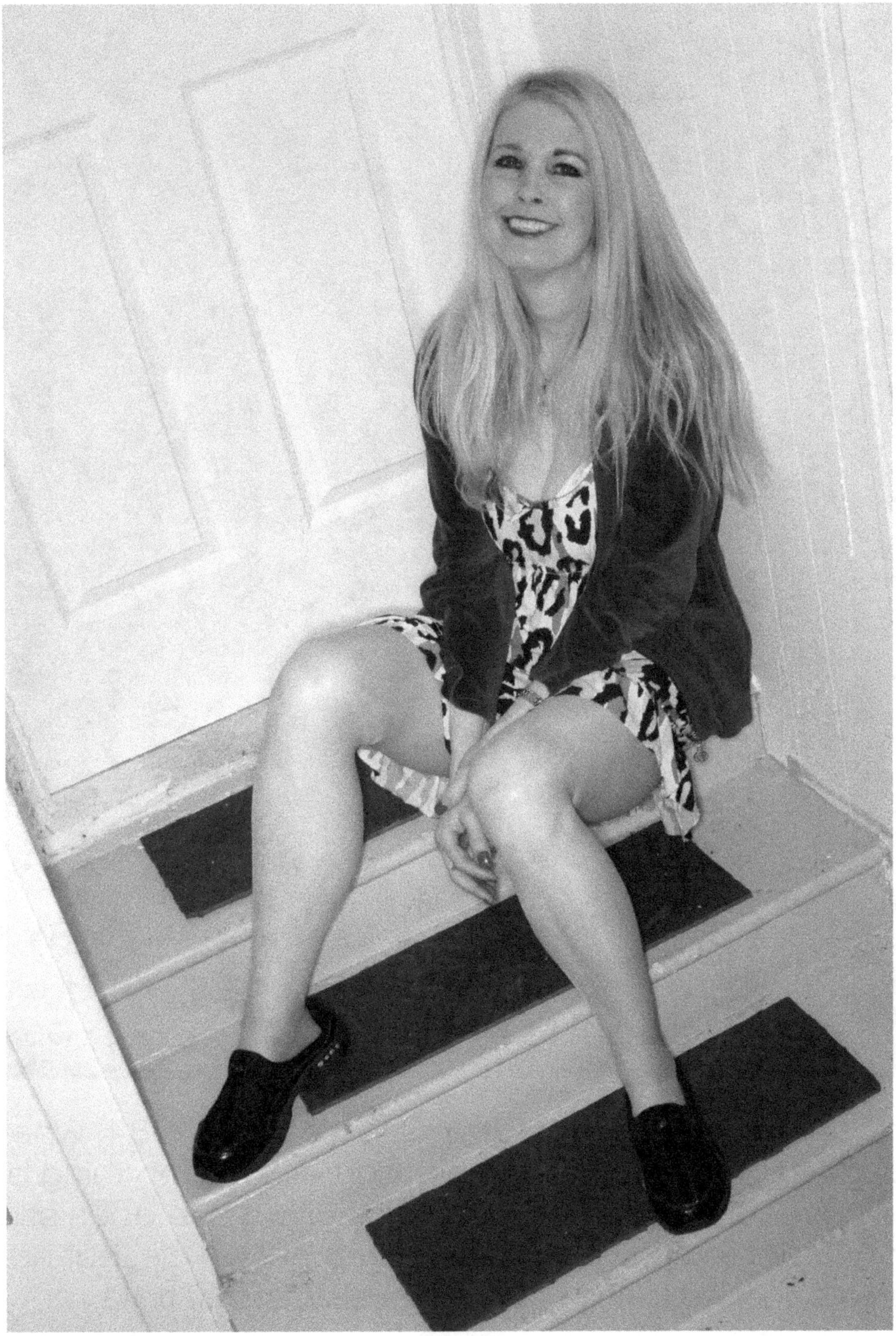

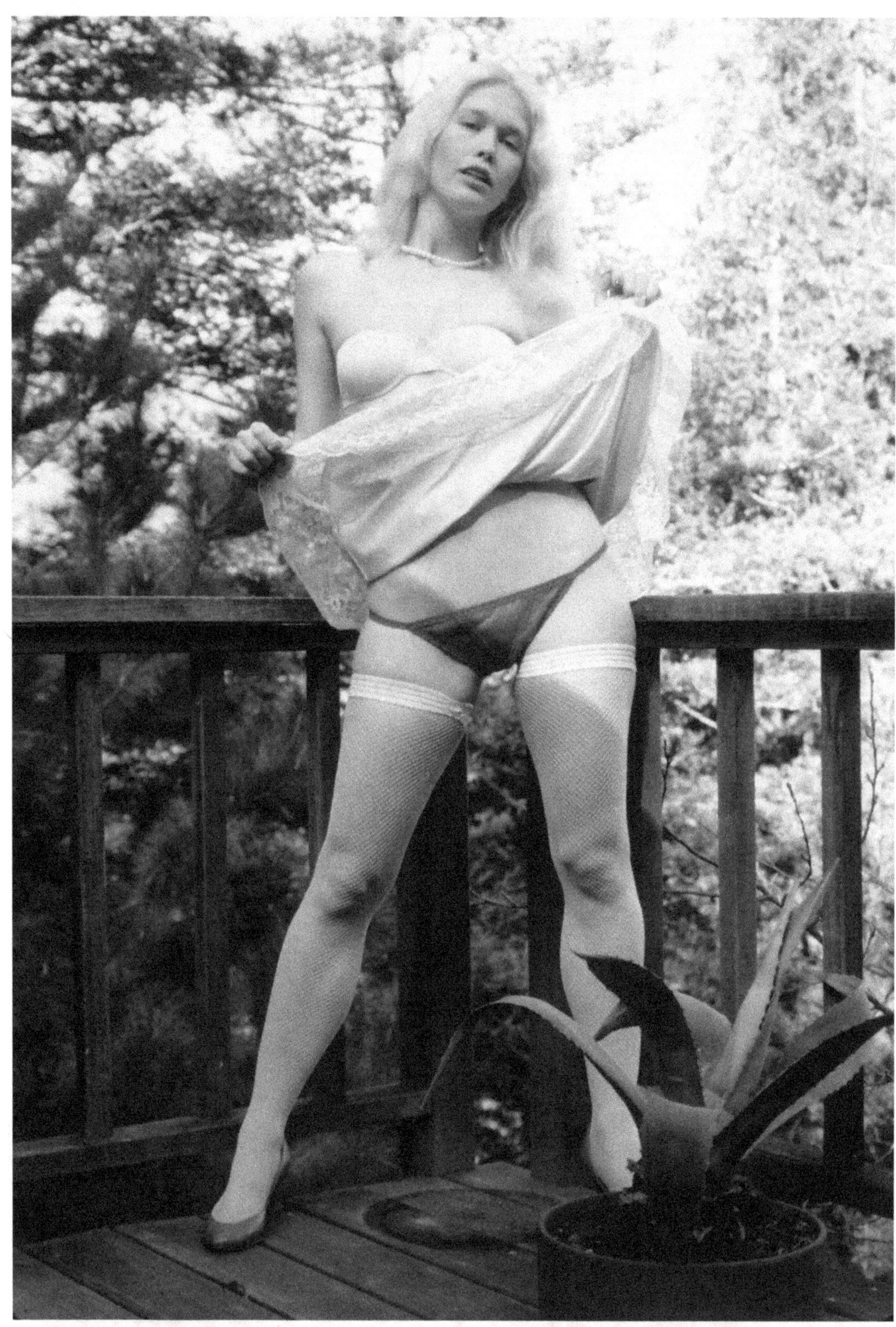

This set of books has taken many years. In 1984, when I wrote Backstage Girls, I was young, scared of everything but knew I'd never die. Now, at 64, I find that my Love does still need me and will still feed me. I can see now that I will die, but am brave. I am brave because being timid is just a waste of time.

Photo by Baron Wolman

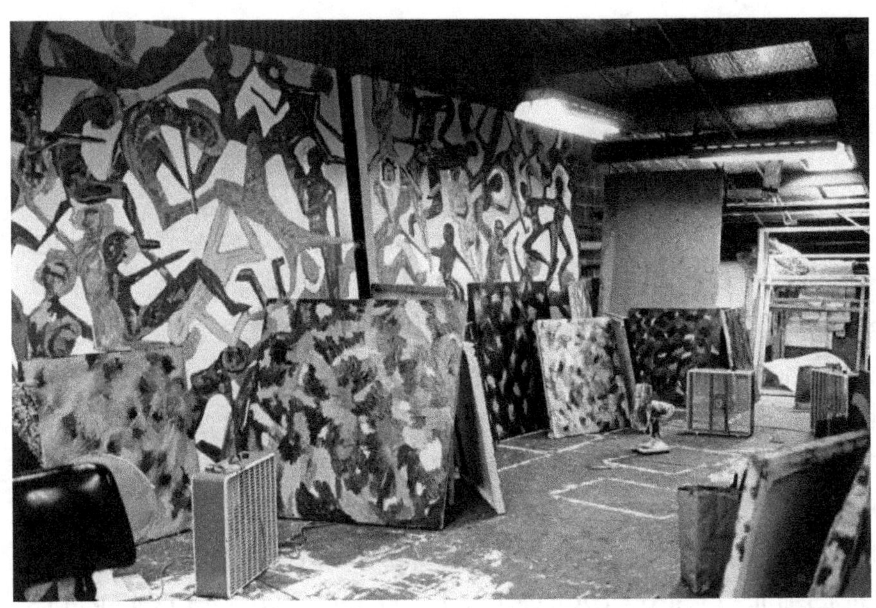

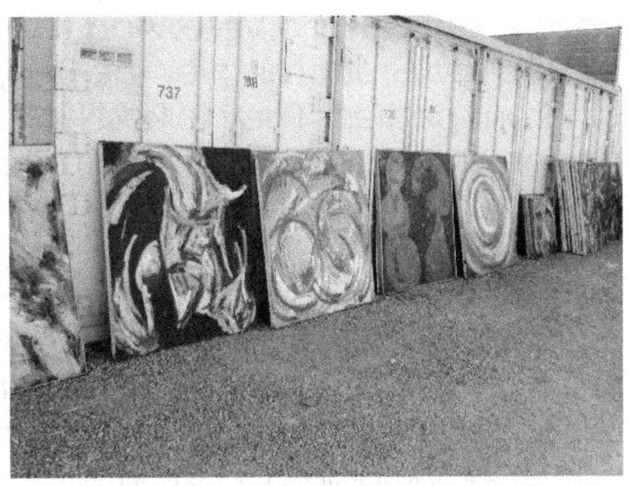

Since Covid, everything in the world has completely changed all at once, for everybody on the planet. But then, everything has always been in a state of flux. I try to be a better person each day. The same, but different. No one can see the morrow; I set goals, but cannot tell you my future. I hope humans can make it through Climate Change. Not much seems to be getting done, this is the greatest threat to humankind, we will die out. The planet will probably survive. Survive better without the polluting human race. It's really hard to stay positive with what's on the nightly news! Understanding that I do not understand much, let alone everything! I try to fill my days with Understanding/Compassion.

When the Pandemic first came, metaphorically I saw it as the Aliens Landing. It is a real chance for the world to be as one. Evil has reared its ugliness to distract us with misinformation and lies, lies, lies. But I am optimistic knowing if we stick with one another, we will see our way through this. We forget how very strong we are, the lies keep getting in the way of sense. We are United. Our very name tells us so. We suffered through a Two Year Old saying he was the man who would be King. I no longer wake up everyday saying, "What new hell is this?" like Dorothy Parker, but he remains a danger. If I could but sweep my brains! Yikes! I am so happy the people got out the Vote. And they did the right thing. The people picked the Stutterer over the Bully. Paul and I each had parents of different parties. They talked Politics over, even when there was disagreement. We all shared the house together. What a concept "reaching across the aisle."

Watching from on high to see millions die, his followers still are dying. The clanging, upset sounds of the last administration are a cacophony of sour notes. The collective orchestra of falsehoods is making an out of tune racket. Not the mellow yet powerful melodies of Union.

Luckily my beautiful California is a Nation/State, and most of us are Vaccinated. Takes so much of the pressure off, the Pandemic has been stressful. I'm certain all of us have felt this; we've all been under pressure - the masks, the uncertainty, the weight gain! Oy vey. I looked up "stress" and read that stress can suppress your immune system. So I breathe through my stress, hoping to save my life! Getting vaccinated and breathing, the solution in this strange new normal.

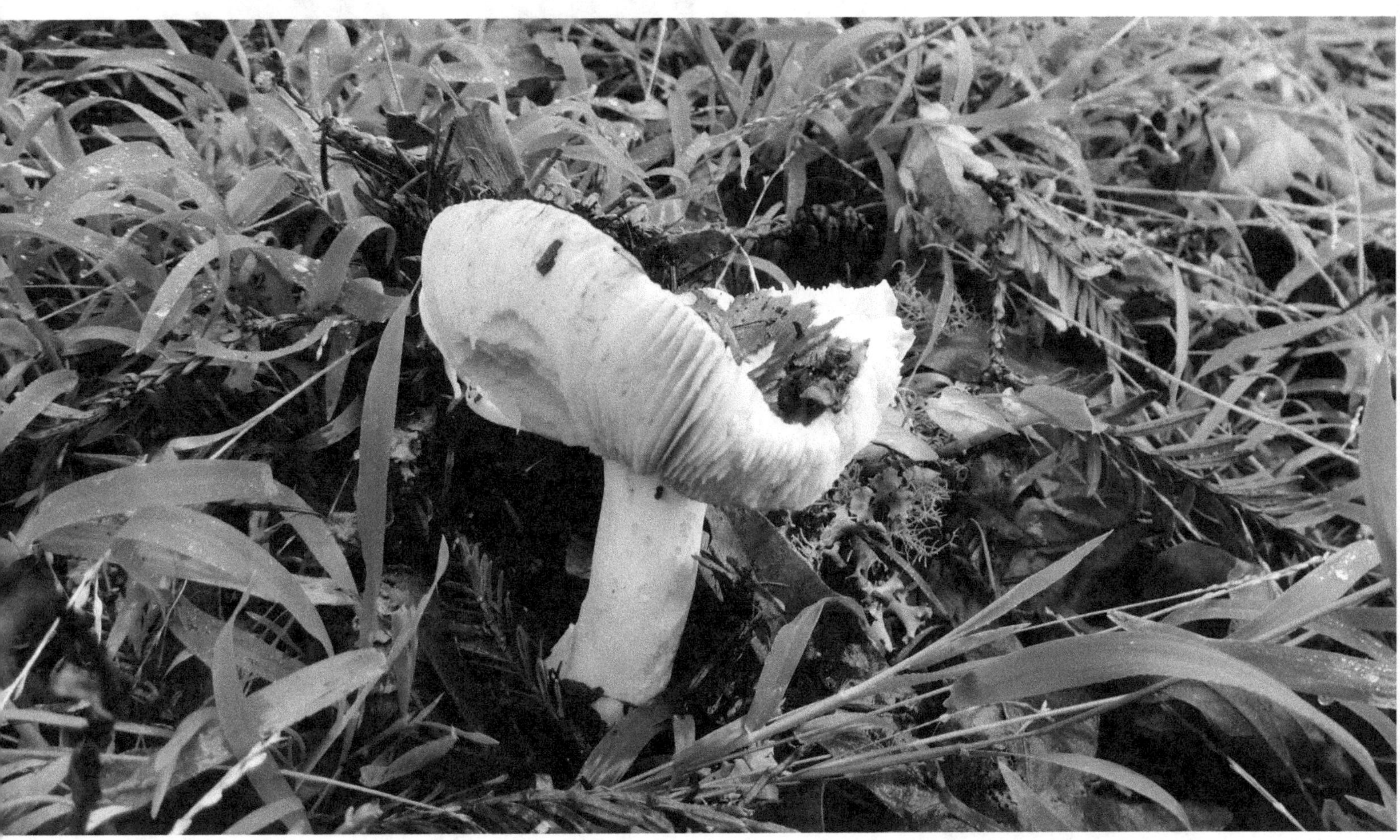

Then why not follow the facts? The Science? For one thing, Russia began a campaign to spread misinformation about the facts relating to vaccines years ago. They've made us (some of us) believe that Science can be questioned. Huh? This is one reason we are founded on a free Press. They are to question and search out the facts and present us with truth. We sure had a nice little Constitution when we used it. Seems like forever ago that we had our First Man in office that was a black man. And boy, the Fascist/ Racists have been rearing their ugly heads ever since. I know there are more like me; many. Otherwise we'd never seen the needed Black Lives Matter revolution. When I was out marching for a cause it was for the ERA, Equal Rights. I'm seeing such turmoil now, I figure I'll be in the streets again to keep Roe vs. Wade. When will we ever learn?

Now that it's obvious that Vaccines work, why are folks not running to save their lives?

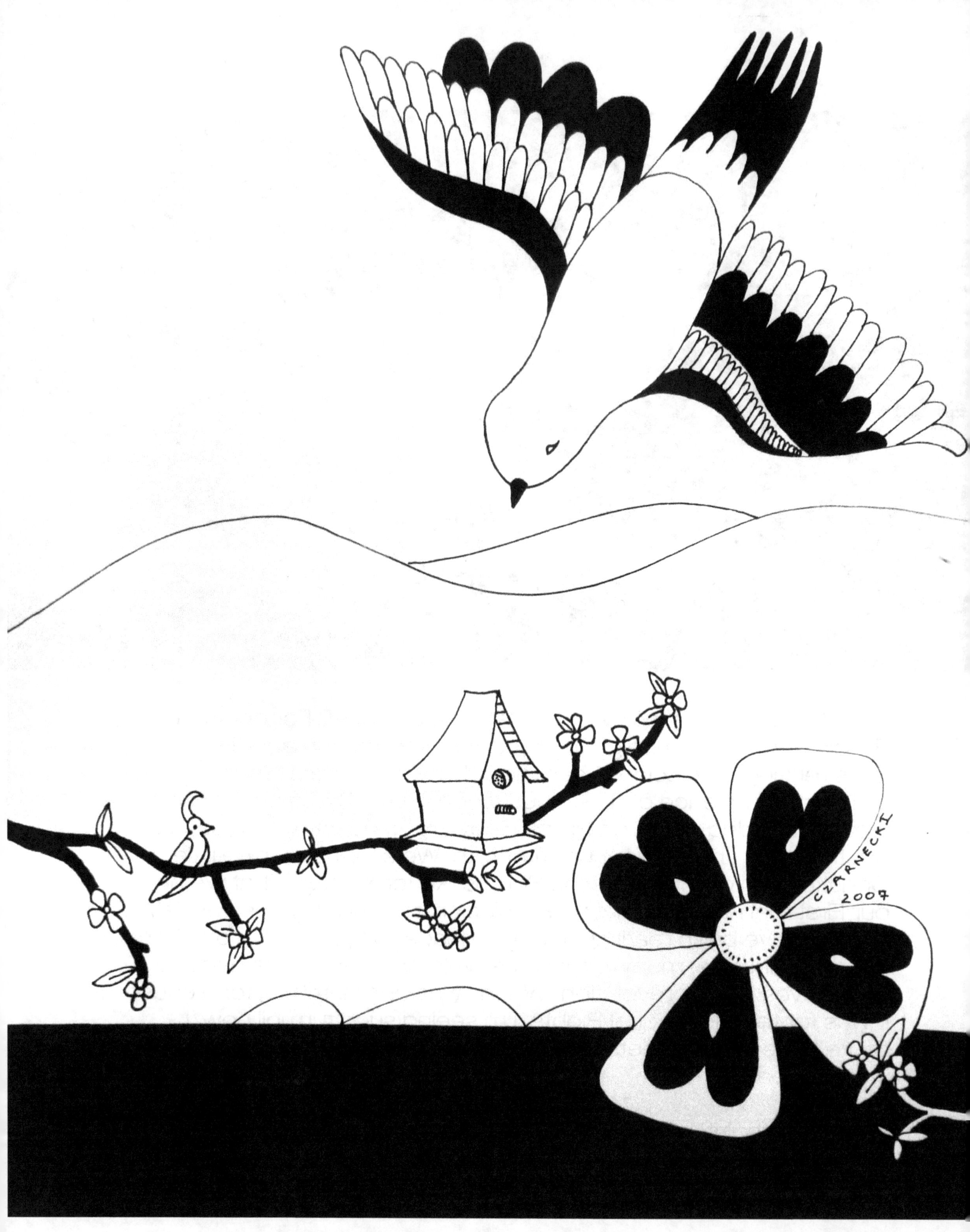
CZARNECKI
2007

I'd thought that once the Orange Clown was Voted out we'd stop hearing his BS. His followers swallowed the Kool-Aid, they gulped up the Big Lie. I want peace and quiet, but they won't shut-up, spreading their lies. Our newly Elected President is working each day to clean up the filthy mess Agent Orange made of our country. In 2017 the GOP gave 2.7 Trillion (with a "T") to the rich by way of tax-cuts. Now we are trying to right this by building back better.

Covid around the planet has slowed everything we depend upon. Since most of our items here in the US have been made in China for some time, when the supply-chain slows, we don't get our goods. This is directly due to the hissy fit, name-calling of the defeated "president". (Note to Editor, please don't capitalize. I voted for Hillary. I have always Resisted.) He taunted the Chinese, penalized them, blamed the virus on them, called them racist names, provoked them. Such Diplomacy. He put tariffs on Chinese goods, which punished the American people, who of course had

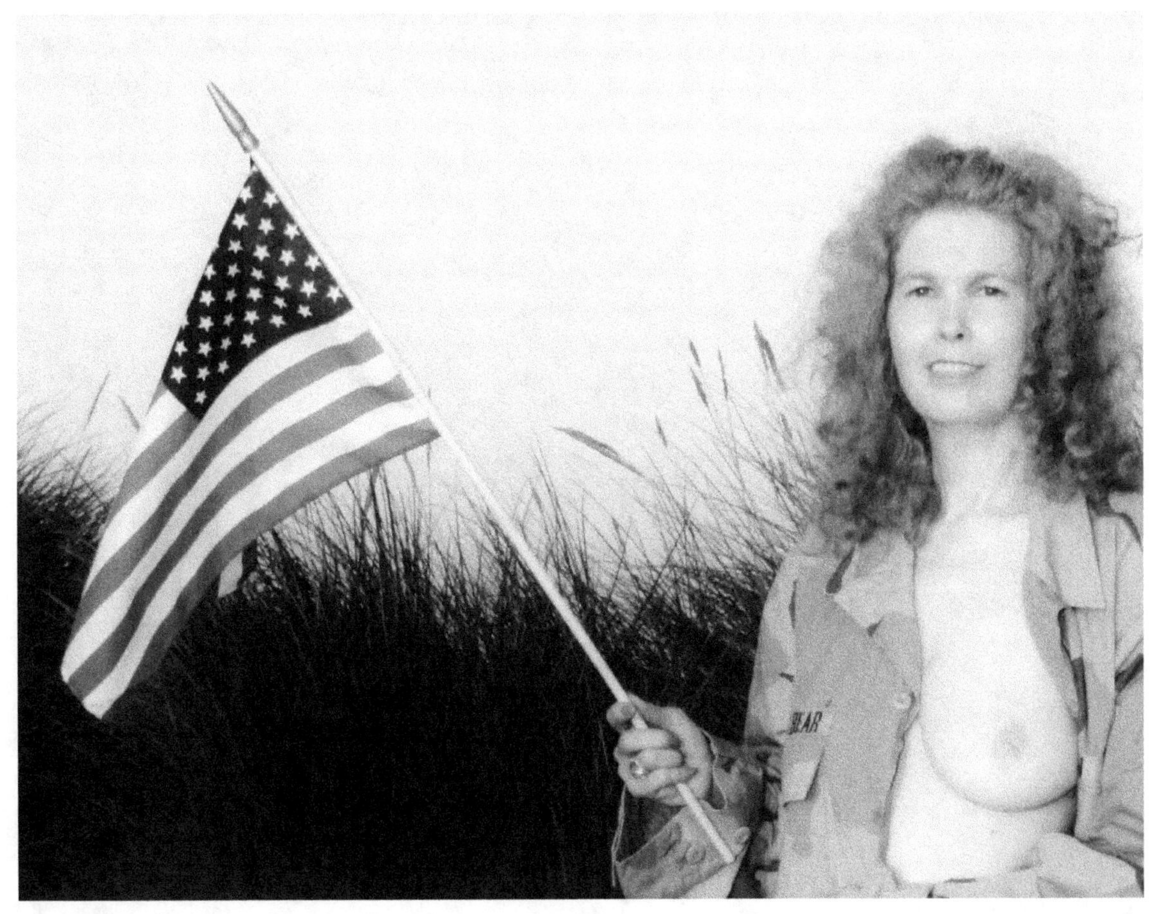

to pay the tariffs as consumers. I am sure it was his racism that bothered me most of all. I would not allow my children to use the language this "president" used!

Paul and I will be leaving the place we've been for the last twenty-six years. I've been so happy here, but am looking forward to a new adventure.

While I have flourished 'neath the dark redwoods I can imagine a home where a cat might dwell. Here, cats are in danger of being eaten.

My skin has been saved from the sun here, the fog is my moisturizer. But I am looking forward to a new place where I could watch veggies grow and plant some flowers that bees would visit. I envision a real studio again; I deserve one!

I need the Universe to send me a Miracle. Miracles are all around us, you just need to reach out and catch one.

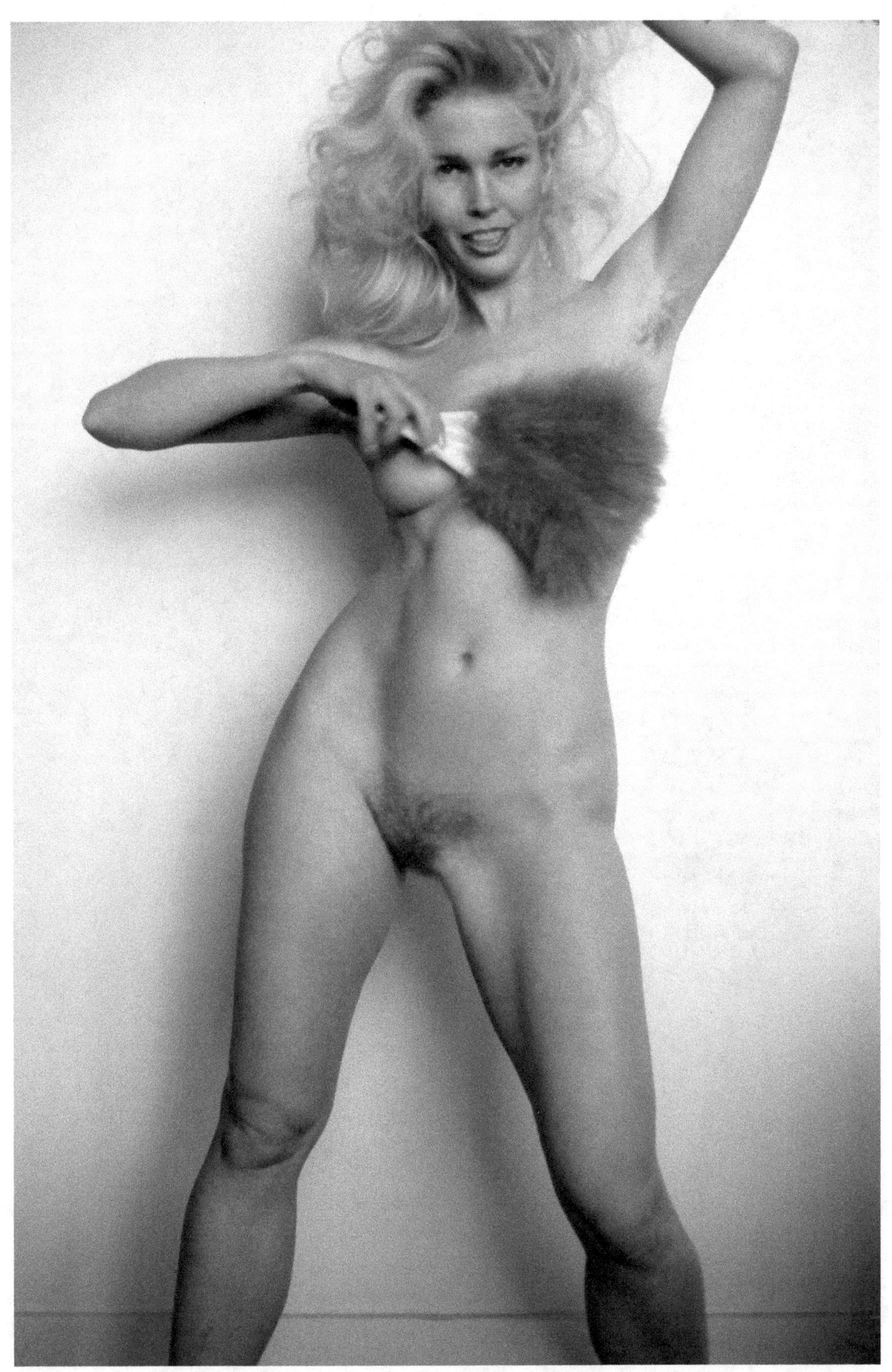

Photo by Baron Wolman

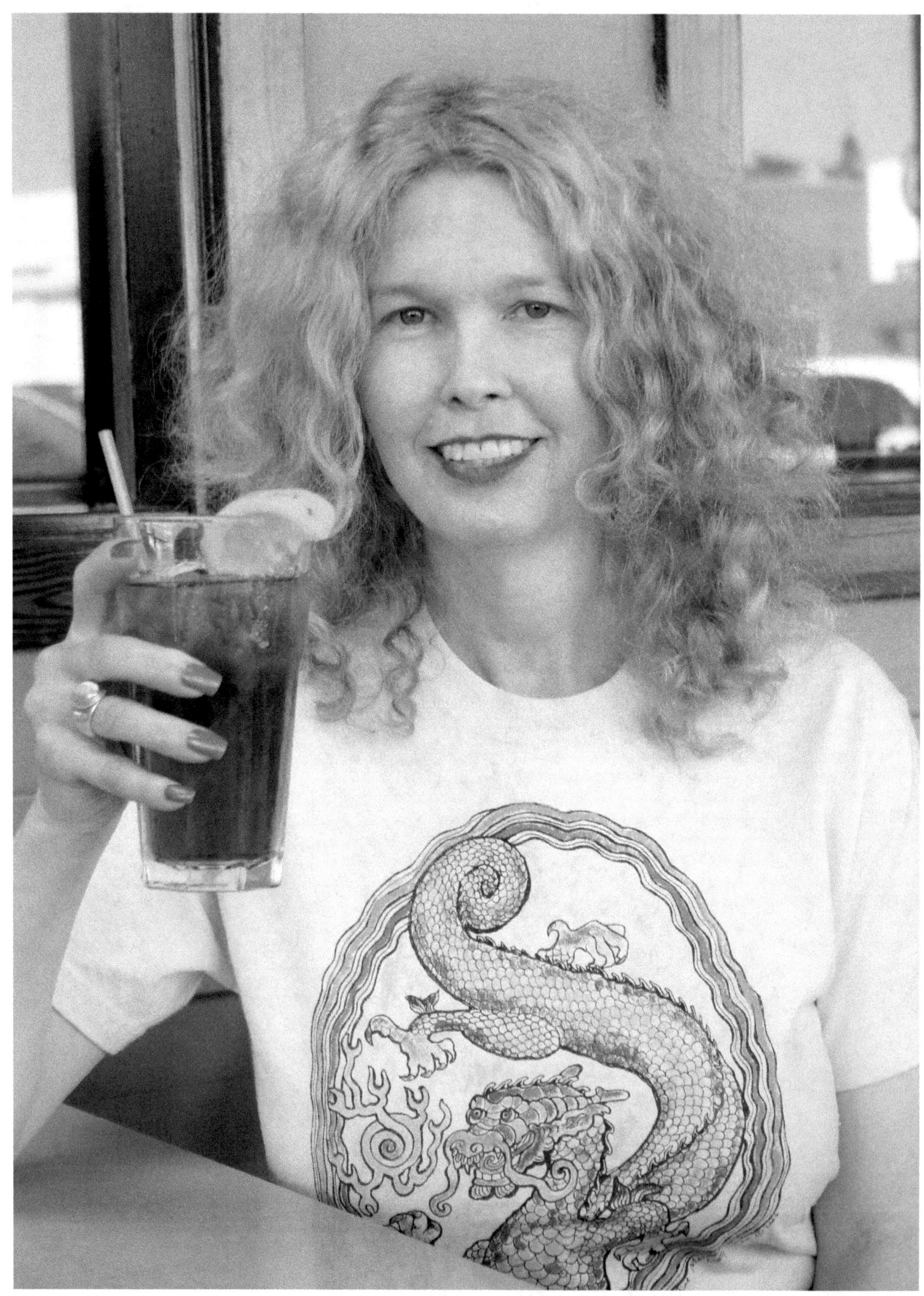

Photo by Steve Zambrano

To create something from nothingness
and to know Love - these have fulfilled me.

I thank the Universe for my life;
even for the obstacles that have made it more interesting.
I only need listen and speak the Truth.

To Life!

L'Chaim!

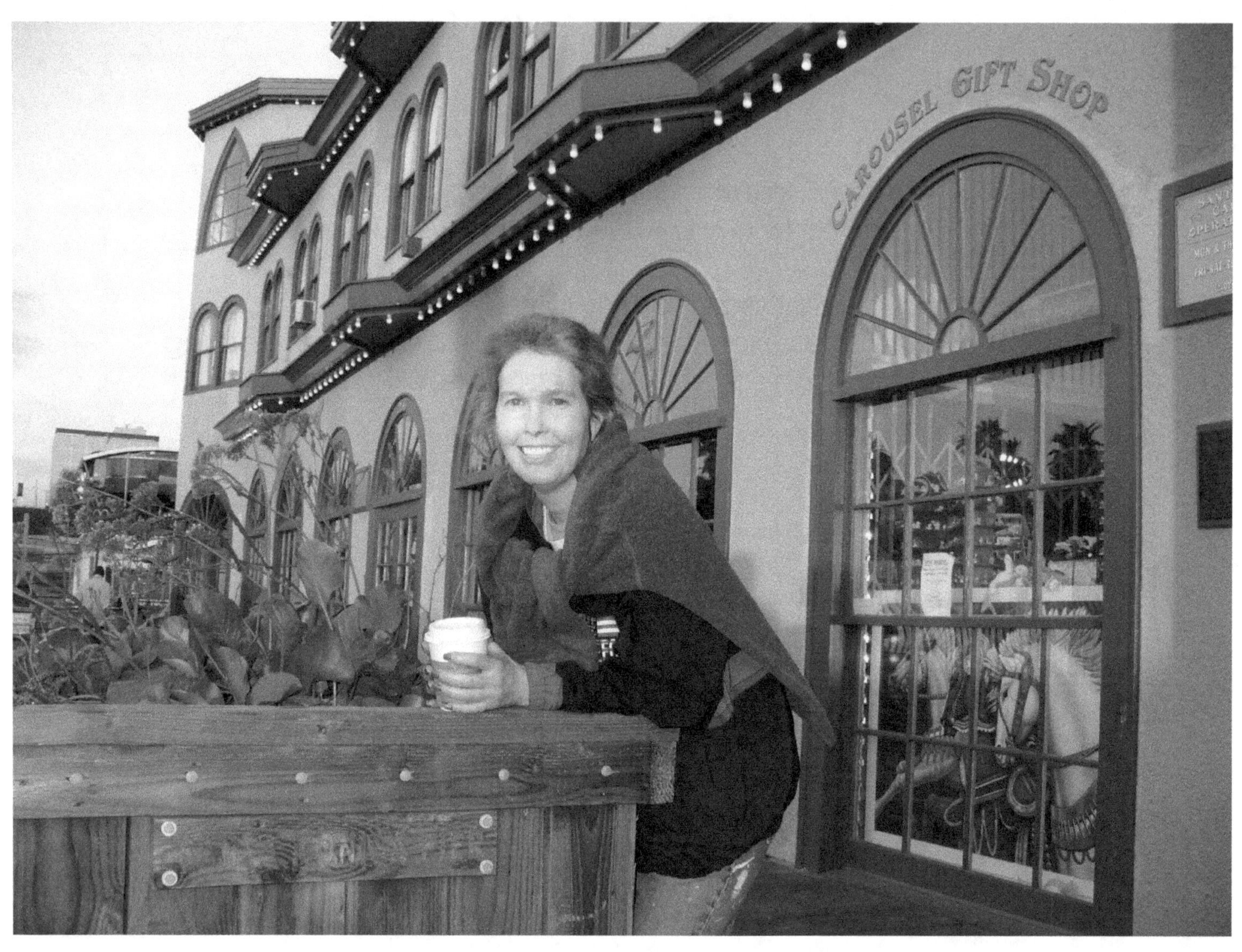

"And in the end, the Love you take
is equal to the Love you make."
- The Beatles

www.ingramcontent.com/pod-product-compliance
Lightning Source LLC
LaVergne TN
LVHW081738100826
845155LV00005B/16
* 9 7 9 8 9 8 5 0 7 9 6 6 1 *